Contents

P9-DVB-191

Preface

Birds have been kept in cages and aviaries for many centuries and, in many ways, they make ideal pets. They are easy to care for, adaptable, and their exotic appearance and lively behavior gives constant delight to their owners. Aviculture provides an opportunity not only to observe and study birds at close range, but also to breed them. If birds are made to feel comfortable, at least, they will show themselves at their finest and are more likely to breed. For this reason, it is important to know about their physical characteristics, habits and general requirements. Their captive conditions must represent, as closely as possible, those to which they are accustomed in the wild. I have kept all but the *Nannopsittaca* species successfully in my aviaries for years, and I have studied all of the species dealt with here, in their wild habitats.

Aviculturists often find themselves having to justify the practice of keeping and breeding birds in captivity, especially to members of animal protection societies. Critics maintain that caged birds are deprived of their freedom and are dependent on the goodwill of their owners, and thus the birds' welfare is subject to human whims, degree of efficiency, and benevolence.

It is undeniable that, in the past, birds which would have been better off in the wild, like the *Nannopsittaca* and most of the *Touit* Parrots, were kept in captivity, and that cruel practices occurred for the amusement of their owners. Present-day bird enthusiasts should therefore try to understand the arguments of people who are opposed to the caging and

The male Spectacled Parrotlet (Forpus conspicillatus) is one of the fascinating little parrots of the genus Forpus. The species lives in colonies, near the edges of lowland evergreen forests and similar lightly wooded habitats, and feeds on seeds, fruits, blossoms, buds, and berries. None of the parrotlet species uses their feet for feeding.

breeding of birds. Both groups of people are motivated by similar feelings, a love of nature in general, and a special affection for birds.

Nowadays, aviculturists play an important role in the conservation of many bird species: think, for example, of the "breed and release" programs (Thick-billed Parrot in Arizona) which many dedicated aviculturists are currently engaged in. With increasing pollution, deforestation, and the drainage of swamps, ponds, rivers, and lakes, the environment is being slowly destroyed, with little consideration for the many forms of life that are thus threatened with extinction. In December 1997 and January 1998, the clearing of forests by burning caused smog and death in several parts of the world as the intense smoke did not dissipate. Few birds can survive this type of destruction!

The Pet Industry Joint Advisory Council (PIJAC) states: "Documentary evidence supports rates of deforestation between 50 and 75 acres per minute, and upwards of 50,000 square miles per year because of agricultural and industrial expansion." Countries primarily affected are in the so-called Third World and underdeveloped areas such as Brazil (20% of rainforest destroyed by commercial cutting and mining); Indonesia (66 million acres classified as "denuded" by uncontrolled commercial cutting); Africa (1 million square kilometers of forest have been eliminated); Mexico (deforestation rate of 40,000 hectares per year, and again, the areas of

The Mexican parrotlet (Forpus cyanopygius) has a fast, deeply undulated flight. While in groups one can hear the buzzing wings. This is a well-proportioned male which has won various prizes at bird shows.

many of our parrots and parrotlets); and Central America (almost two thirds of its lowland and lower montane rain forest have been cleared or severely degraded since 1950—and this area too is the natural habitat of many of our small parrots).

It is scary to know that ". . . the world's rain forests will disappear altogether in 80 years if the present rate of 43,000 square miles per year continues," according to the Animal Welfare Institute. Many countries, however, *are* slowly but surely improving their wildlife resource management, strengthening the provisions of existing wildlife laws, and enforcing laws to protect endangered species. I fully applaud this development.

The overall result of these changes is that the importation of many animals, including birds-of-all-feathers, is being reduced. Most

Wild-colored (or normal) bird on the left, and a cinnamon mutation of the Celestial Parrotlet on the right. Both birds are males.

birds coming into our country are imported, captive-bred species from Europe.

Sympathy for caged birds is entirely misplaced. The great number of nests full of chicks which appear every year in aviaries and specially designed breeding cages shows that cage and aviary birds cannot be suffering unduly from being in captivity. They have many enemies and predators in the wild, human beings included(!), and their natural habitats are slowly being encroached upon by "civilization." Naturalists have studied how birds that once occurred only in forests have moved to parks and later into towns—as have some of our parrotlets and small parrots. Some species, however, totally vanish from sight if they are unable to move on when their habitat is encroached upon.

To believe that birds suffer untold anguish when confined in a cage or aviary is to "humanize" them; human beings suffer in captivity because behind bars or barbed wire they imagine how beautiful freedom would be; but such imagination is possessed only by humans. Animals, hence birds, live mainly for the present. They remain contented and satisfied if they have sufficient food and water, adequate light, plenty of room to move and exercise, opportunity to reproduce, and protection from their enemies and bad weather. Many people think that a bird would jubilantly fly away if its cage or aviary door were opened, but in fact the bird would probably feel rather bewildered, unsure, and inhibited.

Provided that birds are properly cared for, there should be no criticism of keeping them in cages or aviaries. The majority of owners lavish care and attention on their birds, go out of their way to provide them with the most appropriate food, and some create a little piece of nature where birds can build their nests without restraint or disturbance and rear their young with a ready supply of food, aspects we will deal with extensively in this book.

Years ago, as a high school and college student, I became serious about *raising* "simple" bird species. Many people, among them my teachers and professors, who noticed how I went about it, called me a fanatic, or worse. Why should I be so intent about feeding, housing, nest boxes, temperature and humidity on behalf of bird species that could be replaced from any pet store for a couple of quarters? They thought it even stranger when they found out that I made detailed observations about my breeding efforts, went to "far away" countries to observe and study birds in the wild, and published the results in various bird journals.

Nowadays, however, the average bird fancier, as well as the bird expert, have clearly come to a different conclusion. Every right-minded bird fancier endeavors to expand the pet bird stock of this country, so that domestic breeding has completely (or almost completely) eliminated our dependence on import, even from Europe. It is time to roll up our sleeves and develop effective programs to propagate many species in cages and aviaries before it is too late! The parrotlets are excellent examples: ten years ago, they were relatively unknown in the USA, but are now rapidly becoming *one of the most popular* groups of parrots in aviculture due to their beautiful plumage, comical behavior, high intelligence, and *readiness to breed!* Or as Sandee and Robert Molenda of the "International Parrotlet Society" say: "Anyone looking for a large parrot personality in a small parrot body need look no further than the parrotlet. These delightful little parrots can provide many years of devoted companionship as well as a lot of fun!" The same, by the way, applies to all other small parrots we will introduce to you.

NOTE: This book expresses small linear and liquid measurements in their English and metric forms. For the guidance of readers not yet completely familiar with the metric equivalents of English measurements, we are including the following conversion information:

One meter (m) is equal to 1000 millimeters (mm).
One centimeter (cm) is equal to 10 millimeters and is 1/100 of a meter.
One inch is equal to about 2.5 cm or 25 mm.
Four inches equals approximately 100 mm.
Six inches equals about 150 mm.
One foot equals about 305 mm.
Three feet equals about 914 mm.

The number of millimeters divided by ten gives the number of centimeters.

To convert degrees Celsius (or, if you prefer, Centigrade) to degrees Fahrenheit, multiply degrees Celsius by 1.8 and then add 32. (In equation form [°C × 1.8] + 32 = °F.) Some basic conversions are:

0°C = 32°F
10°C = 50°F
20°C = 68°F
30°C = 86°F
100°C = 212°F.

A blue hen of the Celestial Parrotlet. Note the even wing color.

Remember, the time will come, and perhaps sooner than we think, when the breeding stock needed for such propagation will no longer be available because the birds may no longer be around . . . !

It is—I sincerely hope—not too late, yet! It is a good thing that I conducted those experiments with "plain, cheap bird species" years ago, strange as my activities were regarded then. Let us work together to prevent the depredation of nature, so that it will remain dynamic in our time and that of our descendants.

Matthew M. Vriends
Winter 1998/1999

Chapter One

Understanding Parrotlets and Other Miniature Parrots

The Popular Parrotlet

The parrotlet, or *Forpus,* is becoming increasingly popular as a pet because of its diminutive size, charming behavior, and bright, colorful plumage. It is smaller than a parakeet and quieter than some of its raucous cousins in the parrot world. Its inability to scream makes it a favorite avian companion among parrot fanciers who live in close proximity to their neighbors.

The parrotlet has a short, wedge-shaped tail and a proportionately large beak, with a notch in the upper mandible. Sometimes called the "Blue-winged Lovebird of South America," the parrotlet does resemble the well-known Lovebird (*Agapornis,* Selby) native to Africa and the Malagasy Republic, but is not a close relative. It might even seem to be a tiny version of the much larger Amazon Parrot.

In the wild, the parrotlet's range extends from northwestern Mexico through South America as far as northern Argentina and Paraguay. The Pacific Parrotlet can be found along the northwest coast of Peru around Trujillo.

The Yellow-faced Parrotlet (Forpus xanthops) *is found in one remote valley in Peru but is becoming rather popular as a cage and aviary bird in Europe as well as in Canada and the United States.*

1

Forpus Arrives in the United States

Virtually unknown in the United States and Canada until about 15 years ago, the parrotlet has increased in numbers and popularity largely as the result of successful captive-breeding programs. For example, one variety, the Celestial or Pacific Parrotlet, *Forpus coelestis,* was almost unknown outside Europe until the 1960s, but is now well established. The Yellow-faced Parrotlet, *Forpus xanthops,* was unknown here until 1979, and is still relatively rare in the United States, where seven pairs are now involved in a captive-breeding program.

The Spectacled Parrotlet, *Forpus conspicillatus,* first successfully bred in 1932 by Mr. and Mrs. A. R. Hood of California, became popular in Europe in the 1960s and 1970s. In 1992 approximately 20 Spectacled Parrotlets were imported into the United States, and a breeding cooperative was formed to ensure the preservation of a pure gene pool. This well-executed program has resulted in hundreds of Spectacled Parrotlets in the cages and aviaries of American and Canadian aviculturists.

Keeping Parrotlets

Forpus parrotlets are relatively easy to keep in an aviary. Imported wild birds, especially in the first few months, are very nervous, and it is entirely possible that even after a year or two in the aviary they will still fly against the wire or creep, terrified, into a corner at the least provocation. Use gloves if it becomes necessary to catch them, because they can inflict a nasty bite in spite of their small size.

Housing

House each pair in a separate aviary. Keeping more than one pair of the same species together leads to quarreling, which hinders the breeding process—not always a simple matter in the best of circumstances. It is, however, possible to keep them with lovebirds and other nonrelated species. One breeder I know kept a pair of Green-rumped Parrotlets *(F. p. passerinus)* with various finches in a large aviary, approximately 16 feet (5 m) long, for six years. They used a nest box as a dormitory and always went to bed long before their aviary companions retired for the night.

This green pastel male mutation of the Celestial Parrotlet has a beautiful wing design.

Parrotlet Species and Subspecies

Group:	Psittaciformes	—	Parrots
Family:	Aratingidae	—	New World Parrots
Underfamily:	Forpinae	—	Dwarf Parrots or Parrotlets
Genus:	*Forpus*	—	(Boie 1858)

Species	*Subspecies*
Spectacled Parrotlet *Forpus conspicillatus* (Lafresnaye 1848)	*F. c. conspicillatus* (Lafresnaye) *F. c. metae* (Borrero and Camacho) *F. c. caucae* (Chassman)
Mexican Parrotlet *Forpus cyanopygius* (Souancé 1856)	*F. c. cyanopygius* (Souancé) *F. c. pallidus* (Brewster) *F. c. insularis* (Ridgeway)
Blue-winged Parrotlet *Forpus xanthopterygius* (Spix 1824)	*F. x. xanthopterygius* (Spix) *F. x. crassirostris* (Taczanowski) *F. x. flavescens* (Salvadori) *F. x. flavissimus* (Hellmayr) *F. x. olallae* Gyldenstolpe *F. x. spengeli* (Hartlaub)
Pacific Parrotlet *Forpus coelestis* (Lesson 1847)	*F. c. lucida* (Pathe)*
Yellow-faced Parrotlet *Forpus xanthops* (Salvin 1895)	No subspecies recognized
Green-rumped Parrotlet *Forpus passerinus* (Linnaeus 1758)	*F. p. passerinus* (Linnaeus) *F. p. deliciosus* (Ridgeway) *F. p. cyanophanus* (Todd) *F. p. viridissimus* (Lafresnaye) *F. p. cyanochlorus* (Schlegel)
Sclater's Parrotlet *Forpus sclateri* (G. R. Gray 1859)	*F. s. sclateri* (G. R. Gray) *F. s. eidos* (Peters)

* This subspecies, first reported in 1937, has recently been reidentified.

Recently imported birds must be placed in quarantine, checked by an avian veterinarian, and carefully acclimatized. Parrotlets' natural habitat is mild, so they are suscepti-ble to cold and drafts. House them indoors initially, especially in cold climates. Birds that have been locally bred are hardier and can be kept outdoors during the winter in all but

*The male Blue-winged Parrotlet (*Forpus xanthopterygius*).* In some scientific literature this species is called *Forpus crassirostris.*

A gray mutation (male) of the Celestial Parrotlet, and an offspring of the pairing between a blue male and gray-green female.

the coldest climates, providing they have a very well-built, dry, and draft-proof night shelter.

Choosing a Pair

Parrotlets' way of life is similar to that of lovebirds. Pairs mate for life, sleep together, and rear their broods together. Choosing a pair won't be difficult; the sexes can be readily identified. The greens of the male are darker and mixed with blue in his plumage. The females' markings are yellowish green, emerald green, and green.

Note: If you are a novice, ask an experienced breeder to help you choose a female of the correct species. The hens of all species are difficult to tell apart, and you want to avoid hybridization at all costs.

Nest Boxes

The nest boxes should have the following dimensions: The bottom square should measure approximately 11.8 to 13.75 inches (30–35 cm); the height should be 7 to 10 inches (18–25 cm), and the nest entrance should be about 2.4 inches (6 cm) in diameter. The boxes should be made of hard, seasoned wood, and the edges should be strengthened with metal strips. Most species, such as the Pacific Parrotlet, like to roost in the nest box throughout the year.

Because the *Forpus* species do not generally use any nesting materials, it might be desirable to scoop a shallow hollow in the bottom of the nest for the eggs. Complete broods are usually made up of three to six eggs, although there can be as many as eight. Don't inspect the nest, especially if you have an imported pair! The female will not tolerate such intrusions and will promptly desert her eggs. You will rarely, if ever, see the hen during the nesting period, as she remains in the nest box and is provided with food by her spouse. Here, too, there can be problems because, if someone is near, the male will not go inside the nest box.

Brooding Period

The brooding period is three to three and a half weeks. The young fly out when they are approximately five weeks old. Keep an eye on the female since, while she is still feeding one brood, she might "forget" that her children are still relying on her for sustenance, and start laying a new batch of eggs. In the beginning, the entire brood returns to the nest box at night to sleep together.

Feeding Your *Forpus*

Parrotlets' nutritional requirements are the same as lovebirds': white seed (canary grass seed), various types of millet, as well as hemp and small, dark sunflower seeds. Although most parrotlets are not always fond of greens and fruit, it is nevertheless a good idea to offer these. Cuttlefish bone is also essential, especially before and during the breeding period. Most parrotlets accept tasty pellets with gusto. Vitamins should be sprinkled on soft food such as universal or egg foods at least four times a week.

Offer your parrotlets variety in fruits, such as oranges, grapes, and berries—especially blackberries. Give them plenty of greens, which provide essential nutrients.

Note: Parrotlets rarely, if ever, take a water bath but enjoy a roll in

A green pastel female Celestial Parrotlet.

moist grass. Provide them with a patch of grass and simply let it grow. The longer the grass, the better they like it.

Parrotlets at a Glance

Size: Domestic budgerigars or parakeets, in good form and color for presentation at a bird show, are

A somewhat darker gray mutation (male).

about 8.4 inches (21.5 cm) in length; fully grown *Forpus* species, however, have a body length of 4.3 to 5.5 inches (11–14 cm).

Color: Parrotlet species are usually light green with blue patches on the rump and wings of the males. The hens of all species are difficult to tell apart.

Native Habitat: The native range of most parrotlets is northeastern Mexico to northern Argentina. In their range, they inhabit open grassland and lightly wooded areas and are often seen on the ground, where they forage for seeds and other items. The most important foods are berries, fruit, young leaf buds and shoots, grass seeds, grain, and insects. Pairs stay together throughout the year. When danger threatens, they let out a shrill warning call, but otherwise they are relatively quiet birds whose pleasant chatter is quite easy on the ear.

Breeding Behavior: Before and during the breeding season, parrotlets become quite aggressive, mainly toward their own species, but also, in the aviary, toward finches, including canaries, as well as cockatiels, miniature parakeets, and other birds. They especially like to bite the feet and toes of their aviary companions.

Feeding: Offer a seed mixture that includes a daily portion of fresh millet spray, apple, greens, and soft food. Experiment with various fruits. Keep a cuttlefish bone or commercial mineral block in the cage. Provide fresh drinking water every day.

Hanging Parrots

Hanging Parrots *(Loriculus)* are comical birds. They sleep hanging upside down like bats, and sometimes defecate while in the inverted position, an act that can come as a nasty, wet surprise to the unaware visitor who stands too close to the cage. They measure between 4 and 6.5 inches (10–16 cm), and can be kept by fanciers who have limited space.

Description

The beaks of Hanging Parrots are slender and somewhat resemble those of the lories of the genus *Trichoglossus.* Depending on the species, the beak is either red or black. Their wings are sleek and long, but their tails are surprisingly short. The flight of these birds is like that of finches in that it involves rapid beating of the wings, broken at intervals by short pauses with closed wings. They are great acrobats and trapeze artists, taking full advantage of their beaks; in fact, they rarely have their feet on the ground. Consequently, it is important to provide them with a gym consisting of all sorts of climbing bars, swings, and ladders. They are active birds, and chatter constantly. It would be difficult indeed not to be affected by their charm.

When these birds scratch themselves on the head, they lift the foot *over* the wing, unlike most other arboreal parrots, which lift the foot up under the wing. I have seen all

Hanging Parrot Species and Subspecies*

Species	Subspecies
Vernal Hanging Parrot *Loriculus vernalis* (Sparrman 1787)	No subspecies recognized
Ceylon Hanging Parrot *Loriculus beryllinus* (J. R. Foster 1781)	No subspecies recognized
Philippine Hanging Parrot *Loriculus philippensis* (P. L. S. Müller 1776)	*L. p. philippensis* (P. L. S. Müller) *L. p. mindorensis* (Steere) *L. p. bournsi* (McGregor) *L. p. panayensis* (Tweeddale) *L. p. regulus* (Souancé) *L. p. chrysonotus* (Sclater) *L. p. worcesteri* (Steere) *L. p. siquijorensis* (Steere) *L. p. apicalis* (Souancé) *L. p. dohertyi* (Hartert) *L. p. bonapartei* (Souancé)
Blue-crowned Hanging Parrot *Loriculus galgalus* (Linnaeus 1758)	No subspecies recognized
Sulawesi Hanging Parrot *Loriculus stigmatus* (P. L. S. Müller 1843)	No subspecies recognized
Moluccan Hanging Parrot *Loriculus amabilis* (Wallace 1863)	*L. a. amabilis* (Wallace) *L. a. catamene* (Schlegel) *L. a. sclateri* (Wallace) *L. a. ruber* (Meyer and Wiglesworth)
Green Hanging Parrot *Loriculus exilis* (Schlegel 1866)	No subspecies recognized
Wallace's Hanging Parrot *Loriculus flosculus* (Wallace 1863)	No subspecies recognized
Yellow-throated Hanging Parrot *Loriculus pusillus* (G. R. Gray 1859)	No subspecies recognized
Orange-fronted Hanging Parrot *Loriculus aurantiifrons* (Schlegel 1873)	*L. a. batavorum* (Stresemann) *L. a. meeki* (Hartert) *L. a. tener* (Sclater)

* Recognized by Peters (1937) and Forshaw (1989).

The Moluccan Hanging Parrot (Loriculus amabilis) is only 4.3 inches (11 cm), and confined to a handful of islands in the Moluccans where it is the only representative of its genus. There are three sub-species: L. a. amabilis from Halmahera and Bacan (the males from these islands have a red crown and green mantle); L. a. sclateri from Suba; and L. A. ruber from Banggai and Peleng Islands (the latter two have a green crown and an orange or red mantle).

species, with the exception of the Philippine Hanging Parrot, use the foot as a hand.

Hanging Parrots can give the fancier a great deal of pleasure. Unfortunately, however, they are not able to stay outdoors during the winter in our cold regions; in fact, a lightly heated area is recommended.

Feeding and Nesting

Hanging Parrots like to eat all sorts of seeds—weed seeds, oats, millet varieties, canary grass seed, broken hemp, and so on—insects such as ant pupae and mealworms, fruit, greens, and honey water. Fruit is the most important part of their diet, with greens a close second, and then willow twigs, cuttlebone, and grit.

For some time aviculturists thought that this genus was very closely related to the lories and lori-keets; therefore, the diet was rich in carbohydrates (honey, sugar) but low in B-complex vitamins. Others considered a diet of seeds alone satisfactory. Both groups had the wrong idea. These birds must have seeds, fruits, and greens. In the wild, they seem to take many kinds of fruit, seeds, and insects (omnivorous). I have always offered my birds a commercial insectile mixture, ant pupae and such, baby cereals, rich in varied amino acids and vitamins, mixed with evaporated milk, as well as, depending on availability, black-berries, raspberries, elderberries, ripe gooseberries, red currants, rosehips, small white millet, millet spray, honey-soaked wheat bread, red grapes, bananas, figs, oranges, apples, and black sunflower seed. They are also crazy about pellets soaked in fruit juice.

If more than one species is kept together in an aviary, one or more bullies will drive the others away from the food dish, especially when there is not a choice of food dishes. It is therefore recommended that several food dishes be available.

These little parrots build nests, transporting willow and mulberry twigs tucked between the rump and wing feathers just as the lovebird species *(Agapornidae)* do. Roomy nest boxes made of beechwood are ideal. Keep these boxes in the aviary throughout the year, as the birds like to shelter in them when the weather is cold and wet. Fanciers who keep these charming birds indoors do not need to provide them with nest boxes until a few weeks before the start of the breeding season. The boxes should be roomy—like the ones used for Australian grass parakeets—since they often like to hang upside down while taking a nap! Put a perch 2 inches (5 cm) from the roof of the box. Smith (1979) makes the following remark: "The hanging-parrots get both of their colloquial names (for they are sometimes called 'bat-parrots') because they usually hang upside down by their feet to rest and roost. Almost everyone with an experience of keeping any species of arboreal parrots will find that when they are first confined to a fresh enclosure, or when they are uneasy, or disturbed, before settling down to sleep for the night, they will hang from the roof of their accommodation; however the hanging-parrots may well be the only genus that normally suspend themselves to sleep. Hanging-parrots are particularly small and dainty for they weigh somewhere between twenty-

Due to habitat loss the status of the Moluccan Hanging Parrot (Loriculus amabilis) is approximately 20,000 birds, and rapidly declining. In the wild they live in pairs or small flocks, but very often singly too, usually close to flowering trees.

five and perhaps as much as forty grams."

During the winter, Hanging Parrots often disappear into the nest box quite early in the evening and do not reappear until morning.

Breeding

Some fanciers are under the impression that Hanging Parrots are not particularly sociable birds. My

The Blue-crowned Hanging Parrot can easily be housed in roomy cages but like to roam outside their abode. Keep cage, especially the wire sides, scrupulously clean, as this species as well as his family members expel liquid droppings onto the bars.

opinion is that the contrary is true. I have kept them with other hookbills, such as the various Australian grass parakeets (Splendid, Turquoisine, and others) and have yet to have a problem with them. This is not the case, however, where their own species are concerned. It is advisable, therefore, to keep only one pair per cage or aviary.

Although the sexes can generally be determined by small differences in coloring and markings, it is advisable to go to a trusted source when purchasing these birds. In any event, obtain a written agreement, signed and dated, that will allow you to exchange one of your birds if you find that you have purchased two

Like Turquoises and lovebirds, the Blue-crowned Hanging Parrot (Loriculus galgulus) carries bark strips and leaves to the nest tucked under the breast and rump feathers. This is a male; the hen lacks the red bib and has less yellow on the back; the blue crown is somewhat smaller. Members of this genus can be kept together. Rosemary Low recommends a 4.5 by 4.5 by 6 inch (11 × 11 × 15 cm) nest box.

birds of the same sex. DNA testing, which most reputable breeders and aviculturists now conduct before they sell their birds, eliminates any doubt about gender.

The female lays two to four white eggs, which take 20 to 22 days to hatch. Just like those of the parrotlets, the young are naked, with a little down here and there when they hatch.

Fig Parrots and Other Miniature Parrots

Fig Parrots (Tribe *Cyclopsittacini*) are made up of three genera: *Cyclopsitta, Psittaculirostris,* and *Nannopsittacus.* The most important genus to us is *Cyclopsitta* Reichenbach, formerly known as *Opopsitta.*

These colorful dwarf parrots have, over the years, been only sporadically available to hobbyists. Some zoological parks were often successful at breeding these dwarf parrots during the 1960s and 1970s. The London Zoo, for example, had pairs that lived more than ten years.

Size

The members of this genus are very small—5½ to 6 inches (13–14 cm)—and stocky, with a strikingly short tail. A relatively broad bill with a prominent notch in the upper mandible is a typical characteristic of this group of birds. In contrast to the genus *Psittaculirostris,* whose members are larger, the parrots *(Cyclopsitta)* have no elongation of the ear coverts. The cere—the bulge at the base of the upper beak through which the nostrils open—is naked and rather prominent. The tongue is smooth.

Distribution

This genus is found in the New Guinea region including the Aru Islands, the Bismarck Archipelago in Indonesia, and northeastern Australia in southern and northeastern New South Wales. These birds occur up to an altitude of 5,200 feet (1,600 m). In Australia I have observed them along the coast and in the rain forests.

Diet in the Wild

Fig Parrots feed on many kinds of insects, small fruits, berries, wild figs, and nectar. The Coxen's Fig Parrot, native to southern Queensland and northern New South Wales, Australia, is very rare.

Fig Parrot Housing and Feeding

Fig Parrots require a warm aviary or cage—minimum 65 to 70°F (18–30°C)—and the most important foods are berries, figs, insects (especially small mealworms), sprouting birdseed, spray millet, canary grass seed, and other grains. Fruit and sprouted seed should be supplemented with a few drops of a multi-

Fig Parrot Species and Subspecies

Species	Subspecies
Orange-breasted Fig Parrot *Cyclopsitta gulielmitertii* (Schlegel)	*C. g. gulielmitertii* (Schlegel) *C. g. nigrifrons* (Reichenow) *C. g. ramuensis* (Neumann) *C. g. amabilis* (Reichenow) *C. g. suavissima* (Sclater) *C. g. fuscifrons* (Salvadori) *C. g. melanogenia* (Schlegel)
Double-eyed Fig Parrot *Cyclopsitta diophthalma* (Hombron and Jacquinot)	*C. d. diophthalma* (Hombron and Jacquinot) *C. d. coccineifrons* (Sharpe) *C. d. aruensis* (Schlegel) *C. d. virago* (Hartert) *C. d. inseparabilis* (Hartert) *C. d. marshalli* (Iredale) *C. d. macleayana* (Ramsey) *C. d. coxeni* (Gould) (known as Coxen's Fig Parrot)

Fig Parrot Species and Subspecies

Species	Subspecies
Desmarest's Fig Parrot *Psittaculirostris desmarestii* (Desmarest)	*P. d. desmaretii* (Desmarest) *P. d. intermedia* (van Oort) *P. d. occidentalis* (Salvadori) *P. d. blythii* (Wallace) *P. d. godmani* (Ogilvie-Grant) *P. d. cervicalis* (Salvadori and D'Albertis)
Edward's Fig Parrot *Psittaculirostris edwardsii* (Oustalet)	No subspecies recognized
Salvadori's Fig Parrot *Psittaculirostris salvadorii* (Oustalet)	No subspecies recognized

The Edward's Fig Parrot (Psittaculirostris edwardsii) *is found in lowland forests of northeastern New Guinea. The female doesn't have a red breast and belly but a yellowish green one; her purple collar, however, is more extensive. In captivity breeding success is rather limited due to the death of most chicks one or two days after birth—a fact encountered quite often in the genus* Psittaculirostris.

vitamin preparation; vitamin K is particularly important.

Breeding

Coxen's Fig Parrot was first kept and bred by the well-known aviculturist Dr. R. Burkard of Switzerland in 1978. A tunnel about 10 inches (20 cm) long by 1.7 inches (4 cm) wide was dug into a rotting log and completed with a nest hollow. Experience has shown that these and other members of the genus will also accept a small parakeet nest box. Pairs of these small parrots should be kept in an aviary or roomy breeding cage of the type used for lovebirds. Dr. Burkard recommends feeding large quantities of small mealworms. The young fledge in about five weeks and are fully independent after another two weeks. They should then be removed from the cage so that the parents can start on a second (and last) brood. They should not be allowed to breed more than twice a season. Unfortunately, some youngsters starve before fledging for reasons still undetermined.

New Guinea Parrots

The second genus *(Psittaculirostris)* contains three colorful species characterized by a sturdy, frequently keeled beak, a conspicuous cere, elongated ear coverts, and rounded, short tails. These parrots first became available in the late 1970s with the importation of Salvadori's Fig Parrot *(P. salvadorii),* which is discussed in detail on page 164.

Diet

Members of this genus are mainly frugivorous, feeding on various berries and fruits such as figs and bananas, though an adequate supply of insects such as small mealworms and ant pupae is also important both in and out of the breeding season. It is advisable also to provide germinated seeds and several millet varieties throughout the year. It is recommended that a multivitamin supplement be mixed with the fruit or the drinking water. Vitamin K is very important to these lorylike parrots. A good soft food (universal food) is essential during the breeding season. Vitamins and mashed bananas can be mixed into this food, several commercial varieties of which are available.

The Desmarest's Fig Parrot (Psittaculirostris desmarestii) *or Large Fig Parrot (7.1–7.9 inches [18–20 cm]) is a stocky bird from the lowlands and hill forests of western and southern New Guinea. There are various subspecies; very beautiful are the P. d. godmani, with bright yellow elongated ear coverts, and P. d. cervicalis, with an almost entire orange-red head (the female has a green crown). Supply fresh branches and calcium blocks so the birds are able to trim their beaks, which have the tendency to become overgrown.*

All members of the genus are native to New Guinea, where they occur in lowland and thick forest in pairs or small groups.

Pygmy Parrots

The six members of the third genus, *Micropsitta,* are known as the Pygmy Parrots. In spite of numerous attempts by prominent ornithologists, these parrots are difficult to keep

Pygmy Parrots Species and Subspecies

Species	Subspecies
Buff-faced Pygmy Parrot *Micropsitta pusio* (Sclater)	*M. p. pusio* (Sclater) *M. p. harterti* (Mayr) *M. p. stresemanni* (Hartert) *M. p. beccarii* (Salvadori)
Yellow-capped Pygmy Parrot *Micropsitta keiensis* (Salvadori)	*M. k. keiensis* (Salvadori) *M. k. viridipectus* (Rothschild) *M. k. chloroxantha* (Oberholser)
Geelvink Pygmy Parrot *Micropsitta geelvinkiana* (Schlegel)	*M. g. geelvinkiana* (Schlegel) *M. g. misoriensis* (Salvadori)
Meek's Pygmy Parrot *Micropsitta meeki* (Rothschild and Hartert)	*M. m. meeki* (Rothschild and Hartert) *M. m. proxima* (Rothschild and Hartert)
Finsch's Pygmy Parrot *Micropsitta finschii* (Ramsay)	*M. f. finschii* (Ramsay) *M. f. aolae* (Ogilvie-Grant) *M. f. tristrami* (Rothschild and Hartert) *M. f. nanina* (Tristram) *M. f. viridifrons* (Rothschild and Hartert)
Red-breasted Pygmy Parrot *Micropsitta bruijnii* (Salvadori)	*M. b. bruijnii* (Salvadori) *M. b. pileata* (Mayr) *M. b. necopinata* (Hartert) *M. b. rosea* (Mayr)

alive for long in captivity. Pygmy Parrots must be the most colorful of all the parrot species as well as the smallest (3.5 to 4 inches [8.5–10 cm]). The mainly green plumage is decorated with red, blue, yellow, and brown patches; the sexes are different in color. The tail is short and provided with stiff shafts that they use as props when they climb in the trees. Leading Dutch and German ornithologists commonly call them Woodpecker Parrots.

Diet

In the wild these Lilliputian birds occur in New Guinea, the Solomon Islands, Bismarck Archipelago, and St. Mathias and Squally Islands in the Pacific. Examination of these birds has shown that they possess large salivary glands but a small proventriculus—the upper stomach into which food is transported by peristaltic action from the esophagus. It is not unusual for birds that subsist mainly on fruit and insects to have a small proventriculus. They are frequently found breeding and foraging in the nests of arboreal termites. The hen lays two eggs. Ornithologist H. Boreguella reported that in the Solomon Islands, these parrots foraged for small insects and larvae among mushrooms and other fungi growing on trees.

Stress in Captivity

These parrots, unfortunately, seldom live for more than a few hours in captivity. Stress seems to be the cause of death. Aviculturist Rosemary Low, in her book *Parrots, Their Care and Breeding,* states: "Most of the few experiments made to keep these birds alive in captivity have involved very small numbers; however, in one (to me, regrettable) experiment, between 80 and 100 birds were captured at dusk in the hope that when placed in a large aviary together they could be induced to feed. They showed no interest in fruits, soft foods or seeds; they examined termites' nests but did not eat the termites. When termites' nests attached to tree boles were provided, they searched the cracks. Other small parrots placed with them did not induce them to feed; so, 20 hours after capture, when they were showing signs of starvation, they were released."

The Guiaiabero

Only one member of the genus *Bolbopsittacus* is recognized. Native to the Philippines, where it lives in the lowland to an altitude of 1,970 feet (600 m), this species, the Guiaiabero, is closely related to members of the genus *Cyclopsitta,* and some ornithologists prefer to leave it in that "older" genus, categorized by the colors of the plumage, construction of the beak, iris color, and osteology of the skull. The Guiaiabero likes to live among fruit-bearing trees and is common in cultivated plantations. Little is known about the reproductive habits of this species, which is difficult to keep alive in captivity. The few examples kept by

---

The Guiaiabero Subspecies

Species	Subspecies
Guiaiabero	*B. l. lunulatus* (Scopoli)
Bolbopsittacus lunulatus	*B. l. intermedius* (Salvadori)
(Scopoli 1786)	*B. l. callainipictus* (Parkes)
	B. l. mindanensis (Steere)

R. Burkard lived mainly on fruits (bananas, figs, and so on), various berries, insects such as small mealworms, ant pupae, and boiled potatoes. The Guiaiabero is described in greater detail on page 166.

Tiger Parrots

The genus *Psittacella,* frequently called Tiger Parrots by aviculturists, contains four species, all of which live in the dense montane forests of New Guinea to an altitude of 12,000 feet (3,600 m). These little parrots have very short tails. As far as I am aware, some of the Brehm's Tiger Parrots were imported from Australia to the San Diego Zoo in 1966. The barred design of the plumage gave rise to the name, as suggested by J. M. Diamond in his book *Avifauna of the Eastern Highlands of New Guinea.* The plumage and patterns of these birds blend remarkably with the foliage of their habitat, and difficulty in observing them in the wild means that knowledge of their breeding habits and behavior is incomplete. However, we are able to present some interesting observations on page 167.

Blue-rumped Parrots

Blue-rumped Parrots *(Psittinus)* represent only a single species (see page 168). This bird has a stocky body and a short, rounded tail. The

Tiger Parrot Species and Subspecies

Species	Subspecies
Brehm's Parrot *Psittacella brehmii* (Schlegel 1873)	*P. b. brehmii* (Schlegel) *P. b. intermixta* (Hartert) *P. b. harterti* (Mayr) *P. b. pallida* (Mayr)
Painted Parrot *Psittacella picta* (Rothschild)	*P. p. picta* (Rothschild) *P. p. excelsa* (Mayr and Gilliard) *P. p. lorentzi* (van Oort)
Modest Parrot *Psittacella modesta* (Schlegel)	*P. m. modesta* (Schlegel) *P. m. collaris* (Ogilvie-Grant) *P. m. subcollaris* (Rand)
Madarasz' Parrot *Psittacella madaraszi* (Meyer)	*P. m. madaraszi* (Meyer) *P. m. huonensis* (Mayr and Rand) *P. m. hallstromi* (Mayr and Gilliard) *P. m. major* (Rothschild)

Blue-rumped Parrot Subspecies

Species	Subspecies
Blue-rumped Parrot *Psittinus cyanurus* (Forster 1795)	*P. c. cyanurus* (Forster) *P. c. pontius* (Oberholser) *P. c. abbotti* (Richmond)

large beak with notched upper mandible is a striking feature. The cere is naked. The male and female show sexual color dimorphism, and recently fledged young all resemble females for the first week or so but are recognizable by their green heads. The blue color of the forehead develops quickly in young males.

Tepui Parrots

Tepui Parrots *(Nannopsittaca)* also represent only one species (the Tepui Parrot, *N. panychlora*), which is never seen in aviculture; its habits in the wild are also poorly known. For the sake of completeness, I mention the species here. This parrot is closely related to the *Forpus, Touit,* and *Brotogeris* species. The tail is short and squarish, the beak is slender, and the cere naked. The sexes are similar in appearance. In his book *Parrots of the World* Forshaw states: "An undescribed parrotlet, thought to be a new species of *Nannopsittaca,* had been reported from eastern Peru, where flocks of up to twenty or more were observed feeding on *Coussapa* fruits and seeds of bam-

boos (*ICBP Parrotletter,* I: II, 1989). This species is said to be predominantly bright green, with a powder-blue forecrown, flesh-colored bill and feet, and a faint, pale eye ring; apparently there are no differences in the sexes."

Touit Parrots

The Touit Parrot *(Touit)* also has very colorful, extremely small members, of which only one is kept from time to time in captivity. This is the Lilac-tailed Parrotlet, *T. batavica,* from Venezuela, Guyana, Surinam (where I was able to make a close study of it), Trinidad, and Tobago. The body is plump in structure, and accented by a short, stubby tail. The beak is remarkably large in relation to the size of the bird, and quite narrow; the cere is naked. These parrotlets are sexually dimorphic, with the exception of the Lilac-tailed, or Seven-colored, Parrotlet and the Brown-backed Parrotlet, but the differences here are minimal.

Unfortunately we do not know a great deal about these birds; in most cases they live cryptically and are difficult to study.

Touit Parrot Species and Subspecies

Species	Subspecies
Seven-colored Parrotlet *Touit batavica* (Boddaert)	No subspecies recognized
Scarlet-shouldered Parrotlet *Touit huetii* (Temminck)	No subspecies recognized
Red-winged Parrotlet *Touit dilectissima* (Sclater and Salvin)	*T. d. dilectissima* (Sclater and Salvin) *T. d. costaricensis* (Cory)
Sapphire-rumped Parrotlet *Touit purpurata* (Gmelin)	*T. p. purpurata* (Gmelin) *T. p. viridiceps* (Chapman)
Brown-backed Parrotlet *Touit melanonota* (Wied)	No subspecies recognized
Golden-tailed Parrotlet *Touit surda* (Kuhl)	*T. s. surda* (Kuhl) *T. s. ruficauda* (Berla)
Spot-winged Parrotlet *Touit strictoptera* (Sclater)	No subspecies recognized

Small-billed Parrots

The Small-billed Parrots *(Brotogeris)* (see pages 174–181) are extremely charming, well-known birds, both in the wild and in an aviary or large cage. It is no wonder that some of them, especially the Gray-cheeked Parakeet, have become immensely popular.

The birds have long, pointed wings that cover about three quarters of the tail, which is wedge-shaped. Seven species live from southern Mexico to central South America.

Housing

During the breeding season, Small-billed Parrots are extremely hostile to other birds in the aviary, and certainly toward other members of their own species. Outside the breeding season, however, they pose no danger to breeding exotic birds and will, in general, do nothing to bother them; they behave in the same manner even when they are newly out of quarantine.

Observations have revealed that these parrots do not approach the busy tropical birds. A bird alone or with a mate should have a cage that measures at least 28 to 32 inches by 24 inches by 32 inches (70–80 cm long, 60 cm deep, 80 cm high). In their native country, these species are often kept as cage birds, and many are among the most popular birds in the United States and Europe. Unfortunately, they are hunted extensively, not only because of avicultural interest, but also because of the damage they do to banana plantations. It is not surprising, therefore, that these pleasant, lively birds will consider a small piece of banana a real treat.

Gray-cheeked Parakeets

Gray-cheeked Parakeets, among other species, build their nests in termite mounds and in tree hollows. They put down a layer of moist moss on which they lay four to six eggs (20 to 22 mm by 16 to 18 mm). The female incubates them while the male, perched on a nearby post, guards the nest.

A strange phenomenon associated with this species is that they gather in trees at certain times, just as, for example, starlings do when autumn approaches. When they congregate in trees, their constant chatter, especially around early evening, can be heard for miles. With a little patience, you can teach these birds to cry, laugh, and speak.

Breeding

To breed these interesting bird species, a large nest box 14 by 20 inches (35 × 50 cm) is needed; the entrance opening should be 3.2 inches (8 cm) in diameter. The bottom of the nest should be covered with a thick layer of peat moss or pine bedding at least 2.4 to 3.2 inches (6–8 cm) deep and hung as high as possible, facing north.

The Gray-cheeked Parakeet (Brotogeris pyrrhopterus) *makes a handsome pet.*

Diet

The menu for this genus should consist of a variety of fruits (cherries, apples, pears, bananas, bits of pineapple, soaked raisins and currants, oranges), corn, rice, oats, fresh willow buds, various grass seeds and other grains, soft food, small beetles (no dangerous insects or spiders), mealworms, and ant pupae.

Members of the *Brotogeris* genus often had their wings clipped before they were shipped from their native country. Frequently, clipped birds still arrive on the market, and these must be housed separately for some time and given extra nutrition in the form of rice, willow bark, fruits, berries, blossoms, a good commercial budgie-seed mixture, and vegetable matter.

Description

Initially the bird will be very timid and restless. When it has calmed

Small-billed Parrot Species and Subspecies

Species	Subspecies
Plain Parakeet *Brotogeris tirica* (Gmelin)	No subspecies recognized
White-winged Canary-winged Parakeet *Brotogeris versicolurus* (P. L. S. Müller)	*B. v. versicolurus* (P. L. S. Müller) *B. v. chiriri* (Vieillot) *B. v. behni* (Neumann)
Gray-cheeked Parakeet *Brotogeris pyrrhopterus* (Latham)	No subspecies recognized
Orange-chinned Parakeet *Brotogeris jugularis* (P. L. S. Müller)	*B. j. jugularis* (P. L. S. Müller) *B. j. exsul* (Todd)
Cobalt-winged Parakeet *Brotogeris cyanoptera* (Pelzeln)	*B. c. cyanoptera* (Pelzeln) *B. c. gustavi* (Berlepsch) *B. c. beniensis* (Gyldenstolpe)
Golden-winged Parakeet *Brotogeris chrysopterus* (Linnaeus)	*B. c. chrysopterus* (Linnaeus) *B. c. tuipara* (Gmelin) *B. c. chrysosema* (Sclater) *B. c. solimoensis* (Gyldenstolpe) *B. c. tenuifrons* (Friedmann)
Tui Parakeet *Brotogeris sanctithomae* (P. L. S. Müller)	*B. s. sanctithomae* (P. L. S. Müller) *B. s. takatsukasae* (Neumann)

The Orange-chinned or Tovi Parakeet (Brotogeris jugularis) *is also known as the Bee-Bee parakeet, and certainly a well-loved companion with a devoted attitude. The voice is not loud or unpleasant.*

down, and its wings have grown back to proper length, you may introduce it to the aviary.

In spite of their deafening calls, especially when they are not completely used to their surroundings and keeper, these primarily green birds are very popular with fanciers. They all have narrow tails and long, pointed wings that cover the tail. Most of the species like a good bath, and you can give them much pleasure by regularly spraying them lightly with a garden hose. All birds in this genus sleep in a nest box, even outside the breeding season. Since most species rarely come to the ground, you should place their food and water on a platform or shelf at least 5 feet (1.5 m) from the floor.

Thick-billed Parrots

The small, charming Thick-billed Parrots *(Bolborhynchus)* have wedged, long or short pointed tails and thick, stubby beaks, from which their scientific name arises. They are extremely popular in their native lands and in aviculture the world over (see also pages 182–188). They are friendly and peaceful aviary inmates that are not averse to a snow bath—not surprising in view of their natural habitat 8,200 feet (2,500 m) up in the Andes.

The birds nest in earth tunnels about 6.5 feet (2 m) deep with a chamber or two at the end, about 10 inches (25 cm) in diameter. The eggs are laid and incubated in one of these chambers. The Lineolated Parrot is an exception in that it does not burrow but raises its family in a hollow tree limb. Unfortunately, we know little about the behavior of these small hookbills.

It is important that you acquire a true pair. Although the sexes are very similar, surgical sex determination is not recommended. Research has shown that these birds are very sensitive to this procedure, especially *B. orbygnesius* and *B. aymara*. Some species, such as the Lineolated

The Gray-cheeked Parakeet (Brotogeris pyrrhopterus) *was first bred in England by W. Lewis in 1925, and in the U.S. by A. R. Hood ten years later.*

Parakeet and the Barred Parakeet, show a slight dimorphism. The wing, body, and tail feathers of the hen have narrower edges and the back has less black than the male's, or no black at all.

The best way to acquire true pairs is to place a group of the birds together in an aviary and allow them to pair off. Members of this genus usually get along well with their own and related species, so you can do this without much risk.

Breeding

For most species, good breeding results are achieved in nest boxes with a height of 12 inches (30 cm) and a floor area of 8 by 9 inches (20 × 22.5 cm). These boxes are

The female Mountain Parakeet (Bolborhynchus aurifrons) is mainly green with a yellowish green underside.

divided into two parts with a false floor about 6 inches (15 cm) high. The lower chamber can be reached by the birds through an opening 2.75 inches (6 cm) wide in one of the back corners of the false floor. This chamber can be used by the birds as a nursery. A perch 2 inches (5 cm) in diameter and 10 to 18 inches (25–45 cm) long is affixed just below the entrance hole to the upper chamber. Depending upon its width, the perch may be partly or wholly pushed through the back wall of the upper chamber and affixed there so that it cannot move. Place a strip of mesh or affix a few thin nails or large staples on the back wall above and below the opening in the false floor to help the birds enter and leave. I recommend installing a little inspec-

Thick-billed Parrot Species and Subspecies

Species	Subspecies
Sierra Parrot *Bolborhynchus aymara* (d'Orbigny)	No subspecies recognized
Mountain Parakeet *Bolborhynchus aurifrons* (Lesson)	*B. a. aurifrons* (Lesson) *B. a. robertsi* (Carriker) *B. a. margaritae* (Berlioz and Dorst) *B. a. rubrirostris* (Burmeister)
Lineolated Parakeet *Bolborhynchus lineola* (Cassin)	*B. l. lineola* (Cassin) *B. l. tigrinus* (Souancé)
Andean Parakeet *Bolborhynchus orbygnesius* (Souancé)	No subspecies recognized
Rufous-fronted Parrot *Bolborhynchus ferrugineifrons* (Lawrence)	No subspecies recognized

tion door in one of the side panels of the lower chamber. Use a mixture of sawdust, washed aquarium sand, and pine bedding as floor covering.

It is difficult to be precise about the breeding season for birds in this genus. I have had broods in April through July but, occasionally, also in November, December, and January. It is best, however, to encourage the birds to breed from the middle of April to June. This minimizes egg binding, with the aid of a good diet and a proper room temperature (55 to 70°F, [13–21°C]), of course.

Only *B. aurifrons* seems to have a particular courtship procedure; most other species just puff out the neck feathers. Males of the Mountain or Golden-fronted Parakeets show their interest in a partner by increased gnawing on twigs and perches, mutual feeding, and seeking out nest boxes—at least two per pair should be provided—affixed at varying heights and different walls of the aviary and shelter.

Although I have seen copulation take place on the nest box or perch several times—with *B. aurifrons,* even three times on the floor—one can assume that pairing takes place mainly in the nest box. Both birds spend a few days in the nest before the first egg is laid. They sit quietly, gnawing occasionally at the inner walls. They are very sensitive to disturbance at this time but become more tolerant after the clutch is completed. Once the birds start incubating, they are quiet and stop gnawing at the inside of the nest box.

A pair of wild (or normal colored) Lineolated parakeets (Bolborhynchus lineola). Newly hatched young have some white down. They should be close-banded when approximately 12 days old.

The female can sometimes lay an extraordinarily large clutch, but the average is four to five eggs; incubation starts after the second or third egg is laid. The young hatch in 20 to 23 days and leave the nest six to seven weeks later, sometimes a little longer if the weather is cold.

Hens suffering with egg binding can, in my experience, rarely be saved. Do not allow hens under 14 months to mate, because there is the danger of egg binding in these young birds.

Diet

I have found little information in the literature about the correct rearing food. I give my birds whole meal bread soaked in water and squeezed out, plus a daily dish of commercial soft food. Of course, they also get their seed mixture, a ration of budgerigar pellets, and fresh greens and fruits.

Monk or Quaker Parakeets (Myiopsitta monachus) can be very prolific, especially when housed in a spacious aviary. They often construct a large communal nest in a tree or on a heap of brushwood placed on a wooden or wire foundation, using supplied branches, twigs, and other building materials. The birds, however, will utilize sturdy nesting boxes as well.

The Quaker or Monk Parakeet (Myiopsitta monachus) is ready for breeding at one year of age. The blue and yellow mutations are really beautiful but rather high in price.

Quaker or Monk Parakeets

Finally, a few remarks about the monotypic genus *Myiopsitta,* which contains the well-known Quaker or Monk Parakeet. On pages 188–190 we will discuss this perhaps best-known South American Parakeet, which, at the present time, is surviving ferally in various parts of the United States and Europe. This parakeet is extremely interesting in that it constructs rather crude, loosely woven nests. For nesting materials, they use branches and twigs. In the wild, they make their nests in trees, and in the aviary you generally do not need to supply them with nest boxes. They are very attractive when kept in a roomy aviary, or as a pet in the house.

The mainly green plumage of this parrot is set off with a gray breast, cheeks, and forehead. The robust beak is broad, with a rather rounded tip to the upper mandible. The notch in the upper mandible is very distinct; the cere is feathered. Both male and female are alike in color, and even the newly fledged young are difficult to distinguish from the adults.

Monk Parakeet Subspecies

Species	Subspecies
Monk Parakeet *Myiopsitta monachus* (Boddaert)	*M. m. monachus* (Boddaert) *M. m. calita* (Jardine and Selby) *M. m. cotora* (Vieillot) *M. m. luchsi* (Finsch)

Chapter Two
Building and Equipping the Aviary

All parrotlets and miniature par-rots, especially breeding pairs, should be kept in aviaries, although large breeding cages (see page 36) are usually quickly accepted. Experience has proven, however, that all small parrots don't enjoy small compartments; chances are they will attack, kill, or inflict serious injuries on each other. I suggest, therefore, that you use indoor and outdoor flights (aviaries) where possible. Compared with their colleagues in breeding cages, aviary dwellers are in much better physical condition, and the hens are more productive and willing to breed.

It is advisable to place only one pair of the same species in a flight or aviary. Parrotlets, for example, are rather aggressive to their own kind, so if you own more than one pair of the same species, install double wiring between the flights with a space of at least 1.5 inches (3.8 cm). Be sure that the wire stays taut so that the parrotlets cannot reach each other and injure each others' toes and feet. As an alternative, you can erect hard plastic sheets or a wooden partition so that the birds can't see each other.

Parrotlets, and most other minia-ture parrots, can be kept with other *larger* bird species, however, but it is very possible that in the breeding season most of them will become rather aggressive in a mixed bird collection. Rosemary Low states: ". . . I have known them to turn a pair of Cockatiels out of a nest box which would have been ten times too large for the parrotlets."

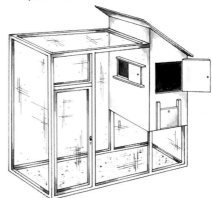

Parrotlets are rather aggressive to their own kind. It is therefore advisable to place only one pair of the same species in an aviary or cage.

The Garden Aviary

Let us first look at a garden aviary, which should consist of both an outer and inner area, respectively called an open flight or run and a closed night shelter.

Location of the Flight

Obviously, a scenic spot with plants, bushes, flowers, and the like, which can be seen from the house, would be ideal. The front of the aviary should, preferably, face south. If this is not possible, then the front should face as close to south as practicable, choosing southeast rather than southwest. Even if the front of the aviary faces south, part of it should still be made of reinforced glass, or sturdy transparent plastic sheets; however, do not use thin plate glass or something similar, for obvious reasons, such as the possibility of breakage. Never use reflective glass as birds like their reflection and have been known to fall in love with their own image. This plays havoc with young breeders.

Breeding aviaries.

Remember that the aviary should be safeguarded against the detrimental effects of the elements, but should be open enough to utilize the beneficial aspects of the environment.

Materials

It is not advisable to use wood exclusively in the building of an aviary that is meant for parrotlets and other miniature parrots; since most varieties are known to gnaw, quite a lot of damage would take place before very long. The foundation should be made of concrete. The frame for the sides of the aviary itself should preferably be made of metal, but it can also be made of wood, provided, of course, that this is made gnaw-proof by covering it with metal sheeting. A brick wall, about 12 to 18 inches (30–46 cm) high should be built on the foundation, upon which the floor is constructed. Concrete would be preferable for the floor, but you can also use creosote-soaked railroad ties. Even ceramic tiles would be useful; they keep rodents out of the aviary and are easily kept clean. Plywood sheets, shingles, or similar materials are the best choice for the walls and divisions inside the aviary, since they will be unaffected by any attempt at gnawing.

The roof can also be made of see-through plastic, and if the shelter has proper, light-emitting windows, a tiled roof is very attractive. The roof should have sufficient slope to allow the runoff of rain and such. If the aviary is built against an existing solid fence or wall, the roof should extend a little way over this structure to prevent rain from accumulating where the fence/wall meets the roof. A strip of asphalt paper can help prevent water problems. Adding a little gutter would certainly be practical, if not entirely necessary.

Other materials needed are good-quality fine wire netting or mesh (use 19G, with a mesh size of 1 by one-half-inch [25 × 12.5 mm]), nails, and glass. For a half-covered flight area, wired glass, shatterproof glass, or plastic is the ideal choice.

Shape and Size

Since it is advisable to keep just one pair, the aviary need not be especially large. The size of a chicken coop is determined by the number of chickens you plan to keep, but with an aviary for parrotlets or miniature parrots, it is the other way around: First determine how large you should make the aviary according to available space and location, and then see how many birds you can keep. If plenty of space is available, you can consider various uniform small aviaries.

The flight should be reasonably longer than the night shelter to provide the birds with adequate exercise space. An average guide is to make the flight four fifths of the entire length of the aviary, although this measurement can be adapted to particular special restrictions.

As far as the shape of the aviary is concerned, we would suggest that following straight lines to match

The Sierra Parakeet (Bolborhynchus aymara), *also called Aymara Parakeet, lives in wooded hills and ravines, sometimes to the altiplano. I have often seen them sitting atop or "inside" low berry bushes and fruit trees.*

those of the aviary's environment will probably be the most suitable. Adding various adornments such as steeples, towers, and so on, often makes an aviary look strange. The aviary will look best when it blends in with its environment by being situated among bushes, shrubs, and flowers that enhance its appearance. Be sure not to make an aviary too low; the height of the front should be about 6 to 8 feet (1.8–2.4 m).

Layout

In general, aviaries consist of three sections; the uncovered flight or run, the covered flight, and the

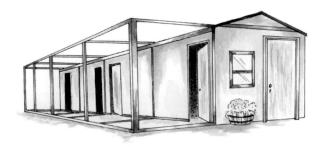

An outdoor aviary with four flights and shelters.

shelter. If the covered part of the flight is open only at the sides, the nest boxes could be hung at the back, thus leaving out the shelter altogether; this may be necessary for reasons of expense or space limitations. The nest boxes require a sprinkling with water every other day during extended dry spells.

Even a freestanding aviary—one that has not been built against an existing fence or garage, for example—can be built without a shelter, by using the nest boxes as such and hanging them out of view in the back, where only the birdkeeper would have easy access to them.

Modern garden aviaries.

This type of aviary has much to recommend it, as it basically consists of two sections, an open and a covered flight, with the nest boxes doubling as night shelters.

The Open Section

Most of the species we deal with in this work cannot spend really cold winters in the unprotected outer area of the aviary. It is, therefore, necessary either to provide the birds with nest boxes or to have a shelter that can be warmed by means of a heat lamp or other mechanism.

In order to give the birds a feeling of freedom, harden them up a little, and maintain their colors, you should give them access to the completely open section of the aviary. As already noted, this is built mostly of wire netting and metal tubing or wooden beams reinforced with metal strips. Without some reinforcement, there would soon be little left of the aviary. If metal strips and the like are not readily available, you can use fine wire mesh or netting for the protection of the woodwork and of any trunks of trees that grow in your aviary.

The Covered Section

This part of the aviary has a watertight roof and perhaps a solid wall made from plywood or tongue-and-groove boards that separates it from the shelter; the remainder of this section consists of wire netting. The floor can be fashioned of earth covered with a 2-inch (5.1-cm) layer of river sand, although cement slabs covered with sand would be preferable. If you use concrete or cement slabs, the shrubbery, of course, will have to be in plant tubs or such. Adding fresh willow twigs every day would be much appreciated by the birds.

Naturally, this section must be fitted with several perches. The most common size is approximately ½ inch (13 mm) in diameter, but it is advisable to vary the size somewhat to allow the birds to pick a perch that is most comfortable for them. They may also like to change their choice from time to time in order for their feet to have a slightly different position, as it becomes tiresome for birds to sit on the same size perch for extended periods of time. More than likely these perches—which should be flat on the top, and are available from any pet shop—will have to be replaced occasionally, again due, of course, to the birds' enormous urge to gnaw.

Making use of wired glass will prevent the birds from doing damage to themselves, as they are unable to see ordinary glass and will fly headfirst into it. Plexiglass can also be used, and is certainly less dangerous than glass if a bird should hit it. It is not advisable to hang nest boxes in the covered section. Hang them either in the open section, or on the back wall where they can be kept wet without disturbing the birds too much.

The Shelter

We strongly recommend that the entrance to the shelter have an outer and inner door to prevent birds escaping when you enter. You open the outer door, enter a small area, and close it before opening the inner door. These doors can be made with wire netting.

The shelter is divided into two parts by means of a shelf-type false floor. The top half is the actual night shelter, while the bottom half is split, vertically, into two parts. One of these is used as the mating room, quarantine station, "punishment" room for troublemakers, observation room, and so on, while the other part is for the storage of spare nest boxes, perches, and containers.

The floors of both these bottom halves should preferably be made from thick plywood, concrete, or tiles; the floor of the actual night shelter should also be made of concrete, but covered with a 2- to 3-inch (5.1–7.6-cm) layer of clean river sand. The sides of the night shelter are made of wire netting, as are those of the inner aviary.

An outdoor aviary consisting of eight single-pair flights: an excellent setup for breeding various parrotlet species, color mutations, or other dwarf parrots.

A properly planned shelter includes provisions for adequate ventilation. This usually involves installation of an inlet, placed low and protected against mice, and an outlet on the opposite wall near the eaves.

Miscellaneous Considerations

Just a few more remarks about aviary building:

• When laying or pouring the foundation, be sure to bury the wire in the earth as this will help to deter rats and mice. Use wire also when pouring the concrete in order to prevent cracks.

• Make sure the roof is built on a slant and extends to all sides.

• Use double wire in making partitions.

• The boards or plywood can be painted with carbolic acid in green

Modern Forpus-breeding facilities. Note the skylight and air ventilator.

or black, but of course everything must be completely dry before introducing birds into the aviary. Whitewashing the interior is a waste of time, and dangerous besides, since most of the whitewashes contain some poisonous elements that would be hazardous to your birds, considering the hookbills' insatiable urge to gnaw.

• An additional convenience is electric lighting, both inside and outside the aviary. When you must perform necessary chores on gloomy days or very early in the morning, electric lighting is almost indispensable to the bird fancier. It is possible to place a powerful light at such a height as to illuminate an entire group of pens from the top. In this way, you can observe the intrusion of any nocturnal creatures and easily dispose of them. Electric bulbs within the aviary should always be wrapped with some form of wire screen—various models are commercially available—so that the birds will not come into direct contact with them.

• If the birds are ever in full artificial light when it is dark outside, it is necessary to include a dimmer in the circuit. A sudden switch from full light to complete darkness can send birds into such panic that it is quite possible they may seriously injure themselves.

• Finally, keep in mind that you should keep a certain amount of extra equipment on hand, because there will be some breakage of materials and these should be immediately replaced.

The Bird Room

Not all miniature parrots can remain in a garden aviary year round; Parrotlets and Fig Parrots, for example, should stay indoors during late fall, winter, and early spring. Only outdoor aviaries with large heated shelters are obvious exceptions. Remember that none of the parrotlets and miniature parrots can be kept in temperatures below 50°F (10°C) and, during the breeding season, when long periods of the day and night are spent in the nest box, below 59°F (15°C).

The bird room is really nothing more than an aviary constructed indoors, such as in an attic room, basement, or any other available space in the house. Construction consists merely of fitting wire screens over the windows, protecting the windowsills with metal strips, and making a little "foyer" by means of an extra wired door to prevent escapes. Four or five mated *Brotogeris* species, for example, can breed here, although dividing the available space into smaller compartments so that each pair has its own lodging would be better.

The Inside Aviary

The indoor or inside aviary can best be described as a small aviary—minimum 6 feet (2 m) long and high and 4 feet (1.25 m) wide—placed in some room of the house or in an attic, around which are usually grouped arrangements of plants and in which are placed young birds, a breeding pair, or, outside the breeding season, various couples. The latter group may give you some trouble; culprits should be taken out of the group. The setup is the same as in an outside aviary.

Many people confuse an indoor aviary with a bird room. A bird room, however, is always an entire room set up only to house birds, for example a mixed pair collection, not used for anything else besides breeding per pair. The indoor aviary, on the other hand, is an aviary placed in a room where there is other activity.

The indoor aviary is currently very popular; there are even a few manufacturers who supply ready-made models, and these certainly meet the necessary requirements. I have seen and worked with indoor aviaries that were truly beautiful and in which successful breeding results were regularly achieved. The bird population seemed to be unconcerned by the children playing nearby on the floor.

Any type of aviary or bird room should always be supplied with plenty of fresh air, or the birds will become quite listless. Also, if the heated air does not have enough humidity, the feathers of the birds can lose their luster, becoming dry and brittle. You can easily supply sufficient humidity merely by letting a pan of boiling water evaporate in some obscure part of the aviary where it will not be disturbed. Since this old-fashioned method presents dangerous aspects, however, I would point out that today various safe humidifiers are commercially available.

Shrubbery

The main requirements for the health of our birds are air and light. The aviary should be as open and airy as possible, without creating crossdrafts, while the sun should be allowed to shine in freely. Ideal plants and bushes for the aviary are, among others, cedar, common privet, which is a favorite treat for cockatiels and various *Brotogeris* species, spirea, snowberry, pine and fir species, weeping willow, tamarack, mahogany, and hazel.

For the covered area we suggest placing a few dead trees with attractive branch formations; in the uncovered area, small trees and bushes are useful, but hardy plants are preferable. Each year you should make an inspection of the existing shrubbery so that you can make any necessary changes and additions. You may ask yourself why you should not provide dead trees, and compensate by giving the birds lots of greens. There is indeed a good reason for this. The shrubbery provides shade as well as edible greens, both of which are necessary to ensure the health of our birds.

Bathing Facilities

Every aviary should be equipped with flat ceramic or heavy plastic saucers to allow the birds to bathe. On colder days, of course, remove these dishes. Make sure that your birds are dry before they retire for the night; they should not have the opportunity to bathe after 4:00 or 5:00 P.M. You could also put a garden sprinkler to good use, as many birds prefer a gentle shower to a tub bath. Ponds with rocks and running water are obviously ideal, but, unfortunately, not something that everyone can afford. Perches, of course, should not be situated above any of these bathing or drinking facilities. The water in the saucers should be changed frequently, at least three times a day.

Water and Seed Dishes

Directions in the feeding chapter (see page 63) pertain to both the fancier who keeps one pair in a cage and the birdkeeper who maintains several aviaries. However, one must realize that a bird living in an aviary has a great deal more room for flying and, therefore, gets a lot more exercise. Consequently, seeds containing fat, such as hemp, small sunflower, linseed, maw, rape, and peanut can be given in greater quantities. Use indestructible seed containers that are easily cleaned, and made so that the birds cannot sit or walk on the seeds. Wooden feeders, of course, would soon be reduced to splinters. Local pet stores can advise you on feeders that are on the market. Saucers made of hard plastic, glass, ceramic, and so on are suitable as well and are most often used both for seed, pellets, and greens, and for water.

The most practical feeders are the boxlike hoppers with glass fronts called self-feeders. These hoppers usually hold enough seed for a number of days. They are often divided into a few narrow compartments in which each kind of seed is given separately, enabling the birds to make their own mixture to suit their needs. Around the bottom of these feeders a detachable tray extends that is designed to catch seeds thrown aside by the birds.

Maintenance
• You must regularly replace the sand sprinkled on the aviary floor.
• You need to turn over the actual soil on a regular basis, the frequency depending on the size of the aviary and the number of inhabitants.
• At least once every spring, you should clean and disinfect all perches
• You must prune all shrubbery and other natural perches whenever necessary, and remove any rotten or dying pieces from the aviary.
• Hose off all woodwork and metal in the aviary, and replace any dead plants.

If at all possible, house your birds in flight cages temporarily during cleaning operations. This gives you the opportunity to thoroughly clean both the interior and exterior and repair any leaks, drafts, faults in the wire, locks (and buy the best lock you can afford because, unfortunately, bird theft is on the rise), or whatever, and bring everything back into top form. Should you decide to winter your birds indoors—and the majority of birds in this book have to spend the cold months indoors—

The Blue-crowned Hanging Parrot (Loriculus galgalus) sleeps hanging upside down like a bat. Never allow this bird to roost in an unprotected outdoor aviary as Hanging Parrots suspended from the roof mesh will attract birds of prey and other predators.

this would be the ideal time to check and repair everything at your leisure. By repeating this procedure each year, it is most unlikely that you will be surprised by a great many problems at any one time. During the winter, when there is no breeding activity anyway, be sure to do a thorough cleaning job on the nest boxes, because these, in particular, are favorite breeding grounds for bacteria and so on, so disease could easily develop a stronghold here. Besides these nest boxes, don't overlook feed hoppers, water dishes, fountains, and birdbaths. You should place the feed and water hoppers in such a way that you have easy access to them without disturbing your birds too much. During the breeding season, in particular, it is desirable to give birds as much peace and quiet as possible so that they can care for their eggs or young virtually undisturbed.

Keep your aviary as clean as you can—both you and your birds will benefit.

Cages

Parrotlets and other dwarf parrots can indeed be housed quite effectively in ordinary living room bird cages, which are available in any pet store. These cages are ideal when keeping these birds as pets, and indeed, these little parrots are extremely pleasant and easy to keep in one's living room or den—and it is very difficult, even for a landlord, to object to their charming chatter. I myself find their vocalization rather amusing; they chatter quite amicably.

When kept in pairs these birds are quite loving to one another. Get the

A simple, roomy, rectangular cage with horizontal bars for parrotlets and similar parrots which can be cleaned easily. The entry to the cage should give easy access to the interior.

biggest possible cage—with close-set bars, so the bird's head doesn't get stuck in between them—to give the birds the maximum freedom of movement: 23.5 by 12 by 16 inches (60 × 30 × 40 cm) and up. The wire must run horizontally so that the birds can climb around it if they like to.

Put a fresh twig from a willow or fruit tree (not cherry) into the cage for the birds to nibble on. This will keep the birds occupied and less inclined to pull out each other's feathers from sheer boredom. Also, supply some toys, made of wood or natural rope such as hemp rope, for example. Don't use round cages—birds get rather nervous in them—and wooden, old-fashioned painted or copper cages. Most paints used for these ornamental cages contain lead, which is deadly for the birds.

Perches

Most commercial cages for pet birds come with a set of perches, hopefully made of hardwood, preferably beech. Softwood can't withstand the gnawing of the birds for any length of time.

• Get perches that are round, but flattened slightly on top, with a diameter of approximately 1 inch (2.5 cm). They should not be too slick; otherwise, birds will have to expend too much effort to stay in place, especially while sleeping.

• Don't supply perches of only one size; some variety is excellent for the foot and toe muscles; therefore, I strongly recommend hardwood manzanita.

• Position perches so that the birds can't foul each other.

• Protect food and water dishes from droppings deposited by perching birds and install perches far enough from the walls to keep birds from damaging their tails.

• Don't put perches so high that the dwarf parrots would have to sit with their heads bent to clear the ceiling.

• Swings are all right in an ornate cage, as well as other toys such as bells, ladders, or unbreakable stainless steel mirrors; however, never clutter the cage unnecessarily with toys. None of these belongs in a breeding cage.

• Don't install too many perches. They decrease the flight space unnecessarily and, if you need to catch a bird, a forest of perches and toys makes the job much harder.

• I recommend removable perches. They are easier to clean, and you can take them out before you try to catch the birds, making the job simpler and quicker. The best arrangement is a so-called *rack,* especially for large cages or aviaries. Birds like racks because they love to congregate if you have a large cage with three or more (never two) couples. You will like them, too, because most of the birds will be on the rack at most times, simplifying the task of determining how things are going for them.

• Parrotlets and other dwarf parrots like to climb. Giving them a ladder minimizes their climbing on the wire mesh walls, which is bad for their tail feathers.

An Ionizer

Ionizers are instruments that purify the air by removing dust particles and other airborne debris as well as viruses and feather dust. In a birdroom, living room, or den where there are several bird cages or indoor aviaries, an ionizer is almost a must. Place it high up and in an unobstructed position. Don't worry, an ionizer is silent when in use and can be plugged into any indoor outlet.

You may remember that high-energy electrons produce negative ions. The high-energy electrons produced at the needle tip of the ionizer collide with molecules in the air and change them into negative ions that shoot out into the birdroom. Dust particles, viruses, and so on, bombarded with these ions, become negative and precipitate out on the earthen surfaces, thus reducing the level of dust in the atmosphere; in other words, the ionizer causes dust and other matter to precipitate out from the air by putting a minute electrical charge on the particles. This may sound rather dangerous, but ionizers are absolutely safe to use.

• In a large cage (or aviary), install one or more solid branches from hardwood trees, especially willow, and fruit trees, except cherry. In an inside aviary or cage, renew branches regularly because they soon get quite unattractive from accumulated droppings. This problem is somewhat

The subspecies male of the Mexican Parrotlet (Forpus cyanopygius insularis) comes from the Tres Marías Islands. The bird is darker (even his bill) and somewhat larger than the nominate form; the upperparts are grayer. The male also has darker turquoise markings than F. c. cyanopygius.

Detail back/wing of the subspecies Forpus cyanopygius insularis.

avoided in outside aviaries because rain helps keep the branches clean. And remember, the plastic perches now often incorporated into various cage models are unsuitable for birds; they should be replaced immediately with different doweling and natural branches.

Breeding Cages

Parrotlets and dwarf parrots can adapt to virtually any type of large cage. They will live happily and even breed in a box, or breeding cage, or in a roomy aviary, inside or outdoors. This is indeed another advantage to delight the fancier and breeder.

Naturally, a proper cage will encourage better breeding results and superior birds. It is therefore wise to select, furnish, and locate a cage properly.

There is only one way to be sure about the parentage of birds—to breed a single pair in a single cage. And since parrotlets and most dwarf parrots like it this way—one to one cage—we should leave it at that.

Location: A cage may not be moist or damp, or put in a moist or damp place. It should be protected from drafts, birds' most dangerous enemy. Outdoors, don't place it on the north side. Don't set it up like a hothouse with too much glass.

Select a quiet location. Birds can accustom themselves to noise, and a parrotlet or dwarf parrot that is used to noise won't be easily upset; however, breeding results are better if you don't set up the cage in the midst of heavy household traffic.

Size: Use a cage with some depth to it; birds feel less cramped when people don't face them nose to beak. Cages should have a greater length than height. Some people with limited space think they can make up in height what they don't furnish in floor space. They are wrong. The natural flight pattern of a bird is horizontal, not vertical. Cages should not be too low, of course, but a long cage or aviary is always preferable to a tall model.

A proper breeding cage for a pair of parrotlets or dwarf parrots is at least 49 inches long, 16 inches wide, and 18 inches high (125 × 40 × 45 cm). These dimensions are not absolute. Bigger, without overdoing it, is better; smaller is possible. After all, there are breeders who breed parrots in a large ornamental cage.

Nest Boxes: Attach nest boxes, when possible, to the outside of the breeding cage. This will preserve the maximum amount of flight space and will permit easy inspection. If you are placing several breeding cages on or next to each other so that there is a common wall between two cages, attach the nest boxes at the front. It's best to have a few extra breeding cages in reserve; then, when a cage needs a thorough cleaning, or you have a chance to buy new birds, you can put them in the extra cages.

Materials: It is possible to build cages yourself; the box, except for the front, of course, should be made out of the best-quality plywood or hardboard on a frame of slats. The

A 1-day-old Celestial Parrotlet (Forpus coelestis). The species was first bred by famous French ornithologist/aviculturist Dr. Jean Delacour in 1958.

bottom should be a tray, made of zinc or hardboard. Cover the bottom with a layer of sharp river sand on top of newspaper or grocery bags. Replace paper and sand regularly, at least twice a week. Cover the front of the breeding cage with wire mesh or mesh fronts. Cage fronts are available commercially in various sizes, ready to install.

Breeding cages for Forpus and other dwarf parrot species.

Chapter Three
Choosing Your Bird

The purchase of a bird requires careful planning; a sensible choice is an important factor in the ultimate enjoyment of the bird. Don't buy a bird that happens to be at the breeder's and catches your fancy without first having thought about its needs and your own goals.

The Healthy Bird

Purchasing birds satisfactorily always was and remains a matter of experience. It is wise to have a look at the stocks of several bird dealers and breeders before making a decision. You should not buy birds that sit with fluffed up feathers because

Before purchasing, make sure the birds are healthy (Forpus coelestis).

this is often an indication that they are not healthy. Always observe birds initially from a distance because, if you get too near to the cage or aviary, they will fly about excitedly. If a bird is healthy, its feathers should lie flush and rather tightly to its body. It should look around observantly and react to the behavior of other birds. All in all, it should make a fresh and lively impression. If you approach it closely, it should try to escape, with the exception of tame birds that usually come to the mesh to see what is going on. If a bird remains still, without looking at you, it is a sign of illness rather than tameness. An active bird, once it gets used to surroundings and care, will eventually become tame.

Checking the Bird's Condition

Before you decide on your purchase, take the bird in your hands. If you do not feel confident enough at first—especially since most hookbills like to bite as their first defense—ask the bird dealer to handle it for you, or protect your hand by wearing a glove. In any case, check its condition. To do this properly, hold the bird in such a way that its back lies in your hand, and use your thumb and index finger to check its breast. If the breastbone sticks out sharply, the bird is too thin and its muscular system inefficient. It would not be a good bird to buy.

A healthy bird has well-developed muscles on both sides of its sternum and only a small edge of the sternum can be felt. Check whether feathers around the vent are dirty because this is often a sign of intestinal upset, with a watery stool as a result, which is difficult to cure without veterinary assistance. If you find this, do not proceed further with the purchase of this or any other bird from that breeding establishment; however, note that if you take a newly imported and untamed bird into your hands, it may pass a watery secretion out of fright. This is a normal reaction and has nothing to do with diarrhea or intestinal problems. Once the bird is used to its new environment, it will become lively. Don't worry if the bird has one or several feathers missing, for example, on its wings or tail. Flying around in cages that often are too small and being frequently handled can impair the plumage, but, with good care, it will recover in the next molt.

When purchasing hookbills, make sure they don't have any bald patches. If they do, you can be almost certain they are feather pickers (pluckers), a habit that is very difficult to eradicate and, in some cases, is even hereditary. It is also

The Celestial or Pacific Parrotlet (Forpus coelestis) *is the most widely available parrotlet in the pet trade. This species should not be kept with other parrotlets, however, as they can be rather aggressive.*

possible that you are dealing with beak and feather disease syndrome, in which case an avian veterinarian should be immediately notified.

Birds should have glossy plumage, clear eyes, healthy feet with claws that are not too long, and a well-formed, well-closing beak. The head should not appear thin. Watch out for nose discharge, coughing and sneezing, shortness of breath, and white crusts on the bill.

The First Few Days

Your new acquisition should be placed in quarantine in a spacious cage for three weeks, in a place that

*In captivity a pair of Sierra or Aymare Parakeets (**Bolborhynchus aymara**) likes to use a nesting box of about 10 by 10 inches (25 × 25 cm), and 1 foot (31 cm) deep.*

has sufficient light but no drafts. Offer the same food as the bird dealer/breeder and supplement this with other food that is suitable for the bird. It is, therefore, essential

Bites

You should be aware of the fact that untamed parrotlets and dwarf parrots are capable of giving painful bites with their powerful, sharp little beaks. This can sometimes happen quite suddenly, when you're least expecting it, but birds don't bite merely for the fun of it; there must be a reason. Always treat your birds quietly and gently and you will discover that, after a short time, they will become tame and trusting, and you will experience a great deal of pleasure in caring for them.

that you know right from the start which food is needed by which bird.

Food and Excreta

A bird cannot be without food for more than 24 hours; therefore, buy only birds that you can get to their final destination within a few hours. The shorter the journey, the better for the bird. If you cannot accommodate your new arrival before evening, leave the lights on for a few hours to give the bird the opportunity to eat and drink. Do not leave the bird in the dark. Give it enough light to adjust to its surroundings; otherwise, it might flutter about restlessly and bump into obstacles, sometimes resulting in very serious injuries.

Food, such as seeds and commercial egg food, should be sprinkled over the cage floor as well as being placed in feeding containers. Many birds will not be used to feeding and drinking from dishes and cups because they are not familiar with them, and will, therefore, instinctively search for food and water on the floor. It is not uncommon for birds to die of hunger because there is no food strewn on the floor, even though the necessary supplies were right in front of their beaks in pots or cups.

Examine the excreta carefully for the first two or three days and let your avian veterinarian examine the stool. The stool must not be too watery. If it is, it is advisable to house the bird in warmer surroundings with a temperature of 86 to 95°F (30–35°C). Contact your avian veterinarian and, in the meantime, give the bird stale wheat bread, soaked in water, with a few drops of an avian vitamin/mineral supplement. Once the bird looks completely healthy again, it can be returned to a more spacious cage, preferably on a sunny and warm morning when it has a chance of familiarizing itself with its new environment and finding food and water.

Responsibilities of Owning a Bird

Owning a bird means a commitment of many years; therefore, consider the following:
• Do we really have time and money for the bird?
• Do we have adequate room for the bird?
• What about its adaptability to the family?
• Do we recognize the positive and negative characteristics of the bird?

A pair of Gray-cheeked Parakeets (Brotogeris pyrrhopterus). *Their flight call is rather shrill and noisy but not unpleasant, and sounds like "stleeeet, stleeeet, stleeeet."*

• Is the bird the ideal pet for our children? What about other pets?
• Do we take a lot of vacations and days off?

The Responsibility of Every Breeder

As long as young, *fledged* parrotlets continue to make begging calls, it is probable that they are still being fed at intervals. If the parents start making obvious moves to nest again, the chicks must be removed in case the father bird should suddenly turn on his sons—this can happen especially in those *Forpus* species with conspicuous blue patches in their plumage, such as the Pacific Parrotlet. Young hens, however, are seldom attacked by their father. For more details see page 77.

Chapter Four

Feeding

Food Requirements

The food requirements of a bird are determined by its physiological condition, its degree of activity, and the demands of the habitat. The most important phenomenon is the requirement for energy that is supplied by the diet. Energy is essential for a bird to be active and to maintain its body temperature at an acceptable level when environmental temperatures are low. Should the body temperature of the bird become too high or too low, its resistance to disease will be reduced and it will be more susceptible to diseases.

Hunger and satisfaction are totally different aspects of feeding requirements; indeed, some foods can satisfy the bird's hunger, but without proper nutrition it could starve to death within 24 hours.

The physiological demands on birds and their resulting dietary requirements are influenced by growth, breeding, rearing young, molting, and the usual stresses of life.

Nonbreeding Birds

An adult nonbreeding bird kept in a cage or an adequate aviary will, in each of these situations, have different food requirements. A lot of activity and a lower temperature will require more energy that must originate from the diet. The number of hours of sunlight also will influence the bird's behavior. The availability of animal protein, such as insects, to

The Green-rumped Parrotlet (Forpus passerinus) is the smallest member of the genus Forpus, weighing barely 22 grams.

seed-eating birds will bring a special enrichment to the diet. Molting birds lose relatively more body heat and thus require more energy. They will also require larger amounts of protein to replace feathers.

Breeding Birds

Birds in breeding condition will require more fat in the diet as reserve energy supplies. During incubation, when they leave the nest infrequently, these fats will ensure that the bird's body temperature remains constant. In order to manufacture the eggs, female birds require extra nutrients. An egg consists of 11 percent shell, 31 percent fat, and 38 percent albumin (proteinous egg white), plus small but important amounts of vitamins and minerals. At first, these substances are drawn from the current food and the body reserves, but in times of shortage they are drawn from the body tissues themselves.

Vitamins and Minerals: It is most important that birds receive a satisfactory quota of vitamins and minerals; a deficiency of one or more of these will lead to deficiency diseases of one sort or another, which can lead to sterility in adult birds, inadequate fertilization, dead nestlings, and loss of resistance to infectious diseases. The calcium required for eggshell manufacture can seriously weaken the bones of the mother bird if she receives an inadequate supply of this mineral both before and during the breeding season. The eggshell consists of approximately

Canary grass seed (Phalaris canariensis), also known as white seed, contains a lot of starch, and experience indicates that an excess has a negative influence on the song of birds. It contains about 14 parts water, 3.5 parts minerals, 11 parts protein, 51 parts carbohydrates, and 1 part fat. It is available commercially in two principal varieties: Maroccan, a large-kerneled variety, and Turkish, with a small kernel. This seed should always be available for cage and aviary birds.

85 percent calcium carbonate. The quality of the eggshell is mainly determined genetically, but is also influenced by the number of eggs produced and the availability of vitamin D_3.

Feeding the Young

Parrotlets and other dwarf parrots are *altricial,* meaning the young stay in the nest for some time while being cared for by the parent. *Precocial* young are those that leave the nest almost immediately after birth; they are usually well covered with down feathers at birth, while hatchling altricial birds usually are naked and take several days to develop down feathers. The quality of food received by parrotlet hatchlings is important for optimum growth and bone and feather development.

In most cases, the parents swallow the food—seed, insects, and so on—first and allow it to soften in the crop before it is regurgitated for the young. Some parrotlike birds deposit the regurgitated food so that the young can take it in the beak. When the hatchlings see other birds eat, they will mimic this behavior.

At fledging time, young altricial birds are not fully grown. Their further optimum development depends on a well-balanced food supply, and this will have a permanent influence on the birds' feeding behavior in later life.

Factors That Influence Birds' Choices of Food

Ground birds such as poultry, quail, and ostriches have more flesh than flying birds have. The increased amount of muscle also requires a

Poppy seed (Papaver somniferum) *comes in a blue (pictured) and a white variety; birds prefer the blue. It has a constipating effect and thus can serve you well when birds run a little loose in their digestion.*

somewhat stronger skeleton to support it. A well-developed pair of legs and feet is also required to support this mass. Flying birds require more energy-producing foods and are relatively much lighter than ground birds, which have a greater requirement for protein.

A bird should like the food that is offered to it. Because we cannot give it exactly the type of food it would get in the wild, we must use a satisfactory substitute. The bird may prefer certain seeds and grains to others. This may be due to the hardness or softness of the seed husk, or to its taste; parrots and parakeets, for example, have a well-developed sense of taste and therefore love the sweet-tasting sunflower seeds above all other seeds and grains. The amount of sugar in the seed, therefore, can influence its acceptability. The shape of the beak or bill and the pattern of the digestive system also will play a role in the choice of food.

Habit

Habit plays an important role in food selection and, if one changes a bird's diet, it should be done very gradually. If, for example, a parrot will eat only sunflower seeds, it will be necessary to change its diet before it suffers from a deficiency disease. It is not stubbornness on the part of the parrot; it is more the fault of its owner, who may lack the knowledge necessary to start the bird off with a greater variety of food. The change to a better seed mixture will take time and must be done with care (see page 46). In Japanese bird-breeding establishments, where birds are hand-reared, the food usually consists of a mixture of boiled rice, soy meal, fish meal, vitamins, and minerals; next, the birds receive a few extra food items for variety and, finally, they are weaned gradually to a seed mixture.

Appearance

Birds also recognize items of food by their appearance. If some birds receive pelleted food in place of a seed mixture, the size of the pellets will play a part in their recognition of the food item. Domestic fowl, for example, initially will refuse pellets that are larger or smaller than their usual rations, even if they are made with exactly the same ingredients. If the usual size is mixed with the other sizes, the chicken will peck up the usual ones first. The memory of the pellet size plays an important role.

The shape and size of the drinking vessel will influence finding and drinking water. The air temperature will influence the amount of water a bird drinks.

Changing Foods

Changing over to rearing food or food concentrates requires care and patience. You can't expect a parent bird to change suddenly to commercial or homemade rearing food just a few days before its brood hatches.

Some species adapt more readily than others to a change in diet. Hob-

A male Spectacled Parrotlet (Forpus conspicullatus) has blue around the eyes, on the upperwing coverts, at the bend of the wing, and on the rump. The female doesn't have any blue and is more yellowish on the forehead and beneath. The rump is somewhat emerald.

byists frequently have great difficulty in getting parrotlets and other dwarf parrots to change their seed mixture. Any change must be done with patience, care, and understanding.

Diet Components

As we have already discussed, we are not sufficiently aware of the natural diets of many wild bird species, especially parrots and parakeets. It is impossible, or at least very difficult, to allow captive birds to forage for their own food.

Research has shown that many parrotlike species feed, in the wild, mainly on seeds and fruits. Some species, for example lories, lorikeets, and the Kea of New Zealand, are special exceptions. The Kea, for example, uses its "pickax" beak to dig up roots, bulbs, and burrowing insects. Many large cockatoos and members of the genus *Platycercus* (Rosellas and so on) eat insects, water snails, and worms in their native Australia and, in captivity, usually will accept small pieces of red meat.

Psittacines (parrots and parakeets) have a characteristic method of feeding. They dehusk the seeds, discard the husks, and peel or skin the fruits. Thus, the digestive system is not troubled with large amounts of indigestible fiber. Because hookbills dehusk their seeds, it is best not to use automatic feeding hoppers exclusively, as the fresh seed will become covered with husks and the birds will have difficulty finding their food. Another well-known feeding habit of many parrots is holding large food items in one of the feet and manipulating it as though feeding from the hand. Exceptions are the parrotlets.

A green pastel mutation of the Celestial Parrotlet, which is recessive and autosomal. This is a male.

Seeds

The majority of psittacines are natural seedeaters. Captive parrots and parakeets often have to make do with the various kinds of commercially available dried, packaged seeds. This is, naturally, far from optimal feeding; in the wild, the birds have the opportunity to seek out all kinds of fruits, leaves, buds, flowers, seeds, grasses, weeds, roots, bulbs, bark, and insects. Thus, captive birds cannot live on seeds alone; they require a lot more.

Parrotlets and dwarf parrots feed mainly on grass seeds such as oats, hemp, millets, wheat, canary grass seed (or white seed as it is often called, especially by canary breeders), and so on. Larger species also take bigger, oily seeds such as small and medium-sized sunflower seeds, safflower seeds, and so on. These oily seeds are very fattening and deficient in various vitamins, especially vitamin A. Unfortunately, birds can soon become addicted to these seeds, especially sunflower seeds, and all too frequently birds may make one of them their staple diet, refusing all other food.

To provide further variety in feeding, give your birds unripe seeds, preferably still in the ear, such as ears of wheat, millet spray, and so on, as they would find it in the wild. Since this is not always available, another possibility is germinated seeds.

Green Food and Fruit

Most parrots are partial to green food and fruit. The neotropical species, such as parrotlets, especially enjoy gnawing greedily on fresh branches of willow, fruit trees, and so on. Many species will devour the buds, fresh twigs, and flowers of trees and plants, and many aviculturists give their birds the seeds of leguminous plants such as peas and beans, either fresh, cooked, frozen (thawed), or canned. Wild Amazons, conures, and parrotlets, for example, will even rob legume plantations, much to the disgust of farmers. For more on greens, see page 60.

Thistle (Niger) seed (Guizotia oleifera) *is very popular among all parrotlets and other small parrots. It contains 18 parts protein, 16 parts carbohydrates, and 43 parts fat. Hence, don't be too generous to birds housed in cages, for obvious reasons.*

Protein

Protein forms approximately 50 percent of the dry weight of the body of any animal; in plants this usually is much less. Proteins are involved in all animal activity. In birds they are important in growth, repair, and maintenance of all tissues including the feathers. In the breeding season, as the young birds grow, protein is of greater importance than in the winter, which is the rest period. Before they take on their new plumage for the winter after the molt, extra protein is essential, because protein is the basis of feathers. Proteins are built up from a great number of little building blocks, the amino acids. Some of these can be made by the bird itself; others must be present in the food. Most plant foods are lacking in proteins, so the necessary animal proteins also must be made available, as in commercial rearing food.

All psittacines require extra protein-containing foods during the breeding season. Excellent sources include meat, such as lean red meat, cooked poultry, pieces of fish without bone, boiled egg with the yolk and white chopped into tiny pieces, small pieces of low-fat cheese, cottage cheese, and yogurt. Raw or pasteurized milk is not recommended, although many birds will take it eagerly, for example, in stale wheat bread soaked in boiled and cooled milk. Some cannot tolerate it too well, and others may be sensitive to the milk's sugar content (lactose).

Carbohydrates

Carbohydrates are necessary for producing energy and are an important part of the diet. In general, they originate in plants. They have no function with regard to growth or repair of cells, but are important for movement and maintaining body temperature. Grains and seeds contain a lot of carbohydrates, usually in the form of starches; sugars are also carbohydrates.

Greens and Fruits

At first, your parrotlets or dwarf parrots may not touch any greens or fruits, as they may never have been given fresh food before, but continue to give them some just the same. In time your birds will get up the courage to try it, and you will find out which foods they like best. Do not give them too much fruit and greens. All of the following greens and fruits are good for your birds:

acacia blossoms
alfalfa
apples
apricots
bananas
beets
blackberries
broccoli
brussels sprouts
carrots
celery
cherries
chickweed
chicory
cucumbers

curly kale
eggplant
endive
grapes
green peas
groundsel
hydroponic sprouted
    oats or barley
kiwi fruit
lettuce (in small
    amounts only)
mango
oranges or tangerines
parsley
pear

pineapple
radish
raisins (soaked
    for approximately
    24 hours)
shepherd's purse
sow thistle
spinach
strawberries
Swiss chard
tomato
turnip greens
watercress
zucchini

Another picture of a green pastel mutation of the male Celestial Parrotlet—just to show you how diverse and variable this mutation can be.

Another beautiful green pastel female Celestial Parrotlet. In this fascinating mutation the females are always lighter than the males.

Fats and Oils

Fats and oils also provide energy and protection, and can be stored as a reserve of food. In the winter, a layer of fat is good for your birds; it will keep them warm and can be used as food in an emergency.

Vitamins

Vitamins in small amounts are important for the maintenance and normal functioning of the body and its organs. They give no energy but are essential to life itself. Cage and aviary birds require various vitamins to enable them to reproduce and grow, and to stay healthy. Vitamins are taken as part of the diet and are used in the breakdown and manufacture of proteins. In nature, vitamins occur in various forms; today, they are also manufactured artificially.

Vitamin A: Unfortunately, birds newly out of quarantine frequently have been kept on a monotonous diet. It is the task of the new owner to introduce these birds to a more varied diet (see page 55, where we talk about the food requirements of the various parrotlets and other dwarf parrot species); in fact, the more varied, the better. Newly imported birds, or birds shipped from European breeders, for example, often are deficient in vitamin A, due to crating, shipping, travel, and other factors. This vitamin is fundamental to the correct function of the body cell metabolism, the maintenance of skin and mucous membranes, and the enhancement of sight. It also has an influence on the respiratory system,

A blue pastel mutation (male) of the Celestial Parrotlet.

and plays a part in the pigmentation of the retina, thus allowing the eye to function well in poor light. Vitamin A is called not only the anti-infection or growth vitamin, but also the antisterility or fertility vitamin.

Minerals

Minerals are inorganic or nonliving materials that the birds need for growth and maintenance of the body. The most important minerals are salts containing calcium, phosphorus, sodium, manganese, copper, potassium, iron, and iodine. Each of these has its own function or functions. The term *trace elements* is often used to describe those minerals of which the birds need smaller quantities.

Grit and Gravel: In addition to the dietary constituents mentioned previously, grit and gravel are important. Grit and cuttlefish bone can help supply the bird's calcium requirements to

A blue pastel mutation (female) of the Celestial Parrotlet.

build bone, eggshells, and so on. This is very important in the breeding season. Small gravel has the function of grinding food in the stomach, making it easier to digest. The gravel is not digested, but passes through the body once it has worn too smooth to continue its job.

Many avian veterinarians and aviculturists tend to disagree on the necessity of a daily supply of grit. This does not mean, however, that seed-eating birds such as parrotlets and other dwarf parrots, both in the wild and in captivity, are not dependent upon small gravel and grit that they pick up from the soil, so that

Essential Compounds Made of Protein

Compound	Function
Actin and myosin	Muscle proteins important in muscular contraction; produced in the body to overcome the toxicity of a specific antigen (a substance that stimulates production of antibodies); in short, they fight diseases.
Collagen	Forms intercellular fibers (holds cells together) and gives strength to tendons, which are tissues connecting a muscle with a bone or part, and ligaments, which are band tissues that connect bones or hold organs in place.
Enzymes	Produce certain chemical changes by catalytic action; serve to convey oxygen to the tissues.
Hormones	Internally secreted compounds formed in endocrine organs that affect the functions of specifically receptive organs or tissues when carried to them by the body fluids.
Keratin	Principal compound of feathers, horn (nails, beak), hair, and the like.
Structural protein	Component of all cell membranes.

Fat-soluble Vitamins

Vitamins	Functions	Sources
A	Metabolism of body cells; maintenance of skin, bone, and mucous membranes; prevention of night blindness; synthesis of visual pigments.	Egg yolk; fresh leafy greens, such as chickweed, spinach, dandelion; yellow and orange vegetables and fruits; fish liver oils.
D_3	Promotes absorption of calcium and phosphorus; prevents egg binding; essential for blood clotting.	Fish liver oils and egg yolk; produced in skin that is exposed to ultraviolet light (sunlight).
E	Prevents oxidation of vitamin A and degeneration of fatty acids; important for development of brain cells, muscles, blood, sexual organs, and the embryo; increases blood circulation.	Wheat germ and wheat germ oils; fruits and vegetables; chickweed, watercress, spinach, and kale; germinated seeds.
K	Promotes blood clotting and liver functions.	Green food; carrot tops; kale; alfalfa; tomatoes; egg yolk; soy oil; fish meal; synthesized by bacteria in the intestine.

their alimentary systems work efficiently in the digestion of seeds and other food. Seed-eating birds have a crop in which the seed is softened before it goes into the gizzard or muscular stomach—the gizzard is an enlargement of the alimentary canal with dense, muscular walls. Without gravel or grit—often ground-up white

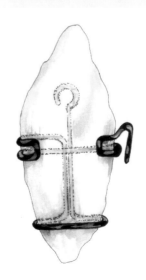

Cuttlebone supplies essential minerals to the birds. The wire holder can be made or purchased. If you gather cuttlebone on the beach, soak it for 24 hours; change the water every 8 hours. Cuttlebone contains about 81.5 percent calcium, and all birds will take it readily, especially before and during the breeding season.

Water-soluble Vitamins

Vitamins	Functions	Sources
B_1 (Thiamin)	Assists in overall growth; metabolic functions; growth of muscles and nervous system.	Germ cells of grain seeds, legumes, yeast, fruits, eggs, liver.
B_2 (Riboflavin)	Egg production; metabolic functions; proper development of skin, feathers, beak, and nails.	Yeast, eggs, green leaves, germ of good-quality seeds.
B_3 (Niacin)	Production of hormones; metabolic functions; proper function of nervous and digestive systems.	Peanuts, corn, whole grains, liver, lean meats.
B_6 (Pyridoxine)	Assists in the production of digestive juices, red blood cells, and antibodies.	Bananas, peanuts, beans, whole grain cereals, egg yolk.
B_{12} (Cyano-cobalamin)	Assists in the production of red blood cells; essential for metabolism.	Fish meal, liver, eggs, insects, vitamin supplements (all plants are low in B_{12}).
Biotin	Assists in the metabolism of various acids and nucleic acid synthesis.	Egg yolk, nuts, greens.
C (Ascorbic acid)	Assists in the metabolism of various acids, healing of wounds, tissue growth, and red blood cell formation; promotes absorption of iron.	Citrus fruits and juices; leafy greens; fresh fruits; cabbage.

oyster shell, as gray or dark shell are believed to contain too much lead—a great deal of the seed remains unground and whole seeds are passed out in the droppings.

Experiments have shown that birds that have no access to grit take greater quantities of food than those that have a supply of grit. Also, the health of the bird declines.

The undigested seeds cause blockages in the intestines and then the only discharge is a whitish, watery substance.

In various commercial brands of grit, redstone, chalk, gravel, and calcareous seaweed or kelp, as well as a little charcoal, are added. In the wild, various birds take little bits of charcoal before going to nest, but the necessity of a daily supply of charcoal is questionable as it is suspected of absorbing vitamins A, B_2, and K from the intestinal tract. If this is correct, it can mean that charcoal can cause vitamin-deficiency disease. Grit also frequently contains crushed quartz, which is a very hard insoluble substance, with sharp edges that grind seed in the gizzard.

Never use grit as a sole source of certain essential minerals that may be contained in it, such as calcium, iron, magnesium, and iodine. In other words, offer a variety of food to ensure that sufficient quantities of minerals are available. An overdose of mineralized grit can cause kidney damage. Most aviculturists supply a separate dish with grit once every other day for approximately one hour, free choice.

Grit is available in various grades: fine or small for finches, canaries, budgerigars, parrotlets, and other dwarf parrots; medium-sized to coarse for large parrots and ornamental fowl.

Calcium: Although calcium is not required by birds throughout the entire year, it is nevertheless recommended that it be made available at all times. The best method of supplying this mineral is with cuttlefish bones, which can be placed here and there near perches. Alternatively, a bowl of grit and dicalcium phosphate can be placed in the cage, breeding cage, or aviary. Parrotlets and other dwarf parrots can be given a piece of cuttlefish bone between the wires or in a holder.

This still rather rare mutation of the Celestial Parrotlet has various colors and I would very much like to call it "green sprinkled" although this recessive and autosomal mutation was first developed in the U.S. and is often called (mainly in Europe, though) "American yellow."

Birds need calcium especially during the breeding season when the eggs are being formed, and during the molt. Calcium is necessary for proper functioning of the heart, muscles, blood, and nervous systems.

Water

Water is essential to birds, whose bodies consist of more than one half water. Not all bird species—various Australian parakeets, for example—drink a lot of water; birds from drier environments can go longer without water as they get their moisture requirements from the food they eat.

The Importance of Calcium, Minerals, and Iodine in Your Bird's Daily Diet

Why Calcium?

It is a well-known fact that minerals should be present in a pet bird's diet; pet birds, however, are most commonly deficient in calcium, mainly because seeds are not a good source of this important mineral. Calcium is essential in the manufacture and maintenance of the skeleton, in blood coagulation (clotting), in the function of sinews and organs such as the heart, and in the formation of the eggshell. Calcium deficiencies can lead to seizures, pathological bone fractures, muscle weakness, egg binding, soft-shelled eggs, and other problems.

Why Vitamin D_3?

Birds can produce vitamin D_3 only if they have access to ultraviolet light. Birds absorb or utilize vitamin D_3; vitamin D_2 cannot be converted into D_3 in their bodies. Vitamin D_3 is synthesized by the ultraviolet fraction of sunlight contacting the bare skin on the face, legs, and feet, and converting a certain skin hormone—the 7-dehydocholesterol—to vitamin D_3. This vitamin is required for calcium absorption from the gut. In other words, even if calcium is provided, it cannot be absorbed by the body if the bird has no access to direct sunlight.

Outdoor pet birds, housed in an aviary, will therefore synthesize their own required vitamin D_3, which is needed for a proper calcium-phosphorus metabolism. Indoor pet birds, however, must have the vitamin supplemented in their daily food through vitamin supplements; they don't have access to direct sunlight as ultraviolet light is filtered out through the window glass. Remember that the majority of the commercial seed mixtures contain D-activated animal sterol—read the label—which is a source of vitamin D_3. Besides, many calcium blocks, often called beak treats, have low levels of vitamin D_3, to make the calcium-phosphorus metabolism possible.

Why Phosphorus?

Phosphorus also plays an important part in the formation and maintenance of the skeletal structure and in bodily metabolism; it may also be an ingredient of protein or fat. A bird's body requires about three times as much calcium as phosphorus.

It is important that a balance exist between these two minerals or the bodily functions will be disturbed, frequently with disastrous consequences. You need not worry too much, however, about phosphorus, since it is contained in adequate amounts in green foods and seeds, especially in bran. Seed husks are also a good source, but they are not eaten by the birds.

Why Iodine?

Pet birds require iodine, although only in very small quantities; iodine is a *trace mineral*. Most of the trace minerals are contained in normal food, including seeds, green food, and drinking water. If the water supply in a certain area is deficient in iodine, however, greens and plants—for example, bird weeds, such as chickweed and dandelion—in that area will also be deficient in iodine.

Many commercial beak treats or mineral blocks contain small levels of iodine, as a shortage of this mineral can cause thyroid gland enlargements, especially in parakeets. The enlarged thyroid gland—called a goiter—presses on the esophagus, a muscular tube that transports food from the mouth to the crop, resulting in regurgitation. Too much iodine will interfere with the normal function of the thyroid gland, leading to feather and skin problems. Other symptoms of iodine deficiency are squeaking, or wheezing breathing, weight loss, and decreased appetite.

Why Mineral Blocks?

Adequate calcium supplements should be available to your pet birds at all times. Another advantage of many commercial beak treats is that they can be stored for years without losing any of their qualities, as long as they are kept clean and dry. When you put a beak treat into a cage or aviary, hang it where there is little danger that it will be contaminated with droppings. If it does become soiled, scrub it with clean water. Also, place it in a covered part of the aviary where it can remain dry. Rain will ruin it.

An Adequate Feeding Regime

Let us briefly look at the feeding regime that has to be followed in order to keep your birds in the best possible condition:

For Medium-sized and Small Conures

• oil-rich seeds, such as small black sunflower seed, safflower, and a little hemp, especially during the winter and in the breeding season, or when birds are kept in unheated accommodations

• leguminous plants, fresh and germinated
• corn (softened and crushed), oats, wheat, various millets (especially millet spray, which is loved by all psittacines), canary grass seed, greens, fruits, fresh twigs, egg food, cottage cheese, yogurt, and so on.

For Small Parrots and Parrotlets

• various small seeds, such as millet varieties and small black sunflower seeds, approximately 70 percent; crushed oats and canary grass seed to 25 percent, and about 5 percent

Sunflower seed (Helianthus annuus) *is available in white, striped, and black. It is rich in albumen (about 15 percent), minerals, and vitamin E.*

mixture of niger seed, hemp, poppy seed, and linseed (flax)

• boiled egg, other animal protein sources, fruit, and greens.

All three groups can be given daily snacks, such as diverse cereals— corn or maize, wheat, bran, rice, shredded wheat, puffed wheat, and millet—pieces of granola bar, and uncooked dry pasta. The latter can be given as a mixture in various shapes and colors; being curious, the birds are bound to try it and soon will eat it greedily (birds *do* see colors).

The above feeding regime is intended to enhance variety in the daily menu.

Hygiene

Hygiene and cleanliness go hand in hand; without the latter, you won't get the former. Good hygiene prevents the spread of disease among captive stock. Utensils should be cleaned daily, preferably in the morning, and empty hulls should be blown off the seed before topping up the containers. Many beginners often make the mistake of putting new seed on top of empty hulls, eventually ending up with a dish of only hulls. I like to spread all the seed out daily on a sheet of newspaper, then blow the hulls away. The new seed is then put in the dish with the remainder from the previous day on top of it. This way the bottom layer of seed never gets old gradually or forms a breeding ground for bacteria or other pests.

Food and water dishes must be cleaned thoroughly at regular intervals, at least once a week. A solution of household bleach and water (1:1) makes an excellent disinfectant— soak the utensils in it for 15 minutes and rinse them thoroughly in clean water afterwards.

Some birdkeepers believe that sick birds don't require food or water. This, of course, is nonsense. Indeed, give a bird its favorite food and try to get it to eat. Once it is eating and drinking, the bird is on its way to recovery. Remember that a bird in a heated hospital cage (see page 95) will become very thirsty, and to prevent dehydration it must have clean, fresh water all the time. Also, the water can be used as an aid in administering medicines and tonics.

Treats and Snacks

There are almost more treats and snacks than there are pet bird species. Some are excellent; others are worthless, regardless of all the promising words and the beautiful, eye-catching packages. So let us go straight to the heart of the matter—for the birds' sake.

What Is a Treat?

In the bird trade, there are all types of treats and snacks with which the birds can be spoiled, mixtures and tidbits containing all kinds of vitamins, hormones, minerals, wheat germ, fancy seeds, often coated with various colors such as pink and blue peanuts, and oats, for example. Reading the labels often means that you may as well take up a study of enzymes, amino acids, trace elements, and the differences between phosphoric and carbonated calcium.

It is a fact that the pet bird fancier, and even the well-meaning aviculturist who fusses with all these tonics and pick-me-ups does not necessarily have, or breed, better birds than the hobbyist or breeder who just makes sure his or her birds get a well-balanced diet. Pet birds do much better on the usual healthy diet consisting of pellets (see page 61), fresh seed mixtures, greens and fruits, cuttlefish bone, and oyster shell.

Niger Seed

If you know your bird's preferences, by all means consider those snacks or treats, and buy honey sticks that have those "goodies." For example, many parrotlet and other dwarf parrot species enjoy niger seed, which is rich in minerals; however, it is also high in fat content, and

A normal (wild-colored) male (front) and a gray-green male (back) of the Celestial Parrotlet.

should be offered only in small quantities. Excessive consumption can cause liver problems, so purchase only seed mixtures for daily use that do not have too much niger seed in them, especially when the birds are housed in small quarters. Focus on those snacks and treats such as sticks, bells, and so on that have a modest amount of niger seed. Most commercial snacks or treats have no, or very few, niger seeds.

Nuts and Fruits

Parrots of all sizes like nuts and fruits, so products with nuts and dehydrated fruits are excellent treats once or twice a week. Too much of these goodies, however, will result in obese birds.

Germinated and Sprouted Seeds

In addition to dry food and treats, most dwarf parrots need and like germinated and sprouted seeds, and during the winter these substitute for green food, although there are dehydrated greens even in sticks and such. Sticks or bells with the proper seed mix can also be considered an excellent "tool" to prevent boredom and stress. Germinated and sprouted seeds contain valuable nutrients, including vitamin E, which is particularly important during the breeding season.

You can make an excellent mixture of seeds and beans for germination. One can indeed call the mixture a snack or treat, as germinated and sprouted seeds should be given only in small quantities three times a week,

The gray-green mutation (male) of the Celestial Parrotlet inherits recessive and autosomal.

as a supplement to the main diet and not in place of it. When intended for the larger parrots, they are excellent; otherwise, omit the beans.

The seeds and beans can be mixed with soft and/or rearing food, which most aviculturists still regard as snacks as well (this is not true, however). These foods are absolutely necessary during the breeding and rearing periods and, in many cases, even throughout the year.

Germinate the following seeds in similar amounts:
• rape seed
• radish seed
• lettuce seed
• white milo seed
• red milo seed

When all these seeds are fresh, germination should take place at the same time when they are mixed together. Follow these rules:
• Soak the seeds in a good quantity of lukewarm water for about 12 hours.
• Rinse the seeds several times in running water, preferably in a stainless-steel strainer.
• Shake the seeds free from the bottom of the strainer and then allow the water to drain off.
• Cover the seeds with a moist cloth and allow to stand in a warm place.
• Shake and rinse seeds regularly in order to prevent fermentation.
• After 24 hours, the shoots will appear.
• Clean the strainer thoroughly after use.

There are various ways to produce sprouts, but a fresh batch must be started every day. Here are two tested methods for sprouting seeds that you can choose from.

1. Mix two parts small-grained millet and one part canary grass seed (white seed) in a large pot. Add water to soak so the seeds will swell. To speed up the process, place the pot on a radiator or in a warm room or outside in the sun. Place the seeds in the strainer and rinse thoroughly under running water two or three times a day. Return them to the pot with fresh water. After 24 hours, the seeds are ready for use. Dry them lightly with a clean towel, then mix in a few drops of a vitamin/mineral preparation. Various excellent brands are commercially available. A few drops of cod liver oil will also be beneficial. This helps the seeds remain moist longer, adds to their nutritional value, and supplies vitamin D.

2. Mix two-thirds small-grained millet, a little large-grained millet, and no more than one-fourth canary grass seed in a pot. Add water to soak so that the seeds can swell, and leave them for 12 hours. Place the seeds in a strainer and rinse thoroughly under running water. Return them to the pot, cover it, and let it sit for another 24 hours. The seeds can then be fed to the birds; however, check the odor of the sprouted seeds. If the batch smells bad, it has not been rinsed often enough or thoroughly enough and should not be used. The next time the seeds are sprouted, rinse them more frequently.

The choice of seeds to be sprouted depends, of course, on the tastes of your birds. So know your birds well; know what they like and dislike. For example: various parrotlets like small-grained millet and canary grass seed, while quaker parrots also enjoy soaked large-grained millet, as do the majority of *Brotogeris* parrots and other conures.

Millet Spray

It is not only the best treat, but *all* seedeating bird species love it, even if they are somewhat under the weather. I'm talking about *millet spray*. It can be given straight from the package and is also available per ear, or it can be sprouted as described above, but it is extremely important to change the water frequently to avoid rot.

Discard the water after 24 hours and set the spikes upright in a sturdy glass container, such as a jam jar, with fresh water. Let the container stand on a radiator for another day, until the sprouts become visible. They can then be fed to the birds.

Golden German millet is one of the many millet (Panicum spp) varieties used in commercial seed mixtures. Other important varieties are red, white, La Plata, Japanese, and Senegal millet. One of the most essential millets is millet spray (Setaria viride, S. italica, etc.) which should be available throughout the year.

Greens

Parakeets, parrotlets, small and large parrots, cockatiels, finches, doves: They should all receive an abundance of fresh green food. This includes chickweed, collard, leaf and bibb lettuce, endive, spinach, cabbage, pieces of carrot and carrot tops, celery leaves, broccoli, dandelion, and so on (see page 48). Most commercial seed mixtures have dehydrated greens and, although the dried greens are not nearly as nutritious as fresh greens, they are better than nothing. Therefore, sticks and bells with greens are good substitutes, as are the "Veggies and Fruit" canned treats that are nitrogen-flushed. In cans and polybags, both usually nitrogen-flushed as well, one can purchase pumpkin seeds, pine nuts, red chili peppers, miniature ears of colorful Indian corn, and carrot tips and slices. They will do

A cinnamon (fallow or Isabelle) male mutation of the Celestial Parrotlet.

nicely, but present your birds *at all times* with fresh greens as well.

Treats of Animal Origin

Practically all pet birds, and certainly parrotlets and other small parrots, like to eat food of animal origin—insects such as termites, ant pupae ("ant eggs"), and similar material—as well as man-made substitutes such as universal food, egg food, and rearing food. Most of these foods are imported from Europe—especially England, the Netherlands, Germany, and Italy.

The amount of animal protein needed on a daily basis, or when young are being raised, varies considerably among bird species. You should have these treats available all year.

Eggs are the cheapest source of animal protein; most rearing foods from Europe are egg-based. Dried mealworms, the larval form of the darkling beetle, are another source of animal protein, as are moths, fly larvae, and enchytrae (white worms), with occasional substitutions of tubifex, red mosquito larvae, and water fleas (Daphnia) for variety. Most pet shops that sell fish and fish supplies carry most of these products. Universal and egg foods may be enriched with finely diced boiled egg and small insects.

Water as a Treat

One last treat: Dissolve some honey or grape sugar (glucose) in the birds' drinking water several times a week. Fruit juice is another acceptable treat, but you have to cover the dishes with wire netting so the birds won't bathe in them.

If the birds' drinking water is highly chlorinated, supply rainwater instead of tap water. Boil it, then cool it for at least three hours before giving it to the birds. You can also use commercially available spring water.

The Avian Pellet

If you keep aviary birds in your home and garden, you must take full responsibility for their care and management. As discussed, this includes providing the best diet possible. The first thing you must do is research the subject and discover the best diet for your birds. The next logical step is to offer the new diet in such a way that the birds will eventually eat it and enjoy it.

Complete Diet

There are three basic types of complete diet for cage and aviary birds. The term *complete diet* is the one commonly used on the packaging label.

1. Pellets, which are homogenous masses of proteins, carbohydrates, minerals, and micronutrients. They sometimes come in various colors and shapes, and are made by a process called extrusion, hence the name *extruded pellet.*

2. Blends of seeds, fortified with pellets or crumbles, which often claim to meet all known nutrient standards for cage and aviary birds.

Willow

The very best treats of all are the small, 2.5-inch-long (6.25-cm) willow branches. The birds like to play with them, nibble at the bark, pull off strips, and eat small pieces. It is the birds' aspirin. Like human aspirin, willow has an active ingredient called *salicin.* People have used willow leaves and bark to relieve pain and inflammation at least since the time of the third-century-B.C. Greek physician Hippocrates. In the early 1950s my father used willow tree bark, leaves, and small branches for his lovebirds; they not only used the bark for nest construction, they were actually eating bark, leaves, branch—the whole thing. We soon found out that all psittacines love willow branches and, since those early days in aviculture, I have been offering my birds willow. It seems that salicin interferes with the production of prostaglandins, hormones made by the body in response to injury. Willow branches, like aspirin, seem to reduce the pain and swelling caused by prostaglandins, among other things.

3. Mixtures of various seeds, which are seed blends without the added pellets or crumbles.

General Characteristics of Avian Pellets

We already know that dietary essentials are food items that are absolutely necessary for a bird's survival. These items are needed to keep the bird in good condition and allow it to perform its biological functions. Such items must be included in the bird's diet, regardless of the type of diet you offer it. As you can imagine, captive birds have little choice in the matter. This makes it all the more important for aviculturists to conscientiously utilize the latest scientific research and determine the best diet to feed their particular species of birds, and then to dutifully follow through and supply the necessary items.

Avian pellets and crumbles are, of course, only one link, although an important one, in this quest to provide captive birds with a complete, nutritionally balanced diet.

Let us take a closer look at the general characteristics of avian pellets and crumbles.

1. Bird pellets and crumbles should contain all the necessary components classified as proteins, carbohydrates, fats, vitamins, minerals, and water, essential for life, production, and reproduction.

2. Bird pellets and crumbles should balance in proteins and carbohydrates.

3. Bird pellets and crumbles are often fruit-flavored. Although many birds are more interested in appearance than taste, all parrots and parakeets do have strong taste sensations. The "right" taste might induce a bird to try the new food.

4. Bird pellets and crumbles often have attractive colors and shapes. The products are created this way because birds, being visual creatures, have color vision and see most colors; therefore, color and shape may play an important role in the bird's acceptance of food.

5. Bird pellets and crumbles are often fortified with a special blend of *Lactobacillus acidophilus* and yeast culture. This is to prevent the depletion of beneficial gut microbes and to maintain normal intestinal conditions.

6. Bird pellets and crumbles are often fortified with an extract from the yucca plant *(Yucca schildigera)*. The production of hydrogen sulfate and ammonia, two odoriferous gases produced by a bird's excretion, is reduced by an extract from this plant, classified by the FDA as a common grass. The yucca plant contains high levels of natural vegetable steroids, commonly referred to as *saponins.* These saponins act biologically to help reduce odors from animal waste.

The Benefits of Pellets

• A good avian pellet or crumble improves avian health, growth, and reproduction.

• Avian pellets and crumbles reduce the incidence of disease and stress because of their nutritional benefits.

• *Lactobacillus acidophilus,* a naturally occurring group of beneficial organisms, may also help to maintain an optimal intestinal pH. It will not prevent disease, but it will strengthen the immune system.

• The yucca plant extract will decrease odors from manure and urine gas.

• Most commercial pellets/crumbles are economical to feed and there is minimal waste. As an additional benefit, there are no seed hulls to clean up.

• One can target the needs of particular birds in specific situations because of the availability of the two general types of pelleted diets: breeder and maintenance.

• Most commercial brands have been used, tested, and corrected for a number of years under varying environmental conditions, demonstrating their effectiveness for all phases of a pet bird's life cycle. They also have been shown to be both palatable and nutritionally sound.

Feeding Instructions— Conversion Method

It is known that cage and aviary birds recognize various foods by their appearance. If birds receive pelleted food in place of a seed mixture, the size of the pellets will play a major role in the acceptability of them.

A bird should like and enjoy the food it is given. We cannot offer it the specific foods it would forage for in the wild, so we must discover and use satisfactory substitutes. As another example, specific types of birds prefer one type of seed over another. The same principle applies to pellets and crumbles. The amount of fruits or the fruit taste in the pellets or crumbles can also influence its acceptability.

Certain special characteristics will often influence a bird's readiness to change its diet. If the birds are of a suspicious nature, they will hesitate to try new foods. Since it is often rather difficult to cajole certain birds to switch from seed mixtures to pelleted foods, great patience, care, and understanding must be exercised.

When first introducing your birds to a pelleted diet, blend the pellets or crumbles with their usual diet, such as seeds, and gradually reduce the seeds and increase the pellets or crumbles over approximately 16 days. This tried and tested method is:

Days 1–4: 25 percent pellets/crumbles and 75 percent current seed mixture.

Days 5–10: 50 percent pellets/crumbles and 50 percent current seed mixture.

Days 11–15: 75 percent pellets/crumbles and 25 percent current seed mixture.

Day 16: 100 percent pellets/crumbles.

Another trick is to moisten the pellets or crumbles with a fruit juice such as apple or orange. This sweetness and fruity flavor may help to make the pellets palatable. Remember that because of the possible growth of bacteria, wet food should be removed after four hours and replaced with clean, dry food. Ideally, after 15 days the birds should be completely converted to the pelleted diet. If you are experiencing difficulty with your birds and were not successful with your first attempt, begin at step one and repeat the process. Sometimes it may take several attempts to successfully convert your birds to pellets or crumbles.

Additions to Pelleted Diets

Most commercial pelleted diets are nutritionally balanced and designed to be fed as a major part of the diet. However, do remember that reasonable portions of fresh vegetables and fruits, as well as fun treats and a variety of birdseeds and nuts, should be offered daily. Be cognizant of the nutritional value of the fruits and vegetables you are offering; for instance, apples and grapes have much less nutritional value than broccoli or carrots. If you are offering apples and grapes, then a broader balance of nutrition would be preferable in terms of your fresh foods.

Breeding Birds' Requirements

Breeding birds have their own special nutritional requirements. It is a wise practice to feed breeding birds a diet of avian pellets or crumbles, fresh nutritional vegetables, and some nuts and seed approximately 60 to 90 days prior to the breeding season.

Management Practices

Consistent and professional management practices are important to the success of the feeding and nutritional program.
• Discard fresh foods and particularly cooked foods daily, or even more often if they are not consumed. This is especially important in hot climates or where the ambient temperatures are likely to spoil foods more quickly.
• Keep food fresh by cleaning and replenishing feeders daily. Some foods, such as pellets, crumbles, and/or seeds, should be available at all times.
• Clean feeders at least every day to prevent mold, and refill with fresh food.
• Keep water bottles and automated watering systems clean and always have fresh water available in a constant supply.
• Store all pellets, crumbles, and seeds in a cool, dry place to maintain maximum nutritional value.
• Once a bird begins to eat a colorful pelleted diet, the droppings will also change color, which is usually a brownish red. Droppings may become somewhat looser due to the extra trips to the drinking dish while eating the rather dry pelleted food.
• In order to offer variety in the diet, feed unripe seeds, preferably still in the ear, such as ears of millet, millet spray, and ears of wheat, just as it would be found in the wild. If this type of food is unavailable, use germinated seed (see page 58) as an excellent alternative.

Remember: A monotonous diet is stressful and boring to cage and aviary birds, and may result in screaming, feather plucking, and unsatisfactory breeding. A well-balanced diet means a diet containing a variety of ingredients.

Chapter Five

Breeding

Because of the increasing popularity of these charming, much-sought-after companion parrots, demand often outstrips supply. It is, therefore, important that aviculturists know how to breed their birds as soon as they become available.

History of Captive Breeding

In the 1920s, most wild-caught parrotlets were imported into Germany, Holland, and Denmark; this gradually increased until the 1950s when almost all of western Europe and England were importing them. Unfortunately, in those early days, priority was never given to the responsible captive breeding of the birds because they were usually easy to obtain or replace; so why would one struggle trying to breed them? Today, however, the situation is quite different. The supply of wild-caught birds from their native countries is dwindling because of importation regulations, so future demands will have to be met by captive breeding. Fortunately, most species are not yet endangered in the wild, yet all parrotlets are listed under Appendix II of the Convention on International Trade in Endangered Species of Wild Flora and Fauna (CITES). Appendix II also lists species that resemble Appendix I species threatened with extinction.

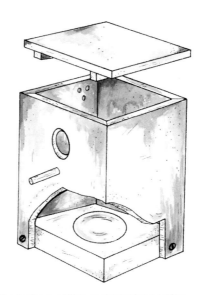

The bottom of this rectangular nesting box is concave to prevent the eggs from rolling to the four corners of the box.

Deciding on the Species

Anyone who is interested in breeding parrotlets must first decide which species he or she wants to keep and breed. It is highly recommended that you start with a minimum of three unrelated pairs of birds per species or subspecies. This must be promoted through bird clubs. The three pairs must not be related in any way, so that the young produced from these pairs also are unrelated; in other words, you will have three groups of unrelated offspring that can then be paired up.

Experience has shown that each pair of birds is better housed in its own breeding cage or, even better, aviary. In this way, it is less difficult to leg-band the young correctly and

to keep an accurate record. Without accurate records—a card system, for example—it is impossible to maintain a healthy, noninterbred series of breeding pairs. Don't forget that many parrotlet species, especially the hens, are quite difficult to distinguish, which can lead to unwanted hybridizations if you take inadequate care. Always take care in determining the species you obtain. Study the illustrations in this book and others such as Forshaw's *Parrots of the World* (3rd edition). Also, ask the advice of experienced, knowledgeable breeders.

Avoiding False Pairings and Inbreeding

Because of the difficulty in determining the various species and, especially, subspecies, beginners should start with three unrelated pairs of Pacific or Celestial Parrotlets *(Forpus coelestis)*. Apart from the rediscovered subspecies *F. c. lucida,* which is rarely commercially available, the Pacific Parrotlet has no subspecies to cause confusion. You must set out to pair up pure birds, so that they, in turn, produce pure homozygous offspring; pairing between nominate and subspecies is taboo! Pacific Parrotlets, moreover, are easy to obtain in America, Canada, and Europe. Several color mutations are available in this species (see page 136). In order to keep specific color mutations pure, they must be paired carefully, and it may sometimes be necessary to inbreed them. For this reason, I would advise begin-

A 32-day-old Celestial Parrotlet.

ners to concentrate first on the normal, wild-colored birds—but be careful that you use genuine wild-colored birds that are not split with a certain color mutation.

Another particularly attractive species, without subspecies, is the easy-to-recognize Yellow-faced Parrotlet *(Forpus xanthops).* This species is extremely colorful and is not difficult to obtain in Europe; in America and Canada it has been intensively imported during the last five years and has been bred widely. The future of this species in aviculture appears to be rosy!

All other species have one or more subspecies, some of which are extremely difficult to distinguish from each other. If you want to breed these species or subspecies, which is quite possible, you must be familiar with the various subspecies, so that false pairings and inbreeding can be avoided. At this point I will stress again that only strict selection of pairs of pure nominate or subspecies can guarantee the continuing existence of the pure forms. For example: a nominate, and not one of its subspecies, hen of the well-known Green-rumped Parrotlet *(F. passerinus)* paired with a cock Blue-winged Parrotlet *(F. xanthopterygius)* will produce offspring that are not only racially impure, but that also closely resemble the father Blue-winged Parrotlet. Inexperienced aviculturists often mistake these offspring for pure Blue-winged Parrotlets. I have known such hybrids to demand high prices when sold as "subspecies of the Blue-winged Parrotlet." Such fraudulent representations have no place in the avicultural community.

Wild-caught or Captive-bred?

It is also advantageous to know if the birds you are considering purchasing are wild-caught or captive-bred. It is not possible to estimate the age of wild-caught birds, and hens must be at least one year old before they can be safely bred. Also, older wild-caught birds are not always anxious to pair up when you place them together in a cage or aviary. Such difficulties are minimized if you use captive-bred stock. I would, therefore, advise beginners to deal only with captive-bred birds, using a trio of unrelated pairs, in order to build a line.

Selecting Breeding Pairs

Parrotlet partners are very faithful and devoted. If one bird flies to a perch or nest box, the other will follow almost immediately. If it flies to feed or drink, the partner will join it without hesitation. The birds frequently mutually preen each other. Though they may have an occasional short altercation, they will soon make up with renewed tenderness. They will separate themselves from other aviary inhabitants, and will chase them away if they get too close. They sleep in their favorite spot, pressed tightly to each other,

Young Celestial Parrotlets with—as turned out later—one cinnamon mutant.

and, when the hen is brooding, the cock will often spend the night with her in the nest box. Parrotlets can correctly be called the "Lovebirds of South America," an analogy to the "Lovebirds of Africa" *(Agapornidae)*. However, before this is at all possible, cock and hen must be willing to pair up in the first place.

The easiest way to pair up birds is to place several unrelated youngsters, which all must be leg-banded, of the same species or subspecies in a flight that is indoors or outdoors, as long as you can keep adequate control, and allow the birds to pair up themselves. This is not always as easy as one may want it to be, as certain undesirable pairings may ensue, such as brother and sister. Once the birds are paired up, it is almost impossible to separate them without causing them an inordinate amount of stress, so you must keep

a close eye on them; once you see which birds have shown an interest in each other, you can remove these individual pairs and place each pair in a roomy breeding cage (see page 36) or aviary. Another simple method is to place two birds of opposite sex together in a breeding cage or other roomy cage and hope that they will show interest in each other. This usually poses no difficulties if previously unpaired young birds are brought together.

Older birds that have already bred, those in which one of the pair has died, or pairs that have shown an unwillingness to breed and need to be remated—for example, in order to maintain a particular color mutation—are, unfortunately, not always ready to accept a new, strange partner. This is especially the case when a bird can still see or hear its old partner, even when they are in different accommodations. You can leave the newly introduced pair together for a few weeks, but if, after two months, the birds have shown no interest in each other, by sitting well apart on their perches and so on, it is advisable to try again with totally new partners and, perhaps, a change of cage or aviary. Needless to say, best results can be obtained when newly formed pairs are not in the position to see, or hear, any of their previous partners—better to be safe than sorry.

As we have already intimated, experience has shown that birds that have spent a long time with one partner and have shown no breeding results will not readily bond with a new mate if they can see or, especially, hear their previous partner. The contact call of both partners, in spite of the fact that they are separated, is enough to cause the birds to ignore, or even drive away the new partner. The newly introduced bird may sit anxiously in a corner or under the food dish. It may even be driven away from the food or water containers by the other bird; therefore, it is important that newly introduced birds not be able to see or hear their previous partners. The best way is to give the "older" bird a young partner that has not previously been paired up—but even this is not always successful. It is, however, the only thing we can try; Mother Nature must do the rest.

Pairing Up

If you possess two birds of opposite sexes that you wish to pair up, then it is best to place them together in a cage or aviary late in the afternoon. The birds will still have enough time to accustom themselves to the new surroundings, to find the food and water dishes—but keep an eye on them—and to find a suitable roost before darkness sets in. The following day, you will be able to see if the birds settled together and tolerate each other. If one of the pair is acting aggressively toward the other, it is best to remove the aggressor from the cage and to try again after three days. In

the meantime, the "underling" will have had time to completely familiarize itself with its surroundings, and will be in a better position to defend itself. In my experience, such a reintroduction rarely results in serious problems and any minor skirmishes will soon diminish. After a week, the pair will be inseparable and will have become real lovebirds. Should they fail to hit it off, then you have no choice but to separate them and try the same process again.

In general, young parrotlets are ready to accept each other within a day, and once they start preening each other you can rest assured that you have a new pair. However, this does not necessarily mean that the pair will start reproducing immediately. You should give them a little time before introducing nest boxes.

Young Vernal Hanging Parrots have black eyes, like the one in the picture, and don't have blue on their chin. It usually takes about a year before young birds are fully matured.

Remember, the best breeding results are likely when each pair is housed singly in its own cage or aviary, without the presence of other birds, including other species. If you have a number of flights next to each other, the adjacent walls should be shielded with vegetation, wood barriers, burlap, or something similar in order to prevent birds from injuring each other through the mesh. Experience has shown that Mexican Parrotlets and Yellow-faced Parrotlets breed most successfully in an aviary, and that applies also to other species, but most of them will also breed successfully in a roomy breeding cage (see page 36).

Nesting Facilities

Wild parrotlets are not particularly fussy with regard to nesting sites; they seem to be easily pleased. In

This tall wooden nesting box can be used for parrotlets and all conure species. Attach some big staples to the inside of the front panel to make it easy for the birds to leave the nest.

the wild, I have found nests in hollow fence posts and holes in walls, as well as in tree hollows. My cage birds are always given a choice: a hollow birch stump or other "natural" nest box, or a nest box made with planks. Strangely, perhaps, preference is often shown for the latter. The main advantage of a homemade nest box is that the eggs are seldom damaged, even when the parent birds storm tempestuously inside, which they do frequently, and scare the living daylights out of the inexperienced breeder. Nest boxes made with 1-inch-thick (2.5-cm) oak or beech are best as this wood is durable enough to withstand the gnawing of the birds for some time. Such boxes provide more room for the nestlings, and for the father bird when he spends the night with his spouse. Vertical nest boxes do not provide adequate space, so horizontal models are better. Also, the latter are easier to service when, for example, you may want to hold the hen back with a piece of cardboard in order to remove the babies if you wish to hand-feed them. Unrestrained hens, unfortunately, may have the habit of attacking their young if you try to remove them from the nest. You should make sure that the nest box floor is provided with a shallow cavity, so that the eggs cannot roll about and can be fully covered by the brooding bird.

Natural nest boxes also, as you will imagine, have their good points; the interior will stay warm for longer than a board nest box. However, because the natural nest box cools slowly and gradually, which may be a problem in the warmer days of summer, it could cause desiccation of the egg membranes. Natural nest boxes are quite decorative in the cage or aviary, but they are so heavy as to be almost unhandleable. Examination of the interior is also difficult to perform without sending the birds into a fit.

Material

As nesting material, you should provide strips of fresh willow bark and moist humus that can be collected from rotting tree stumps. I don't recommend cedar bedding, wood shavings, or sawdust, as small particles can lodge in the eyes of the nestlings, or adults, and promote various infections. And that is without mentioning respiratory problems.

From the above, you will have realized that parrotlets don't collect their own nesting material as the lovebirds of Africa do. You must place the nest material in the boxes yourself, pressing it down into the cavity with your fist.

Don't be surprised if the birds, especially the Green-rumped Parrotlets, push the nesting material you have supplied into one corner of the nest box, or even turn it out altogether. The nesting material must be returned because youngsters reared on the bare floor can develop orthopedic problems. Species such as the Mexican Parrotlet have a habit of pushing their eggs beneath the nesting material. In such cases you have

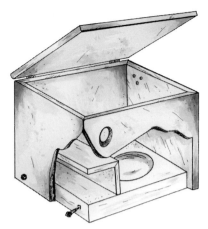

A square nesting box which is easily constructed at home. Due to the little inside "step" breakage of eggs or damage to young birds is minimized.

provided too much nesting material, and you should remove enough to expose the eggs so that the birds can brood properly. Take note of the habits of the various pairs so that you know how much nest material to

A hollowed-out log as a nesting box. It can easily be made by sawing a log down the center, hollowing out the two halves, and then refixing with dowel and glue.

provide for the next round of breeding. Fairly coarse humus is good as it is difficult for the birds to bury the eggs, as is the case with pine bedding or sawdust.

Size and Placement of the Nest Box

The dimensions of the nest box are: height 7 to 10 inches (18–25 cm); width and depth 11.8 to 13.75 inches (30–35 cm); diameter of entrance hole 1.6 to 2.4 inches (4–6 cm). The entrance hole is best situated in the upper right-hand corner, with the nest cavity on the left side of the floor. A few pieces of batten attached to the inside of the box just below the entrance hole will make a type of ladder to enable the birds to get in and out easily. If you have battery breeding cages, which are several cages stacked together in a breeding room, it is necessary to mount the nest boxes on the outside of the cages to leave as much room as possible *inside* the cages; in small cages, parrotlets are more likely to squabble than in runs or aviaries.

A pair of Celestial Parrotlets (Forpus coelestis). *In the wild they live in mostly dry wooded habitats (thorny scrubs, deciduous forests, cactus scrubs, banana plantations, etc.).*

The nest boxes are best fixed to the front upper corner of the cages, with the entrance holes facing the cage backs. In aviaries, where we can use natural or manufactured nest boxes, the boxes can be affixed as high up as possible in a light area. If possible, the entrance holes should face south. All of the nest boxes must be hung at the same height; if you don't do this, you will notice that the birds will choose the highest boxes, making the lower boxes a waste of time and expense.

Incubation and Rearing

If you possess a harmonious pair and provide them with a roomy breeding cage or aviary, with the right kind of nest box, chances of successful breeding are high as long as the temperature doesn't fall below 59°F (15°C) and the humidity lower than 70 percent. A stimulus at breeding time is the addition of vitamin E to the soft food that is fed almost exclusively to the young for the first few weeks. A good commercial vitamin/mineral supplement is adequate. This soft food can be given throughout the year, but if you want to use it just as rearing food, you must be sure that the parents have access to it at least six to eight weeks before the breeding season commences.

Crop Milk

Parrotlets feed their young from their crops. This starts on the day of hatching and continues until the young fledge at about three weeks of age. At first this so-called crop milk is a very thin mixture. As a rule, the cock feeds the hen with partially digested food from his crop and she, in turn, digests it further and mixes it with the crop milk before feeding it to the young. It is obvious that the food taken by the male must be of high quality. Various commercial soft foods are available for lovebirds and parakeets, and these are ideal for parrotlets as well. For the first week, you can experiment with various brands before using that brand that the birds obviously prefer. From the first day, mix in a good vitamin/mineral supplement (containing vitamin E) with the soft food. Offer the food at least twice a day. To make the food more attractive, mix into each five ounces of food, one dessertspoonful of honey, half a dessertspoonful of very finely grated (blended) carrot, and a touch of carbonate powder.

Courting Display

In aviaries and runs, nest boxes are usually inspected (by the parents-to-be) at night; boxes in breeding cages can be inspected also during the day, especially late afternoon and evening. The cock bird takes the initiative and tries to entice the hen into the nest box. After the courtship display, and once the pair stays for prolonged periods in the nest box and the male feeds the hen

Rearing-food Recipe

The following is my own rearing food recipe for parrotlets and other dwarf parrots, which I use for both birds in outdoor aviaries as well as those in cages indoors:

- 9 ounces (250 g) rusk flour or fine bread crumbs (wheat)
- 4.2 ounces (120 g) hard-boiled eggs
- 3.5 ounces (100 g) cooked fish (whiting or similar)
- 1 teaspoon (5 ml) glucose powder
- 1 teaspoon (5 ml) sustagen, a product that contains vitamins, minerals, proteins, and carbohydrates
- 1 teaspoon (5 ml) pollen, available in health stores
- 1 teaspoon (5 ml) brewer's yeast
- ¼ teaspoon (1 ml) multivitamins.

To the above mixture, add approximately two cups (1 lb [500 g]) of strained meat and vegetable baby food, available in cans of about 4.6 ounces (130 g), and 3 cups (750 ml) of water, and mix it all together in a blender. The resulting mixture should be placed in airtight containers and stored in the refrigerator, not longer than four days, or frozen for up to a month.

with regurgitated food, you can consider that the pairing is clinched. The first egg can be expected in a few days. However, don't think that the cock feeding the hen is necessarily a sign of imminent breeding; this can occur at any time, both in captivity and in the wild.

Under normal circumstances it is the cock bird that begins the courting display. The wings are held out from the body at the elbows, while the remainder of the wings are pressed tightly against the body. This behavior is repeated slowly, but the wings can also be quickly raised and lowered as though the bird is trembling. The wing movements are usually accompanied by bowing movements toward the hen. The hen, in response, may drum her beak against the branch or perch on which she is sitting. The male also may perform this beak drumming at times.

Occasionally, the cock may approach the hen with tripping steps, but this is only possible when

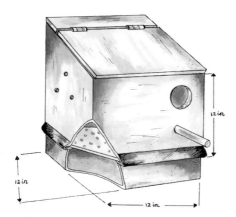

Square nesting box, especially designed for parrotlets and other small parrots. The box has a perforated bottom and is placed over a tray containing water. Water vapor can pass through the holes in the zinc bottom and thus keep the shell membrane of the eggs moist to ensure hatching.

there is adequate room on the branch or perch. Sometimes the whole dance may be performed on top of the nest box or, rarely, on the ground. In the wild, I have never observed the courtship display performed on the ground in any species. If the hen is ready to mate, she will make little bows, and raise her tail. The cock will then raise one of his feet onto her back while using one of his wings to hold her body; the second foot is held fast to the perch in order to maintain balance. Copulation is thus not via back-sitting, but sideways, for parrots a somewhat unusual posture.

Egg Laying

Eggs are usually laid every second day, but sometimes a hen may lay daily; I have observed this in Mexican and Yellow-faced Parrotlets. The usual clutch contains five to six eggs, rarely more, and seldom fewer than four. Exceptions include the Pacific Parrotlet, which can lay up to ten fertile eggs.

Incubation is carried out by the hen and usually begins after the appearance of the second egg, so that the young hatch in the order in which the eggs were laid. Therefore, there can be a considerable time difference between the laying of the first and last eggs, especially in large clutches; however, under normal conditions, eggs take about 21 days to hatch. As we have stated, the hen broods alone and, during incubation, rarely leaves the nest; in this time she is fed regularly by the cock bird. During the day, the cock stays close to the nest box, ready to fiercely defend it should danger threaten; this is particularly applicable to wild birds. The cock frequently spends the night in the nest box with the hen and, occasionally, may brood the eggs for several hours. Some hens, however, will not allow this to happen.

Brooding hens have white, fluid droppings that they usually pass only once a day, when they leave the nest box to feed. This is the best time for the breeder/fancier to inspect the nest. Should the clutch be too large, that is to say, at least six eggs, the eggs should be candled to assess any that may be infertile. *Infertile eggs must be removed.* A clutch of five eggs is ideal for brooding. With more than five, one or more of the eggs may not be covered during brooding, will cool down, and the embryo will die. As the eggs are frequently turned, interchanged, and moved by the hen, this can mean that a high percentage of embryos can be lost when the clutch is too large.

The Young

On hatching, the deaf, blind, lightly downed chicks frequently herald their arrival during the day with their loud cries; the young of Blue-winged, Green-rumped, and Spectacled Parrotlets are especially lively, and create pandemonious sounds a

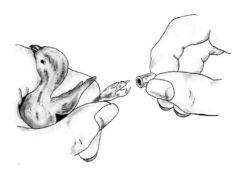

Banding; step one: With thumb and first finger of the hand in which the bird is held, gather the three long toes together, holding them in the proper position by the ball of the foot.

few hours after hatching. From that time, the nest must not be disturbed for the first few days. It is important to supply adequate rearing food, millet spray, germinated seeds, and finely chopped greens at this stage.

Banding

At the age of about eight days the young will be large enough to be banded. With the help of a little saliva, or petroleum jelly—after banding, wipe clean with a piece of

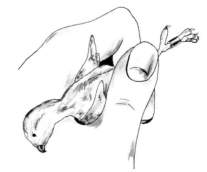

Banding; step two: Slide the band over the toes, then pass it over the ball of the foot, gradually sliding it up the leg.

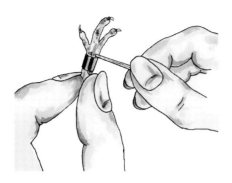

Banding; step three: To release the small back toe, which now lays against the leg by the band, insert a pointed matchstick between the toe and leg, and carefully ease the toe through the band.

wadding—hold the two front toes and the longer of the rear toes to the front, leaving the shorter rear toe to the rear. The diameter of the band is just a little greater than the joint, and slips easily over it. You can pull the small rear toe through the band with a sharpened matchstick. Check after three or four days to see if the band

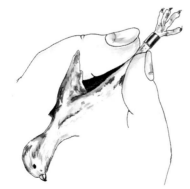

Banding; fourth and final step: The band is now correctly positioned around the young bird's leg. **Nevertheless keep an eye on all banded (ringed) chicks as the parents often try to remove the bands, obviously resulting in mutilated youngsters!**

is still in position. It is advisable to darken the band with a black felt-tipped pen in case the hen tries to turn it out of the nest, complete with its wearer. The inner diameter of the band should be 0.15 inches (4 mm) in most cases, but for larger species such as Yellow-faced Parrotlets, Pacific Parrotlets, and Mexican Parrotlets, a budgerigar band of 0.16 inches (4.2 mm) diameter is better.

Feathers

If all goes well, the young will have their first feathers after 12 to 14 days; at 20 days of age the whole body is feathered, and after another 10 days, they will have their complete juvenile plumage. The young will leave the nest at 32 to 35 days.

Hand-rearing

Many breeders remove the young from the nest after about two weeks in order to hand-rear them. The young must be placed in a brooder in which a constant temperature of 89°F (31.7°C) can be maintained. If the chicks begin to gasp and look uncomfortable, lower the temperature to 84 or 85°F (28.9 or 29.4°C). If they seem to be too cold, in which case they usually huddle close together, raise the temperature to 91°F (32.8°C). Spectacled Parrotlet and Green-rumped Parrotlet chicks are especially susceptible to cold.

The birds must be hand-fed at four-hour intervals; begin at 7:30 A.M. and finish at 11:30 P.M. Should the chicks be younger than two weeks, it will be necessary to feed them at two-hour intervals.

The best utensil for hand-feeding is either a bent spoon or a syringe. Make sure that each chick has its own spoon or syringe, and always make sure that utensils are thoroughly washed and disinfected between each feeding session. At ten days old, a feeding of 0.068 fluid ounces (2 cubic cm) is adequate; this can gradually be increased to 0.204 fluid ounces (6 cubic cm) per feed at three weeks of age.

By the time the young are five to six weeks old, they will be showing interest in solid food. I like to offer them dry or soaked millet sprays, finely chopped greens, germinated seeds, fruit such as chopped apple, berries, and so on, and whole-grain bread crumbs in the brooder. Sandee and Robert Molenda also recommend small seeds such as those given to finches and cockatiels, pellets, cooked rice, and pasta. They scatter dry food over the bottom of the brooder and place cooked foods in shallow dishes.

The brooder temperature needs to be gradually lowered; when the young are fully feathered, the temperature should equal room temperature. At five weeks of age, the young are placed in a large cage with low-fixed perches; all of the food except the millet spray should be placed in flat dishes on the floor of the cage. At six weeks of age, the young should be completely weaned. The Spectacles and Blue-wings are exceptions and require an extra two weeks before they are independent. After three weeks, the young cocks, which have blue in the wings and tail, can be separated from the hens; for Spectacles, Blue-wings, and Mexicans this can be a little later, even as late as after the first molt. According to the Molendas, color enhancement continues after the first molt, often up to the age of two years.

Hand-reared chicks must also, of course, be close-banded, and records must be kept regarding their parents, date of birth, and medical data. It is advisable to use colored bands on the birds so that you can easily distinguish which chick is from which parent and thus make it simpler for later pairings, bearing in mind that you must avoid inbreeding.

Leaving the Nest

As soon as the young have left the nest, they will begin to seek out their own food. This will consist initially of soft food and germinated seeds, especially from millet spray. They learn to feed from their parents, which continually make pecking motions as though they were about to take up food. The young copy the parents and, in a short time, learn how to feed themselves; however, they will still allow themselves to be fed by the parents, which will let this continue sometimes for one to four weeks. For this reason, it is not advisable to remove the chicks from their parents too early, even if it seems they are no longer being fed.

Chapter Six

Health Care

While most parrotlets and other dwarf parrots are reasonably hardy birds, they will soon succumb to sickness if their care and nutrition are not the best. It is essential, therefore, that you place great emphasis on the correct housing, feeding, and other aspects of their care. By taking the time and trouble to get things right in the first place, you can avoid disasters.

The Canary-winged Parakeet (Brotogeris versicolurus chiriri) *has brilliant shades of canary yellow on the edges of the wings.*

Bird diseases often have a short duration and if symptoms are not noticed in their early stages, the chances of successful treatment and cure will be severely diminished. Therefore, by carefully familiarizing yourself with all of your birds and studying their individual traits and behaviors, you will be in a much better position to quickly recognize any possible problems.

For example, if a bird should suddenly start perching in spots it normally avoids, you can conclude that there is something not quite right. The same thing can be said when a bird starts messing up its food. One very obvious pointer is when a bird sits moping in some corner of the cage or aviary, with its feathers puffed out and looking extremely sorry for itself. Healthy birds normally perch on one foot only; if a bird sits on both feet, with its eyes partly shut, it is probably coming down with some ailment.

Preventive Care

Personal hygiene is a very important aspect of bird care, especially when dealing with sick birds. You could possibly be the cause of passing an infectious disease from one bird to the next, perhaps even infecting your whole stock, if you don't take the necessary precautions. Wash your hands thoroughly after every treatment or contact. I am often quite astounded at how some people fail to observe this simple but important rule. Just imagine if you were dealing with an outbreak of psittacosis or a similar disease—you could infect all your other birds, and perhaps even yourself or members of your family. It is best to wear frequently laundered overalls and rubber gloves when dealing with sick birds. The overalls can be worn in the sick room and removed as you leave. Even your rubber gloves must be disinfected between uses.

A basic hospital cage. Various designs are also commercially available.

Health Problems and Injuries

Aspergillosis

This unpleasant condition is brought about by the respiration of spores, particularly those of the fungus *Aspergillosis fumigatus.* Certain plants, such as those belonging to the genus *Asperula,* can help bring about this fungal infection. Moldy bread, seeds, chaff, musty hay, straw, rotten wood, corncob bedding, and the like can also cause aspergillosis. The spores produce poisonous toxins that damage tissues in the lungs, nostrils, head cavi-

ties, air sacs, trachea, syrinx (voice box), and bronchi, promoting a buildup of a yellow cheeselike pus that will, of course, interfere seriously with breathing. An infected bird loses all interest in food, weakening it severely in a short time. Gasping, with open beak, the bird may stretch out its neck and shake its head frequently, as if trying to dislodge the blockage. No particularly satisfactory remedy has yet been found for this disease, though medications used include ketoconazole, Amphotericin-B, flucytosine, and rifampicin. It is best to take a bird suffering from this disease to an avian veterinarian.

To avoid this disease it is very important to supply only fresh seeds, never old or moldy ones. Don't give spilled seeds a chance to become moldy; clean the aviary regularly and always remove all old, spilled food. Try to prevent dust and plant spores from blowing into your aviary, particularly in spring and fall. This is especially important if you live near a lumberyard or any place where hay is stored; wet or damp hay is particularly dangerous. After any outbreak of this infection, all bird areas must be thoroughly scrubbed, rinsed, and dried before applying a solution of 1 percent copper sulfate over all surfaces. Allow this to dry before returning the birds to their cages or aviaries.

Coccidiosis

This disease is caused by *Coccidia,* minute protozoan parasites that may occasionally infect parrotlets and other dwarf parrots. The infection occurs in the intestines and is spread via the droppings. Any bird that eats food or drinks water contaminated with these infected droppings will thus also contract the disease. Birds may sometimes be infected for a long time before any symptoms are noticed. Should you notice a gradual decrease in appetite and loss of weight, coupled with loose, often bloody droppings, you must immediately isolate the bird and consult an avian veterinarian. If coccidiosis is confirmed, sulfa drugs may be administered. Recently imported birds should be routinely checked for this disease. Good hygiene and sanitation are the finest prophylactic measures. Other treatments, including amprolium, nitrofurazone, Bactrium, or Tribrissin, are not always satisfactory.

Colds

A number of respiratory difficulties can be classed generally as colds. All of them are infections of one or more parts of the respiratory tract and can have various causes. Drafts, low temperatures, vitamin A deficiency, stress, and exposure to various fungi, bacteria, or viruses are some of them. Symptoms of respiratory diseases are usually fairly obvious and include rapid, audible respiration, open beak, gasping, wheezing, sneezing, and coughing, coupled with nasal discharges and loss of appetite. The sick bird will usually sit moping in one corner of the cage, with its eyes partly closed and its feathers ruffled out.

Such cases require immediate treatment. Place the bird in a warm environment, preferably a hospital cage (see page 95), and minimize stress. Nasal discharges should be gently swabbed away with a cotton ball. Use a vaporizer spray, available at most drugstores, to spray a fine mist of lukewarm water into the cage; this will help moisten and soothe the lining of the bird's air passages. As is usually the case, it is best to consult an avian veterinarian, as well as to rethink your methods of housing, feeding, and general care.

Diarrhea

Diarrhea is an indication that something is wrong with your parrots' digestive systems. Intestinal upsets can be caused by a number of different infective organisms, as well as food that is spoiled or even contains toxins. Other causes of diarrhea include obesity, respiratory infection, excessive heat, or an excess of protein in the diet.

Warm weather coupled with poor ventilation in the birds' quarters can also help to cause intestinal problems, as can cold, drafty conditions. Temperature extremes, especially when there are sudden changes, can always be considered a threat to the birds' health. In outdoor aviaries, cold water often is a problem during the winter months, especially in the harsher climates. In extreme cold, the drinking water will freeze over and, unless you are very vigilant, your birds may be without drinking water for hours.

Visible symptoms of impaired intestinal function include lethargy, "hunching," and watery, often foul-smelling, or unusually colored droppings. In serious cases, the bird may take to the floor and sit in a corner with its head tucked under its wing. Although it may drink quite a bit, it will have little appetite for food.

All cases of intestinal disturbances are best referred to an avian veterinarian, but there are a few home remedies you can try yourself. I have personally enjoyed some success with chamomile tea. The sick bird can also be given boiled rice, oat flakes, millet spray, peanut butter, and canned baby food. You can try providing rice water in place of the usual drinking water, or you can use the well-known commercial preparations Kaopectate or Pepto-Bismol in a dosage of one to two drops every four hours, using a feeding syringe or a plastic medicine dropper.

As with other ailments, it is best to place the sick bird in a hospital cage, with the temperature maintained at about 90°F (32°C). Together with the antibiotics or other medication prescribed by the veterinarian, the quiet and warmth will help the bird recover quickly.

Remember that diarrhea is a pointer to many avian diseases, or it may be caused simply by a case of mild indigestion if there are no other symptoms. To be on the safe side, it is always best to consult your avian veterinarian when a case of diarrhea occurs.

Accidental Poisoning

Intestinal problems can also arise from accidental poisoning. Spoiled food or other poisonous substances can be a great danger. Insecticides such as Lindane and DDT should never be used in the vicinity of cages or aviaries, or near your stores of foodstuffs. If you suspect poisoning in your birds, place them in warm quarters. Feed them with green food and put a little bicarbonate of soda in the drinking water, about .035 ounce (1 g) per glass of water, but do not continue this for more than three days. Other good purges include fresh milk or a few drops of Pepto-Bismol.

Excessive amounts of protein in the diet can cause a special type of poisoning, especially during the breeding season. Too much egg food or soft food is often the cause. Such foods must be provided as a minor supplement to the usual food and *not* as a replacement for it. Birds affected by excessive dietary protein will suddenly show typical signs of poisoning, becoming lethargic, having difficulty with breathing, and possibly losing the ability to fly properly. This may be accompanied by severe diarrhea, which can be fatal.

E. coli Infection

This infection is caused by a gram-negative bacterium (*Escheridia coli* or simply *E. coli*) and can pose serious problems in parrotlets and other dwarf parrots as well as many other bird species. *E. coli* can also be carried by humans and other animals; however, don't let anyone tell you that *E. coli* are normal residents of a bird's digestive system. They are certainly *not,* and, if they spread to other internal organs, they can quickly be fatal.

Good hygiene is the best preventive measure. Wash your hands every time you deal with your birds, especially when moving them from one cage or aviary to the next. Prevent fecal contamination of foodstuffs and work areas, and clean cages and furnishings frequently and thoroughly.

E. coli infection can be treated by administering three to four drops of Kaopectate or Pepto-Bismol to the sick bird every four hours with a plastic medicine dropper. This treatment coats and soothes the inflamed linings of the digestive tract. If rapid improvement is not observed within 24 hours, consult a veterinarian, who may prescribe alternative treatment.

Egg Binding

Egg binding means that the female is ready to lay her egg, but cannot do so due to various factors, such as inadequate husbandry, bad diet, cold weather, and so on. It rarely occurs in birds that are properly housed and fed. An egg-bound hen will look sick, will sit hunched up, usually on the floor, rarely in the nest box, and is, in most cases, quite easy to catch in the hand. By carefully feeling her lower abdomen, you will be able to locate the egg that is stuck.

Under normal, healthy circumstances, the egg spends no more than 24 hours in the wide section of the ovary leading to the cloaca and in the cloaca itself. When the egg is ready to be laid, muscular contractions of the oviduct push the egg into the cloaca, and then, in a short time, entirely out of the body. The muscles involved may malfunction as a result of chilling, overbreeding, breeding when too young or too old, being out of condition, or dietary deficiencies, especially an insufficiency of calcium or various vitamins. Such malfunctions may cause the egg to be retained in the body, however hard the bird may try to lay it.

"Wind" eggs are either shell-less or have very soft shells. This also arises from either a lack of calcium or an inability for calcium to be deposited properly on the egg surface during its development. Such eggs cause egg binding because the muscles involved are unable to get a proper grip on the soft mass of the egg.

Under normal circumstances, egg binding is entirely preventable. You must, of course, plan to ensure that your birds get their optimum dietary requirements well in advance of the breeding season. A balanced diet, including an adequate supply of germinated seeds and green food, will go a long way toward preventing this condition. Wind eggs can be prevented by making sure that the birds get adequate calcium supplementation, especially calcium phosphate. Cuttlebone should be available at all times, and during the breeding season a little wheat bread soaked in water and squeezed out, a little grated cheese, and mineral blocks will help.

It is advisable not to start your birds breeding too early in the season as the temperature and/or humidity may not be ideal for correct egg development. In the colder areas it is best not to start your breeding regime until late March to mid-April.

Treatment: Egg binding, fortunately, can be treated successfully if you act quickly. A plastic dropper can be used to insert a few drops of mineral oil in the cloaca so that the passage path of the egg is lubricated. The bird should then be transferred to a hospital cage that is maintained at a temperature of about 90°F (32°C) with an infrared lamp. The warmth should help the bird to recover. In severe cases or in any cases where you are so inclined, a good avian veterinarian can be consulted. The veterinarian may be able to stimulate egg laying by injections of certain drugs. In very severe cases, the egg may have to be removed surgically. Eggs removed by surgery or medication should not be used for incubation.

Egg Pecking

Birds occasionally develop a habit of pecking and damaging eggs in the nest. If you find any of your birds doing this, they should be removed from the cage/aviary and not used again for breeding. The cause of egg pecking is not known, but it can be suspected that a lack of certain substances in the diet may be at fault. Proper husbandry and diet should eliminate the chances of your bird developing such an unpleasant habit.

Eye Diseases

Parrotlets and other dwarf parrots may occasionally be subject to various types of eye infections, which in most cases arise as a complication accompanying respiratory or other infections. The causative organism of the main disease may affect the eyes. A deficiency of vitamin A, allergies from dust or aerosol sprays, and so on can also cause eye problems. The infected eyes are normally held partially closed and there may be a discharge and inflammation of the eye rims (blepharitis).
• Bacterial eye infections can arise as a result of unhygienic conditions, especially perches contaminated with feces. Birds often wipe their beaks on perches and, in so doing, can transfer any bacterial contamination to one or both eyes, another rea-

son for practicing strict hygiene. Birds shipped together in overcrowded conditions are especially prone to eye conditions because of their close proximity with other birds. You need only one infected eye to start with and the condition can spread to all the birds in the cage.

• A bird with an infected eye or eyes should be placed in a warm environment, preferably a hospital cage. You should rinse both eyes with a 5-percent boric acid solution, or apply an antibiotic ophthalmic ointment such as Neosporin or Neopolycin two or three times per day. Treatment usually results in rapid recovery but, if in doubt, consult your veterinarian.

• *Knemidokoptes* mites (see Scaly Face, page 92) can also indirectly affect eyelids and eyes when the typical scabs occur in areas around the eyes. The scabs and the edges of the eye can be treated with an ophthalmic penicillin ointment.

• Wartlike lumps appearing on the eyelids can be caused by a deficiency of vitamin A. Improvement of the diet will cure these, but don't confuse the symptom with that of psittacine pox, which produces similar warts. This contagious disease requires veterinary treatment.

Unfortunately, untreated serious eye diseases can lead ultimately to blindness in one or both eyes. Heavy tear discharge plus a milky whitening of the eye is a pointer to developing blindness. Blind or partially blind birds can be kept alive in a small cage. The food and water dishes should, at first, be placed on the cage floor, and the blind bird will eventually adjust.

Feather Cysts

These may occasionally occur in our little psittacines. Not to be confused with tumors, these growths are caused by a feather shaft growing inside a feather follicle. The feather curls up beneath the skin and does not emerge, gradually developing into a cyst as it enlarges. If opened up, the cyst will be found to contain a cheeselike substance. An untreated cyst will eventually break open, or the bird itself may peck the cyst open, with the danger of secondary infection. The exudate from the cyst hardens on air contact and forms a scab that is attached to the feather as it continues to grow. The scab will eventually drop off.

It is recommended that birds with several feather cysts have them removed surgically by an avian veterinarian. Any bleeding can be stopped by using styptic wadding or by fine cauterization. In the case of large cysts, the wound may need to be sutured. Antibiotic treatment usually follows such operations.

Feather Plucking

This usually occurs towards the end of a molt. The growth of new feathers may cause irritation in the bird, resulting in scratching and then feather plucking. Once a bird gets into the habit of feather plucking, it often continues to do so, apparently out of boredom, as there seems to be no other plausible reason. Quaker

Parakeets, especially, sometimes become habitual feather pluckers, though it may occur in most birds from time to time. In some cases the birds may strip themselves almost naked.

The bird usually starts by plucking out a few old feathers that must be removed—at least the bird thinks so. It may then advance to new, perhaps undeveloped feathers. This produces itching and possibly pleasurable sensations, after which there is no end. Feathers may be gnawed off at the base, leaving just stumps. Such stumps may interfere with the growth of new feathers so they must be removed. To do this, hold the wing firmly with one hand and pull the feather stumps out at right angles. Make sure you have some kind of styptic preparation handy in case of bleeding. In some cases the bird itself may initiate bleeding while it is gnawing at the base of its feathers. The worst cases normally occur in the wings or in the tail. Loss of too much blood will weaken the bird so you must be vigilant and take the necessary action.

It seems that most cases of feather plucking in conures, in particular, especially in the United States, are accompanied by an infection of giardiasis, an intestinal protozoan parasite that causes pruritis, which is intense irritation of the undamaged skin. It is this irritation that leads to the feather plucking.

Discouraging Feather Plucking: Feather plucking can be discouraged by giving the birds things to keep them occupied. Pieces of sisal rope, twigs from fruit trees, willow, privet, and so on will provide them with hours of gnawing pleasure thus take their "minds" off the feather-plucking habit. Improvement in the diet by the addition of minerals, proteins, vitamins, and amino acids will also help. Willow twigs contain lignine, an amino acid that can be effective in curing feather pluckers.

Certain environmental factors also may encourage feather plucking. Low temperatures, high humidity, and poor lighting and ventilation may all contribute. Make sure your birds are kept in the best possible surroundings. Provide bathing water regularly. On hot days, a fine spray from a hose will do wonders for the birds. Do not clutter up your aviaries with plants, utensils, and so on. Make sure the birds have adequate flying space.

Serious feather pluckers will need to be fitted with an Elizabethan collar, which can be made from stout cardboard and fixed around the neck so that the bird cannot reach its body with its beak, but can still feed and drink. This may seem a somewhat drastic step to take, but such collars often cure the bird of its feather plucking in a few weeks. Hormonal imbalance may be a cause of feather plucking in some birds. If all else fails, your veterinarian may recommend an injection of an appropriate hormone preparation that often does the trick.

Removing Damaged Feathers: Because feather plucking can lead to cannibalism, it is important to remove damaged feathers; new feathers will replace them in a few weeks. If the damaged feathers are left on the bird, it will continue to gnaw them until it injures its skin, causing bleeding and possible secondary infection. Some conures and parrotlets may develop the habit of plucking their young in the nest. It is not unusual in such cases to see fledglings totally bald on the head, neck, and upper back. In severe cases, the flight and tail feathers may be plucked out, with possible damage to the feather follicles. Replacement feathers will grow in an abnormally twisted manner.

You could try using one of the commercially available sprays that have a nasty taste and claim to stop the adults from plucking their young; however, some adults are persistent in plucking the feathers of their young and, in such cases, it is best to remove the young and hand-feed them or foster them to better parents. If no foster parents are available, the young can be separated from their parents in a cage with mesh wide enough for the parents to feed their young through it.

Fractures

Bone fractures in the leg or wing can be avoided by handling birds carefully and protecting them from howling dogs and prowling cats that may cause the birds to panic and injure themselves. If a fracture should occur, consult an avian veterinarian.

If this is not possible, you can try treating a broken leg yourself. Line up the severed sections and splint the fracture on either side of the leg with a couple of thin sticks, such as matches, or pieces of bamboo skewer. Keep the splints in place by winding gauze around them and securing with surgical tape. The gauze should be wound fairly tightly; the site of the fracture should have as little movement as possible.

Another, better method is to use strips of gauze that have been immersed in a thin suspension of plaster of paris. Wrap the leg twice, line it up properly, then hold it until the plaster sets before wrapping a few more strips around it. Remember that it is always better to refer such cases to a veterinarian, if possible.

Torn Muscles: A torn muscle may sometimes be mistaken for a fracture. It may occur in a bird that struggles to release itself after it has been caught up in some snag such as wire mesh, especially if the bird has overgrown nails. Torn muscles are slow to heal. You could try to immobilize the affected leg with a bandage, keeping it stable while nature takes its course.

Wing Injuries: Wing injuries can best be bandaged with gauze. Cut a slit in the gauze, then put the folded wing through the slit. Wrap gauze around the body and secure it to the leg to stop it from slipping off. Make sure it is tight, without squeezing the bird. This treatment will enable the wing to heal in a reasonable position, but the bird may not be able to fly properly afterwards.

All fracture cases should be kept in a hospital cage in a quiet spot until the healing is complete. No perches should be used and the floor should be covered with a soft material such as peat moss. Be sure to provide additional vitamins and minerals throughout the healing process.

Frostbite

Frostbite of the toes may occur on cold winter days or nights, especially if the birds hang onto the wire mesh for too long. This can happen if the birds are startled, especially at night. Perches that are too thin may also cause problems because the birds' toes cannot be adequately protected by the feathers. Make sure your roosting perches are sufficiently thick. It is a good idea to provide sleeping boxes with an insulating layer of peat moss on the floor.

Frostbite causes the infected toe to darken, stiffen, and eventually drop off. There is little you can do about it, though you can consult your veterinarian, who may supply a soothing salve. In most cases, frostbite poses no real problems to the bird other than loss of one or more toe tips; however, keep a close eye on cases and, at the first sign of infection at the site of the frostbite, treat the wound with noncaustic iodine.

Goiter

Caused by a deficiency of iodine in the diet, goiter symptoms include an enlarged thyroid gland that can be seen as a large swelling at the front of the neck. A large goiter may press against the crop and windpipe and interfere with the bird's functions. The bird will quickly become breathless from normal activity and, breathing heavily, may drop to the ground, often with outspread wings and a pendulous crop and neck. Breathing may be accompanied by wheezing or squeaking. To help itself breathe more easily, the bird may rest its beak against the bars of the cage or on a parallel perch or branch.

Fortunately, goiter is no longer the problem it was at one time. Commercial cage sand and many mineral blocks contain sufficient iodine to prevent the condition, but the problem may still occur in areas where drinking water is deficient in iodine.

Untreated, a goiter can cause complications such as cerebral infection, asphyxiation, heart failure, or severe weakness due to an inability to feed properly. The condition will eventually be fatal if no action is taken. Treat the condition by administration of iodine glycerin—one part tincture of iodine to five parts glycerin—in the beak by means of a plastic medicine dropper. A couple of drops, two or three times a day over three days, often works wonders. If the condition persists consult a veterinarian.

Mites

Several species of mites, which are small arachnid parasites, can cause problems in birds. Feather mites consist of three types that live on the skin as well as on the feathers.

1. *Syringophilus bipectioratus,* which feeds on feather and skin debris. This species is not a danger in itself, other than the fact that it may cause irritation that can lead to feather plucking.

2. *Dermoglyphus elongatus,* which poses more of a problem because it burrows into the follicle and/or shaft of the feathers.

3. The common red bird mite, *Dermannysus gallinae,* which does not normally live on the bird's body, but lurks in cracks and crevices around cages and aviaries, coming out at night to suck blood from the birds.

Smaller than a pinhead, a single mite obviously cannot take much blood at a time, but they tend to multiply into enormous numbers, and can severely affect the health of your birds, both by causing anemia from blood loss and stress due to the intense irritation of their bites. They can be particularly stressful to brooding birds and nestlings. Mites are also capable of transmitting pathogenic diseases from bird to bird.

Mites can be introduced into your aviary by such wild birds as pigeons, sparrows, and others sitting on the aviary roof, or may be brought in with new additions to your collection, especially if the newcomers have been previously kept in crowded conditions. Good cage and aviary hygiene, and facilities for the birds to bathe, will go a long way toward preventing mite infestations. Always keep a close watch for mites in your collection. You may need a magnifying glass to find them. One way of detecting red bird mites is to place a white cloth over a cage at night. The next morning, if mites are present, they will be seen as tiny red dots gathered together in the creases of the cloth. The cloth should be placed in boiling water to kill the mites, and it can then be used again. In cases of a mite infestation, all areas in and around cages and aviaries, nest boxes, and so on should be thoroughly cleaned before spraying with an appropriate miticide. Several makes of insecticidal spray, safe for use in bird aviaries, are available commercially. The birds themselves can be treated with the appropriate application. Information on what to use may be obtained from pet stores or from your veterinarian.

Molting

Molting in birds is not a disease condition but a natural process in which old, worn feathers are replaced by new ones gradually over a period each year. Parrotlike birds, in fact, molt during the whole year, with the high point coming after the breeding season when the young have become independent. Molting is thus closely associated with sex-hormonal changes in the body at the appropriate times. A normal, problem-free molt is also dependent on the season, the temperature, the humidity, and the bird's diet. The molt is usually more intense after a warm spring than it is during colder and wetter periods. Some birds may be so eager to molt that they continually fluff out the feathers, shake them, and even go so far as to pluck them out with the beak, clearly deriving some relief from doing this. Molting time, however, is a restful period for most birds and activity is kept at a minimum. Research has shown that a bird's body temperature is somewhat higher than normal during the molt, but may sink during an unsatisfactory molt.

During the molting period, birds require a diet rich in protein—feathers consist of 88 percent protein. They are also more susceptible to bone fractures at this time, owing to resorption of calcium from the bone tissue. As new feathers are formed from protein, there is the possibility that a bird receiving inadequate food will use them to supplement its diet.

Abnormal Molts: Abnormal molts occur when a bird loses too many feathers at once and has difficulty replacing them, or when the bird molts in the wrong season. These abnormal molts are usually caused by extreme environmental factors such as unusually high or low temperatures, or sudden weather changes. Shock, disease, or fear may also trigger abnormalities in the molt. A thyroid problem is another fairly common cause of abnormal molt. Your veterinarian will advise you on whether a dietary supplement is required.

Shock Molt: Shock molt can be avoided by making sure your birds are not subjected to sudden changes, loud disturbances, or the sudden appearance of predatory animals such as cats, owls, and weasels. Even mice and rats can pose a problem, especially if they gain access to an aviary at night. I have frequently seen birds contract shock molt after being removed at night to be treated for a totally different disease. With shock molt, the bird often loses its tail feathers and smaller body feathers, but rarely loses its wing feathers. Tail feather shedding can be compared with autotomy or tail shedding, a defensive measure in many lizard species. A predator ends up with a wriggling tail in the case of lizards, or a mouthful of feathers while the bird makes its escape.

Permanent Molt: Dwarf parrots, parrotlets, or conures may very occasionally suffer from what is described as a permanent molt. This is usually caused by a dietary malfunction, especially when there is a deficiency of amino acids in the diet. In such cases the normal molt may also be incomplete. Correction of the diet will usually solve the problem. Plant and animal proteins are necessary and a good vitamin/mineral supplement should be given two or three times per week. The birds must be comfortably housed and protected from extremes of weather. Supplementary heating and lighting may be provided in the colder months and the birds will benefit greatly. Lamps such as Vita-Lite (a fluorescent lamp) provide a broad spectrum of color as well as the vital ultraviolet rays that birds may miss out on with lack of natural sunlight. Ultraviolet rays play an important part in many biological functions, especially with regard to the production of vitamins in the body and the proper absorption of calcium into the bone tissues. It is especially recommended that birds with inadequate access to natural sunlight, such as those kept indoors, be provided with Vita-Lite or a similar product.

Obesity

Obesity simply means being too fat. Being overweight is a well-known cause of health problems in humans and the same applies to other animals, including parrotlets and other small parrots. In most cases, obesity in birds is caused by a badly planned diet and lack of exercise. Becoming fat is a fairly slow process; however, when a bird becomes so fat it can hardly fly, or even sit on its perch, things have already gone too far. The bird may sit on the cage floor, lethargic and panting heavily. The normal sleek outlines of a healthy bird become blurred and the body becomes heavy and cylindrical. If you look at the skin beneath the feathers, you will see the yellow color of the fat shining through.

Obesity will decrease a bird's life span if nothing is done about it. Apart from a proper diet, the bird needs plenty of exercise to keep it in good shape. If you realize that a bird is getting too fat, you must adjust the diet and make sure it gets plenty of exercise. In larger aviaries, birds normally get adequate exercise by flying from perch to perch, but for caged birds this is barely possible. That is why it is necessary to let your caged bird out for at least an hour every day, so that it can fly around the room or other secure area. Larger cages, perches spaced further apart, and providing sisal ropes and spray millet will also help the birds to be more active. Do not over-supply fatty foods, especially seeds high in oil, and make sure the birds get a good portion of fresh greens and fruits in their diet.

Preen Gland Problems

Infections of the preen gland may result in an abscess, which may be seen as a marked swelling on the base of the tail. A suffering bird will peck and scratch at the site of the abscess and may even pluck out some of the feathers. Eventually, the abscess may burst, leaving signs of blood on perches and other areas in the cage or aviary. The conscientious birdkeeper will not let the problem advance to this stage. Overproduction of the preening secretion usually precedes such an infection, so the symptoms can be somewhat relieved by gently squeezing out the gland at frequent intervals. If this does not help, it will be necessary to consult your avian veterinarian, who will incise the abscess and squeeze out the contents. This is followed by an application of antibiotics. Sometimes a tumor occurs in the preen gland. These tumors are usually benign and can be surgically removed by a veterinarian.

Psittacosis

Psittacosis is a disease of parrot-like birds, but can also occur in other birds, where it is known as *ornithosis.* It rarely occurs in parrotlets and other dwarf parrots. The disease is caused by an obligate intracellular parasite *(Chlamydia psittaci),* which is distinguished from all other microorganisms by its unique growth cycle. Psittacosis is usually associated with unhygienic conditions and may be brought in with imported birds, especially smuggled birds. Be wary of purchasing birds that look dirty; they may seem healthy, but careful examination may reveal that they are infected.

Because psittacosis shows a variety of symptoms, diagnosis can be difficult, especially in the early stages. It usually starts with obvious respiratory problems such as a mucous discharge from the nostrils, coughing, sneezing, wheezing, and so on. The bird becomes lethargic and may have diarrhea. Eventually, the bird will have cramps and lameness before dying.

There is a mild form of this disease that can be completely cured with the right treatment by a veterinarian, but be aware that recovered birds can sometimes continue to carry the organism that can be infective to other birds and humans. Any case of the disease poses a hazard and must be referred to a veterinarian or to the U.S. Public Health Service.

In humans, the disease usually starts with cold symptoms and may progress to a lung infection. The advent of antibiotics has removed the danger, provided you get timely diagnosis and treatment. During the mid-1960s, many countries placed strong restrictions on the importation of psittacine birds because of the risk of psittacosis to humans. In general, imported parrots must be quarantined for 30 days on arrival and are given a preventive treatment of chlortetracycline. The same drug is used in infected birds for a period of 45 days.

Salmonella

Salmonella is caused by rodlike bacteria that cause many fatalities in young hookbills. Symptoms include diarrhea, painful joints, and nervous disorders. The bacteria are passed on via the droppings of infected birds, or via the saliva, such as when parent birds are feeding their young. Salmonella organisms can also enter the eggs.

Salmonella occurs in four forms, all of which can occur together.

1. *Intestinal form:* The bacteria enter the wall of the intestine, resulting in diarrhea. The droppings are foul-smelling, soupy, green, or brown, surrounded by slime and containing undigested food particles; a green color in the droppings can indicate a gallbladder infection— consult a veterinarian immediately.

2. *Joint form:* A strong intestinal infection can result in the bacteria gaining entry to the bloodstream and infecting all parts of the system, including the bone joints. The results are pain and severe swelling. The infected bird attempts to relieve the pain by not using its wings or feet.

3. *Organ form:* Once in the bloodstream, the bacteria can invade all internal organs, especially the liver, kidneys, pancreas, heart, and various glands. The sick bird becomes lethargic and mopes in a corner, breathless and becoming nearsighted.

4. *Nervous form:* If salmonella invades the spinal column and nervous system, it will cause loss of balance and crippling. Typical symptoms include holding the head in an awkward position, fouling of the cloaca, and cramplike contractions of the toes.

Parrots infected with salmonella will develop serious intestinal problems within three to four days and, once the bacteria invade the bloodstream, fatalities can occur quickly, especially in young birds. Older birds acquire some immunity and may incubate the disease over a long period, but if they are not adequately cured, they will become carriers, capable of infecting other birds via their oviducts and their droppings.

Heavy losses of young birds in the breeding season are a sign of salmonellosis in the stock. A veterinarian should be called immediately to examine blood samples and dead birds.

Scaly Face

Scaly face is caused by a burrowing mite, *Knemidokoptes pilae,* which attacks the skin area around the eyes and beak and also, in serious cases, the legs and toes. These little arachnoidal parasites burrow into the outer layers of the skin, where they lay their eggs. If untreated, the resulting rough, scaly growths will gradually increase, and severe deformities of the beak will occur. The condition will spread among the birds if no remedial action is taken.

Benzyl benzoate, petroleum jelly, or glycerin can be applied to the crusty, honeycomblike scales. Mineral oil can also be used, but be careful to apply it only to the affected area and don't drip any on the plumage; use a cotton-tipped applicator. Serious cases should be referred to a veterinarian for specialized treatment.

Any scaly scabs that come away should be removed and burned, if possible. Clean and disinfect all areas in cages and aviaries to reduce the possibilities of further infection. Though not a particularly dangerous infection, it is troublesome and ugly, so take great care to prevent it. Though particularly common in budgerigars, the disease is, fortunately, rare in parrotlets and other dwarf parrots.

Sour Crop

Sour crop occurs when the crop exit is blocked by something the bird has eaten, such as a small feather. Unable to continue through the system, the crop contents start to ferment, producing gases, especially carbon dioxide. The crop soon becomes inflated with gas and the bird vomits up copious quantities of frothy fluid. Its head and beak become stained with the mucal discharge. To relieve the condition, hold the bird with the head down; gently massage the crop to drive out the gas and some of the accumulated fluid, which is mainly water. Keep the bird warm, and offer it some water to which a little potassium permanganate has been added. In severe cases, consult an avian veterinarian.

Worms

The type of worms we are discussing here are those parasites that infest the intestines. It is especially difficult to avoid worm infections in birds kept in outdoor aviaries as new infections are continually being brought in by the droppings of wild birds.

Roundworm (Ascaris) eggs are picked up with food that has been contaminated by the droppings of infected birds. They hatch in the bird's intestines as white larvae, and develop into adulthood, feeding on the contents of the host's intestines as they grow. With large infestations in the gut, the bird loses much of the nutrients it takes in by feeding, so weakness, loss of weight, and anemia will soon set in. The infection may be accompanied by diarrhea or constipation. When the adult worms lay their eggs, these are again passed out in the droppings, ready to infect more birds, or to reinfect the patient. Worm infections can be detected

from fecal samples. It may pay to have samples of your birds' droppings tested at regular intervals by a veterinary laboratory service. The veterinarian usually prescribes piperazine or levamisole, which will cure the infection. Good cage and aviary hygiene will help prevent infestations.

Threadworms (Capillaria) are spread in a similar manner to roundworms and may develop in the crop or the intestines. Loss of weight and diarrhea are typical symptoms. An infection can also be detected from a stool sample and treatment is usually similar to that described for roundworms. A good disinfectant to use on aviary floors and elsewhere is a 9 percent solution of Clorox. This will kill any worm eggs present, but note that this disinfectant may be corrosive to bare metal. After disinfecting, rinse all areas thoroughly with clean water before allowing the birds to go back into the aviary/flight.

Caring for a Sick Bird

Sometimes, indications of sickness in parrotlets or dwarf parrots are barely perceptible, but even the smallest indication that there is a problem must not be ignored. Even if you are wrong with your diagnosis, you will have lost nothing other than a little time.

Isolation

If you think one of your birds is showing signs of illness, your first

Essential Emergency Items

Although serious illness or accidents almost always require the advice and care of an avian veterinarian, you will be better equipped to cope with emergencies if the following items, next to your first aid kit, are available:

• Heat source. Infrared lamp (60- to 100-watt bulb); heating pad.

• Hospital cage. Several commercial models are available. Ask your avian veterinarian or pet store manager for advice.

• Environmental thermometer. Buy one that's easy to read, so you can accurately monitor the temperature in the hospital cage.

• Adhesive or masking tape. Use ½-inch (13-mm) width; this should be in your first aid kit.

• Gauze bandage and gauze sponges; they should also be placed in your first aid kit

• Sterile gauze pads, cotton-tipped swabs (Q-tips), rubbing alcohol, needle-nose pliers or tweezers, sharp scissors with rounded ends, and Latex gloves; these items belong in a first aid kit.

• Feeding tubes. Use 8F or 10F tubes, which many avian veterinarians carry. Ask the veterinarian to demonstrate the technique of tube-feeding or consult *Hand-feeding and Raising Baby Birds* (see page 191). Ask your veterinarian or an experienced aviculturist/breeder to demonstrate the various techniques of hand-feeding and tube-feeding.

• Syringes or plastic—not glass—medicine droppers for oral administering application; tubes and syringes should be placed in your first aid kit.

• Clorox. In a dilution of 6 ounces (177 ml) per gallon (3.8 L) of water, excellent for cleaning concrete floors, but may be corrosive to metal.

• Gevral Protein. For appetite loss. Always mix with Mull Soy, which is also a good source of essential vitamins and minerals. Use one part Gevral Protein to three parts Mull Soy; tube-feed ½ to ¾ fluid dram (2–3 ml) two to three times daily. Ask your avian veterinarian for more details.

• Kaopectate or Pepto-Bismol. For loose droppings and regurgitation; soothes and coats the digestive tract; helps to form a solid stool. Dosage: two to three drops every four hours, administered with a plastic medicine dropper.

• Karo Syrup. For dehydration and as a provider of quick energy. Add four drops to 1 quart (1 L) of water. Administer eight to ten drops slowly in the mouth every 20 to 30 minutes with a plastic medicine dropper.

• Maalox or Digel. For crop disorders; soothes the inflammation and eliminates gas. Dosage: two to three drops every four hours.

• Monsel solution. "Quick Stop," a clotting agent available in the better pet stores, or cornstarch; one of these belongs in the first aid kit. For bleeding. Don't use styptic powder for areas near the beak.

• Milk of Magnesia. For constipation. Dosage: Three to five drops in the mouth with a plastic dropper, twice daily for two days. Don't use Milk of Magnesia if your bird has kidney problems or heart disease; consult your avian veterinarian.

• Mineral oil. For constipation, crop impaction, egg binding. Dosage: two to three drops in the mouth with a plastic dropper. Be very careful when administering oil as it can cause pneumonia if it enters the breathing tubes and lungs.

• Goodwinol, mineral oil, Scalex, Eurax, Vaseline. For scaly face and/or scaly legs and feet.

• Betadine, Domeboro Solution, A & D Ointment, Neosporin, Neopolycin, Mycitracin, Aquasol A. For skin irritations. Domeboro is used on wet dressing: Dissolve 1 teaspoon or 1 tablet in a pint of water. A & D is an excellent remedy for small areas; Neosporin, Neopolycin, and Mycitracin contain antibiotics; Aquasol A is a cream and contains vitamin A. All these ointments and creams can be applied to the affected skin twice daily.

• Lugol's Iodine Solution. For thyroid enlargement. Dosage: $\frac{1}{2}$ teaspoon of Lugol with 1 ounce of water. Place one drop of this mixture in 1 ounce of drinking water for $2\frac{1}{2}$ weeks.

priority must be to isolate it from any other birds you may have. This quick action could save your whole stock from an outbreak of a virulent contagious disease. Should a disease be confirmed, the next step is to thoroughly clean and disinfect the cages and areas around it, as well as all feeders, water dishes, utensils, perches, and so on. It is also a good idea to boost the nutrition of all your birds by introducing a good tonic or multivitamin/mineral supplement to their favorite food or drink, following the manufacturer's instructions.

Consulting a Veterinarian

Many internal diseases are difficult to diagnose and treat yourself, so it is highly recommended that you consult a good avian veterinarian. In the case of contagious diseases, the veterinarian will usually prescribe antibiotic treatment, administered via the drinking water. Any bird that dies suddenly or in spite of treatment should be sent to a veterinary laboratory for a postmortem examination to ascertain the cause of its death. In the case of a severe contagious disease, the necessary prophylactic steps can then be taken to ensure the welfare of your other birds.

Hospital Cages

The sick bird should be placed in a separate cage, preferably a hospital cage in which only the front is open, the back, top, and sides being enclosed. The cage should preferably have a wire base to allow the bird's droppings to fall through into a tray beneath and thus prevent the possibility of the bird further contaminating itself. To maintain warmth, the front of the cage can be covered with a cloth. By using an infrared lamp suspended above the cage you can create a constant temperature of 85 to 90°F (29–32°C) in the interior. A thermometer is placed in the cage, and the lamp is raised or lowered until the desired temperature is maintained. Once the bird recovers, the temperature must be *gradually* lowered back to room temperature by raising the lamp a couple of inches a time at two- to three-hour intervals, and eventually switching it off. As you don't want your bird to catch a cold on top of its other problems, it is essential that drafts be avoided.

Several makes of bird hospital cages are available in the pet market, but it is quite easy to make one yourself with a little know-how. The conscientious aviculturist will, of course, have a hospital cage ready for emergencies rather than wait for a bird to get sick and then have to panic-buy or -construct.

A simple box about 28 inches high, 16 inches wide, and 20 inches deep (70 × 40 × 50 cm) can be made with plywood or similar material. Install three or four light sockets in the roof of the cage to take ordinary 60-watt bulbs, each of which can be operated individually. It is advisable to screen the lights from the bird by inserting a panel. The bulbs will allow you a range of internal cage temperatures, depending on how many you switch on. The front of the cage can be of glass, fitted into a hinged frame or simply slid into some runners affixed to the sides of the cage front. An additional small door should be made in one of the side walls so that you have access to feed and water the bird. A continual supply of fresh water is particularly important because the warm temperature in the cage will make the bird very thirsty.

A sliding tray is placed in the base of the cage, below the glass door, and this is covered with a wire screen so that bird droppings can fall through into the tray. Use bird sand or newspaper in the tray to make it easier to clean.

An easy-to-read thermometer should be affixed to the center of the rear wall of the cage, away from any of the light bulbs. As the cage is almost completely enclosed, you must supply a means of ventilation without producing cold drafts. A few small holes drilled in the upper side walls will do the trick.

After use, the hospital cage obviously must be thoroughly cleaned and disinfected. Be sure you unplug all electrical appliances before using liquids in the cage. It is a good idea to dry the wet cage outside in the sunlight.

Disease Signs and Symptoms

It is important to have a general idea of what to look for with regard to illness in birds. Conscientious birdkeepers will, of course, thoroughly check their cages and/or aviaries at regular intervals, preferably at least weekly, for signs of parasites. If you catch a parasite infestation in time, you will avoid more serious problems later on. You should regularly inspect the birds themselves for signs of parasites. Hold the bird firmly but gently in the hand and blow its feathers aside; a magnifying glass can be used to detect smaller parasites such as mites. If the feathers have a brushlike appearance, you must take immediate action (see page 87). If the bird shows signs of losing weight—if its breastbone sticks out, for example—or if it becomes overweight and has difficulty in moving, it must be isolated for individual treatment.

Signs of respiratory infections include runny nostrils, labored breathing, wheezing, and squeaky breathing. If the bird is gasping, with its beak open, this could be a sign of aspergillosis (see page 79).
• Check the eyes for inflamed rims.
• Feel the legs and wings carefully to see if they are normal.
• Examine beneath the wings and the rest of the body for signs of tumors, wounds, or other skin blemishes.
• One important part you can check regularly is its vent. Wet or dirty feathers around the vent indicate the possibility of diarrhea caused by one of several types of intestinal diseases.

If the bird has apparently recovered from whatever was affecting it, it should not be immediately placed

At the right a wild (normal-colored) Green-rumped Parrotlet, and at the left a dark green mutation which is dominant and autosomal. The latter has a so-called single dark factor.

back in its cage or aviary. Having been kept in a warmer environment for a period of time will mean that a sudden change to cooler temperatures could give the bird too much of a shock. It is therefore important to lower the temperature of the hospital cage or the sick room back to normal room temperature very gradually.

Be aware that a bird can starve to death in 24 to 48 hours; this applies particularly to sick birds that may be off their feed anyway. Try to alleviate this by giving them their favorite foods and adequate fresh water. Many birds have died from starvation rather than the disease that caused them to fast in the first place.

Chapter Seven
Taming and Training

Contrary to many opinions, it is not important how a psittacine is colored and marked when you are looking for a parrot, large or small, to tame or train. Of course, individual differences exist and some birds learn more easily than others, but appearance has nothing to do with it. It is also untrue that only males can learn to talk; I have known females with tricks and vocabularies that many male parrots would envy. If you want to own a talking parrot, look for a young bird, because they are more open to "suggestions," and will want to imitate the trainer without much ceremony. To achieve success, the bird should be isolated from other birds and kept with its owners. A young, hand-reared parrot makes the best pet. Such birds like to be cuddled and handled and will sooner or later imitate the various sounds they hear, including those of other birds. So, don't give the bird the opportunity to pick up sounds you don't want it to repeat, and the bird will then concentrate on learning what you want to teach it.

Welcome Home

When you decide to purchase a young bird, or hand-raise one yourself, important questions may come up, namely:

1. How will you transport a young purchased parrotlet, which will have to be independent, eating and drinking on its own, to its new abode?

2. How will you proceed in order to accustom the bird, either purchased or one you hand-reared, to its new surroundings?

The Gray-cheeked Parakeet (Brotogeris pyrrhopterus) *is still the most popular of the* Brotogeris *species in our fancy.*

Traveling Cages

Never collect your new pet from a bird dealer in an ornamental, round cage. These cages are generally far too big, and even if you were to wrap the cage in newspaper or packing paper, the bird would flutter around in it wildly, risking injuries. Also, once you get home, you will have an extremely tired and especially nervous young bird, of no use for training for some time. Therefore, transport your new parrotlet in a so-called traveling cage; a box, usually made of thick cardboard or hardboard, with some ventilation holes or with a piece of insect screening. Of course, it's possible to make such a cage yourself: The front side consists mainly of small-mesh wire netting; the rest is made of wood and should measure 10 by 8 by 8 inches (25 × 20 × 20 cm) for small parrot species. If you use a cardboard box, be careful that the ventilation holes are not covered by labels, wrapping paper, or any other obstruction. On the bottom, throw sufficient seed and also— especially for a long journey— provide some moist wheat bread, so that the bird will not get too thirsty. Don't worry that the bird may not be able to find the seed in the darkness of the traveling cage. During our study sojourns in Africa, South America, Indonesia, and Australia, we regularly saw parrots, parakeets, and many other birds foraging during the evening and at night, even when there was little moonlight. Also, with most of our psittacines we are able to establish that the birds searched for food at night. From this we may conclude that transporting parrotlets and other small parrots over a longer distance is feasible. As long as the birds have been provided with seed and fruit—pieces of apple, and such—they can be carried by car, airplane, or train in the traveling cages, providing the time between departure and arrival does not exceed three hours.

Settling In

On arrival home, make sure all doors, windows, and other openings have been secured, that there are no open flames, that the gas or electric stove is not on, and that fans have been turned off. Once all that has been checked, you can remove your parrotlet from the traveling cage and place it in its new home, perhaps an ornamental cage. The easiest way to do this is to place the open doors of the two cages together; the bird will usually change cages on its own, but don't try to rush things.

If possible, try to make sure the newcomer is settled into its new home before noon, so that it has plenty of daylight left for it to adjust to its new cage and surroundings. It will then be able to find the various perches with ease and choose one as a permanent sleeping place. Parrots that are placed in their new home during the evening will flutter and scramble about restlessly at night and injuries are likely to occur.

The majority of newly purchased birds will come from an aviary or a large flight; others will come from breeding cages or even from the well-known barred parrot cages, and will, therefore, be accustomed to seed cups and drinking fountains. Still, you must keep a sharp eye on the newcomer—from a distance—and check on whether it has been able to find the seed and water cup quickly. Most birds learned this at their previous owner's home, or in your own aviary or cage, but just to be sure, scatter some seeds, or pellets, depending on what the bird is used to, on the bottom of the new cage. A bird will instinctively search for food on the ground and, therefore, doesn't have to starve. Even though a full seed cup might be right above its beak, if the bird is not acquainted with similar utensils—and hand-fed parrots might not be—it might take some time for it to figure out what their purpose is and what's in them. Also, the fact that the parrotlet wants to eat quietly after a very tiring journey is easy to understand. If your new bird isn't able to find food immediately, that won't exactly be beneficial to its peace of mind!

Once the parrotlet has found its food, then "trailing" the seed in the direct proximity of the seed cup will no longer be necessary and you can stop scattering seed on the cage floor.

When to Start Training

Ideally, you should start training as soon as possible when the bird is still young, although even older birds can learn a lot if you work intensively with them. Many trainers raise their young birds by hand once they are independent.

When a young hand-raised parrotlet doesn't come into close contact with other birds, it sees its keeper as its real father or mother, and will irrevocably accept him or her as a member of the same species, however unkind that may sound.

In their behavioral patterns, many animals show a tendency to accept the first object they see as a parent and member of the species, especially when there are no other congeners or other animals around. Ducks, hatching from the egg, follow the first object that moves; if that happens to be a human, they will follow it. Biology shows many examples of this behavior; therefore, as you will probably have realized by now, taming and training parrots isn't so difficult as long as you do it with patience and devotion. Because the keeper/aviculturist/fancier is seen as a father or mother, and because the bird's behavioral pattern is formed in large part by copying set examples, certain games are very easy to learn for a young parrot.

Of course, a parrot should never be allowed to spend its whole life in the solitary confinement of a cage without any special attention from its keeper. Petting, conversation, and personal interplay greatly enhance the human/bird relationship. Tame, trained parrots may be kept together. If you have untamed birds, keep them away from the trained ones; if you have one trained bird, give it a lot of daily attention, but it is best to keep it away from other birds because it sees its keeper as a friend and a member of its species.

Personally, I find it better to keep all trained birds separate. This isn't absolutely necessary, however, as I have previously explained. Of course you can let trained birds perform as a group, but as soon as the performance is over, separate them again; in this way you can prevent the birds from taking over each other's tricks.

Training with a T-Shaped Perch

A T-shaped perch most resembles a natural resting place and, therefore, is an excellent training tool. Many bird trainers prefer using a finger during the first training sessions; others prefer a T-shaped perch. Such a perch must never be too smooth and, if it is, it can be made rough with sandpaper. Of course you should make sure there are no splinters left on it.

Note: Perhaps you already know that birds cannot determine by appearance whether they are dealing with males or females. Through behavior, birds almost immediately recognize gender, for example, the generally greater aggressiveness of males when they look at each other. On the other hand, when a hen looks at a male, she will slant her head to one side or look away and more or less ignore the male, or, if she is interested in him, she will watch him closely while making nodding and bowing movements, her tail spread like a fan, and producing small chattering sounds with her beak. You will probably say that this all sounds very interesting, but it doesn't have anything to do with our subject, the T-shaped perch, but it does. The fact is that it's a serious mistake to point a perch, finger, or hand straight at a sitting bird and slowly approach it. This resembles an approaching aggressive male parrot.

Approaching Your Parrot

The only way to approach a parrot with a T perch—or even with your hand or finger—is from the side and very, very slowly. As soon as the parrot perceives the perch, it is already close to it and it will want to perch on it; now you can make the bird sit on the perch by pressing it softly against the abdomen at the height of the feet. If the bird spots the perch sooner than you mean it to, move it slowly away from the bird's immediate reach and start anew by bringing the perch toward the bird from the side. It is not necessary to start all over from the other corner of the room; start right where you were standing when the bird perceived the T perch. If it again backs away from the perch, wait until it has calmed down before making a new attempt. Again, you stay right where you were with the previous attempt.

Getting the Bird out of the Cage

The same procedure can be followed to get the bird out of the cage without using the hand/finger method, but with the help of the T perch. Do not take the T perch out of the cage until the parrot has learned to accept it as part of the cage furniture. Most cages have a detachable bottom for easy cleaning, so the T perch can be laid on the floor or placed against the bars. Sometimes it appears, with this method, that the parrotlet reacts better and easier when approached from behind; the perch is moved across the back and head and under the abdomen in a semicircle and, subsequently, the bird is forced onto the perch by the light upward pressure. Again, this upward pressure may be strong, so that if there is no reaction, the bird is more or less slowly lifted from its seat. If the bird starts nodding nervously and appears to be getting jumpy, wait a few minutes until it has calmed down again, or else you risk having the parrot fluttering and scrambling about its cage restlessly, which will only make it more upset and perhaps even afraid of the T perch. Obviously, this is far from desirable.

Talking to Your Bird

During the whole training period, talk to your bird. It doesn't really matter what you say, as long as you say something, especially his or her name. The human voice often calms the bird and inspires trust. Don't give up the lesson unless the bird has made some progress, no matter how small it may be. In the case mentioned above, go on till the parrotlet has placed itself on the T perch, and after some well-meant, encouraging words, back to its usual perch. This is accomplished by pressing the T perch against the abdomen, right next to the feet. This can sometimes be very tiresome for the trainer and it may take some time, but giving up is out of the question. The bird should learn *something* in the session, even if it is only a little; otherwise, the rest of the training will become a difficult and tiresome occupation that you won't enjoy very much, and neither will the parrotlet.

A Second Perch

When, after many lessons, your parrotlet steps onto your finger, hand, or T perch without hesitation, you can teach it, now that it is outside the cage, to climb onto the index finger of the other hand, or onto a second T perch. You must not forget to talk to your bird and praise it if it reacts correctly. Personally, I first let the bird step once or twice onto my finger or hand, or to the second T perch, in this new lesson. If the parrotlet has performed it properly once or twice, put it back into the cage, which it considers a "safe harbor."

After having learned something new—however simple that may seem to you—the bird will be enthusiastic, even though it may not be immediately apparent; therefore, to calm it down, return it to its cage for a little while. After about half an hour, repeat the process; now let the bird step back and forth four or five times. While perched on your finger or the T perch, it will probably look around the room inquisitively, and even fly around the room a bit, but there is no real harm in that. If the bird is well trained, it will return to your finger, the T perch, or its cage when you want it to.

Distractions

In any case, I think it would be sensible not to have anything in the room that can distract its attention, such as a radio, TV set, and so on. Once the bird is accustomed to stepping from finger or perch back into its cage, the moment has arrived to slowly walk your pupil, perched deftly on either hand, finger, or perch, around the room while talking to it. If this has gone well, put the bird back in its cage for half an hour and then try again. A bit of advice: Raise your extended finger, hand, or perch a little above your own height if you can; a bird prefers to go to roost as high as possible as this makes it feel safe.

The Ladder

Now start using the second T perch, your forefinger, or the hand itself. Make the parrotlet step from one perch to the other or from one forefinger to the other, in a similar way, by lightly pressing its abdomen. At the same time, imitate a staircase by holding the right-hand perch a bit lower than the left-hand perch; the same applies to your finger or hand. Now make the bird go up or down as you please, as if it were climbing a ladder.

The first time you try this, the young bird will usually start flying around, but if you calmly put it in its cage and try again after half an hour, you'll eventually succeed. Don't make the parrotlet nervous; if it flutters to the ground, approach it slowly, hold out your forefinger and quietly wait for it to accept it. Follow the same procedure with a T perch or your hand. Speak to the bird and don't rush things. If it flies or walks away, take your time until it calms down and starts taking in its surroundings inquisitively; then approach it again, while speaking to it calmly and in a quiet voice. Should it unexpectedly be necessary to catch the bird without delay, throw a towel or sweater or something similar over it. Don't try to catch it in your bare hands, because a nervous parrotlet will bite under all circumstances.

Introducing a ladder should be easy enough. I have found that I obtain the best results when I perform these lessons in front of a large mirror; the bird sees itself, wants to imitate itself, and tries its very best to captivate its reflection. More than once, a bird was so intent on acting up for its double in the mirror that it seriously fell in love with itself. There's nothing wrong with that, as long as you give the bird enough attention and leave it alone during its romantic spells.

Removing Food

At least one hour before beginning initial training sessions, remove the food cups from the cage. Once the bird is used to your hand, you may hand-feed it. First try some millet or some other seed it likes, and snap the cricket—the well-known toy that makes a snapping sound when you press the tongue—as soon as it accepts the food. Every time you give it something especially delicious, make the same snapping sound and, before long, the bird will associate the sound with the food it likes so well.

Tricks

You are probably aware that all animals learn through associations. The Russian scientist Pavlov demonstrated this with dogs; every time they were fed, a bell sounded. After some time, the dogs would start salivating when the bell was rung, even without being fed. In other words, Pavlov had taught the dogs to associate the sound of the bell with food. In view of our training, this is an important detail. Reward the bird for everything it does well. Soon it will associate a well-performed trick with a food reward and be aware that that reward is a consequence of its action.

What kind of reward? You could try some millet spray. That's sensible and delicious for any parrot species. Birds often get a bit bored when they are in training or during a performance. It may seem as if they can't keep their minds on the subject at hand. The best way to revive their attention is to use the cricket. The birds immediately react to this sound and show a rekindled interest in the game; of course, you should reward them for their efforts with a few tasty seeds.

What games and tricks can you teach your bird? There are many possibilities, of course, and the bird itself will discover and even design games and tricks on its own. One of my parrotlets clearly enjoyed taking a coin from my desk and letting it drop into an empty ashtray. Once the penny lay in the ashtray, the bird would return for a second coin and repeat this performance until there were no coins left. Then it would transfer all the coins to the edge of the desk and drop them on the floor. When it had finished this task as well, it would fly to the floor, take each coin into its beak, and take them again to the ashtray. If it was willing to repeat the whole proce-

Holding a Parrot

The best way to hold a parrotlet or other small parrot is to let the bird's back rest against the palm of your hand, the head between your thumb and your middle finger, your forefinger over its head, as if it were a helmet, your ring finger on a level with its stomach, your little finger behind its legs or in line with its tail.

dure more than twice, to the delight of my granddaughter, I would provide a food reward in the ashtray and summon it with my cricket to take a well-deserved rest. If it was tired of the game, it would come and sit on my shoulder or head, pleased as punch.

Clipping Wings

Clipping a few flight feathers to prevent the bird from escaping before it is completely tame is a part of the taming and training process about which I don't hold a very definite opinion. I have worked with birds—primarily larger species—that have had their wings clipped, as well as with mainly small birds that have not, and I really couldn't say which birds were easier to work with.

If you treat your parrotlet in a calm and controlled manner, it will, in my opinion, not make a great difference which way you go, and, of course, it may depend on the spirit of various individual birds. I would, therefore, advise that you start training the birds without clipping their wings. If, however, your pupil proves rather obstinate, clipping a few flight feathers is a good idea.

If you are for clipping, always do it on both wings, using a pair of sharp scissors. Clipping a bird's wings won't hurt it and, after the next molt, the feathers will be replaced by new ones. If the bird isn't fully trained when it starts growing new feathers, you could consider another clipping.

Children and Parrots

It's hard to say who gets the most fun out of the companionship: the parrot or the child. From what I said earlier, it should be clear that parrotlets and other dwarf parrots are very affectionate and always willing to play games. Because they are easily tamed and because they can quite literally imitate the human voice and many other sounds, these birds are a constant delight to children as well as to adults.

On the practical side, parrots can be an asset to a child's education by teaching children the wonders of Nature. Furthermore, by letting them take care of the animals, they develop a love for and a respect for all living things. Taking care of and caring for birds can give a great deal of spiritual and physical satisfaction.

Talking Parrots

As soon as your parrotlet or other dwarf parrot is hand-tame, start considering speech lessons. If the bird has been raised by hand, directly from the nest, taming and training, as well as learning certain words and/or short sentences, should be fairly easy. You must always realize, however, that not every bird raised from the nest will become an excellent speaker. Teaching parrots, even those a few years old, is possible as long as the trainer works with patience and perseverance. Before starting speech lessons, it is important that the bird feels completely at ease with its keeper. During training it is important to be sure that the bird is not put off or even frightened by other noises or activities. Children playing boisterously nearby, loud radios, TVs, and so on are not conducive to speech training in parrots.

If the bird you are training to talk has a fright during the first few days, only kindness will win back its trust and secure its undivided attention for the things you wish to teach it. Don't expect the bird to start talking in only a few days; it can sometimes mean several weeks of hard work. New birds should, therefore, always be placed near people so that they can observe routine human activity.

Don't place them too nearby, of course, and make sure that household noises and happenings are not allowed to frighten them or make them nervous. Remember that birds that are given only their daily food and drink, and that are otherwise left to themselves, will never grow tame and will certainly not learn to talk. Constant attention and kindness are needed to develop that important bond between human and bird, and to make the bird trust and love you. If you cannot succeed in this with your parrots, it will be very difficult to tame them and teach them to talk.

Intelligence

It should be obvious to most people that a bird that talks or performs tricks only imitates. Animals cannot reason; they cannot "think" in the literal sense of the word, even though the opposite may seem to be the case. The parrot is taught to imitate and to repeat, or to do things that have attracted its attention and piqued its curiosity. The bird can be taught only to repeat certain sentences and to use the right answer at the most suitable moments. A bird is not taught to say *"good night"* at 6:00 A.M. or to say *"good-bye"* when someone comes for a visit. The bird is taught to say certain words and/or sentences at the appropriate times of the day. It has been proven, however, by various animal behaviorists and physiologists that certain birds do have some kind of reasoning and are able to "understand" various tests and requests, and even, in some cases, to understand numbers and recognize colors.

Male or Female?

I firmly believe, and I have repeated this often, that the sex of your bird makes no difference to the outcome of its training. Both sexes are equally able to learn to speak and to perform tricks. I have often found that the more responsive birds were the trainer's favorites or special pupils and nothing more; in no way could the trainer tell the sex of the birds. This is different in the case of the fancier. Then the sex is very important. Only one conclusion is possible here: Children and women have the best voices for speech training. The pitch of children's and women's voices makes them easier for parrots to imitate.

Covering the Cage

There is a tendency to cover the cage of a student with a cloth or a newspaper or a commercial cage cover during the first lessons. I don't think that this has a positive result; I have always thought that the bird likes to see and to hear the trainer. This statement is naturally based on personal experience and, if the bird learns better and faster when it is screened from the outside world, act accordingly. Covering the sides and rear of the cage, however, appears to increase the bird's concentration in the majority of cases, because distraction is obviously limited to a minimum.

Inappropriate Language

Some trainers like to teach their birds all kinds of violent expressions, curses, and inappropriate language. This is very childish. Remember, obscene language may be used by the bird at embarrassing times and in awkward places. I'm not saying that the teaching of curses and such

words is difficult; I believe that teaching many of these words is simplified because of their often sharp intonation and unusual combination of sounds. In my opinion, however, this is a very poor excuse for teaching birds things that they cannot possibly understand, and that might offend some people, and that have a detrimental effect on the children.

Training Methods

Many a fancier occupied with teaching speech to parrots has concluded that the process usually takes less time than expected. Children do not learn to speak within a few months; it often takes more than two years before infants formulate anything understandable or sensible. Therefore, you must first develop patience if you want to teach parrots to speak—patience *and* love.

• Don't punish the bird if it is not interested, but treat it with love and affection. Experience has taught many trainers that mornings are best for speech lessons, while parrotlets and other dwarf parrots can also be successfully trained between 7:00 and 9:00 P.M.

• If desired, the cage may, except for the front side, be screened and the trainer may place himself or herself where the bird can hear but not see him or her, for the bird's concentration is greater than when it can see the trainer's every movement.

• The words or the short expression must be uttered clearly in the same pitch and always at the same speed. Don't say any other expression or other words during the lesson than those the bird must learn to repeat. After every 15 minutes, take a five-minute break so the words may sink in. Make sure that there are no sounds during these breaks; it is sensible for the trainer not to speak with anyone within hearing distance of the parrot and not to sing or whistle a tune to a song on the radio. After the break, start again with the same expressions, words, or whatever you've selected as the subject matter of teaching.

• In the evening, perform the training in the same way. Don't praise the bird until it has mastered certain words or expressions faultlessly, so that certain sounds and impurities are not taken into the word that should be learned.

• Apart from the specific speech lessons, it will do no harm to say the word or expression regularly upon entering the room where the parrot is kept. The morning greeting as well as your "good night" when you turn off the light to go to bed is part of the teaching material.

• If, after some time, all your attention and instruction do not work, you will need to try a different method. Train in a half-darkened room twice a day, for no longer than half an hour per session. Sit with the bird in such a way that it can hear you, but not see you. Sooner or later you will discover that the bird will start repeating the words it has learned. Never lose patience or punish the bird.

Punishing usually has the opposite effect—the bird will have had enough of speech lessons, and its confidence will be shattered. You can, with a single gesture or word, turn a sweet and gentle parrot into a nervous and aggressive creature that is no longer tractable.

Under all circumstances be aware that you are working with animals that ask only for your greatest love and that, if it is given to them undividedly, will reward you with strong devotion and affection.

Using Bird Psychology in Training

As already stated, when teaching a parrotlet or dwarf parrot simple phrases like *"good morning"* or *"good-bye,"* you should practice such expressions when they are most appropriate. The association of time and deed—here, the spoken word—is remarkably strong with parrots, parakeets, mynah birds, crows, and related bird species. Seldom will a bird say an expression out of context if taught properly. When a bird is taught to say the name of a certain flower or a certain type of food, and you practice this when the bird is looking at the flower or is fed the food, it will soon learn to repeat the name of the flower or the name of the food when it sees it. It is also remarkable that parrots find it easy to learn to pronounce the names of members of the family and use them properly.

Many fanciers think that training and teaching parrots to speak can be done at the same time. Personally, I think that it is better first to domesticate them, to tame the animals, and then to teach them to speak, but, nevertheless, many trainers who give their birds speech lessons and tame them simultaneously are very successful.

1. The most common method of taming a bird and teaching it to talk at the same time is as follows: Remove food containers from the cage as soon as the new bird arrives and hope that it has had enough food in transit. I prefer giving the newly arrived parrot a few hours to get used to the cage, surroundings, and food, and then remove the food and water trays temporarily.

2. Early in the morning of the second day, the newcomer is fed by hand all the proper treats it is entitled to. Don't forget to use the expression or words you intend the parrotlet or dwarf parrot to learn. Every time you work with the bird, offer it food. Do this until the parrot faultlessly repeats what you say.

3. When the bird is ready for a second expression or a few new words, go about it as above. Eventually the trainer, not food, will be the main stimulus; the bird will happily learn other words when the trainer is present. By this time you should be able to give the parrot its daily food allotment without additional hand-feeding. Your presence, at this point, should be enough for your friend to perform its entire repertoire. Rewarding the bird now and then with a proper treat is, of course, advisable.

Often, a bird stops talking as soon as you come to its cage. The bird uses, more or less, what it has learned to lure you to it, and once you are there it will look at you with its shrewd eyes and remain silent. If you are about to go away again, it will undoubtedly surprise you with a torrent of words and expressions, with the sole purpose of changing your mind and making you stay.

I should point out that it is not wise to stop the lessons after a few words or expressions have been taught, as the first few words are the most difficult to teach. Once the parrot has taken to learning words, teaching it new words or expressions is, of course, child's play.

You will continually have to give the parrot your full attention and love, and you will have to continue in the usual concentrated way. If a review appears necessary, provide one directly. Developing a good talking parrot requires considerable effort.

Tape Recorders

I have heard several tapes and phonograph records with detailed instructions on how to train parrots and other bird species, and how to teach them to speak. If you want your bird to learn quickly, a tape or record like that can be very handy, especially if you have limited time to train the animal yourself, but obviously the most rewarding issue, the bonding with the bird, you miss out on.

With a tape recorder at your disposal, you can have enormous success as you can, for example, record the first expression or the first words you would like the bird to repeat; it requires only one extra tape on which you record the lesson needed. Later, after your personal lesson, you can play this tape as often as you like or, better still, until the parrot can repeat certain words faultlessly. While the bird listens and, hopefully, tries to repeat what it hears, you can leave the parrot on its own and do what you like. A parrot imitates not only the words, but also the intonation and the pitch, and it will, therefore, be fully concentrating while not completely realizing whether you are present or not. Again, it is essential that you present your personal lessons in order to create the bond so important for the happiness of the bird.

After a while, your parrot will no longer limit itself to words or short expressions, but with just as great an effort will try to imitate the whistling of other birds or the bark of your dog. I have known parrots that could faultlessly imitate the creaking sound of the wheelbarrow, the squeak of a badly oiled door, and Grandfather's smoker's cough. A sound can be picked up by the bird as long as the sound that can be imitated catches the bird's attention for long enough and often enough, so take care!

Teaching birds to talk or training them to do all sorts of tricks does not involve any cruelty to the bird, for in the 40-odd years that I have worked with animals, both as a hobby and in my work as a biolo-gist/ornithologist, it has become clear to me that both the bird and the trainer are having a pleasant time together, creating the bond that is one of the most rewarding experiences one may encounter.

Parrots and Technology

Parrots can learn words, expressions, songs, and even whole sentences that have to be spoken at the right moment. Most parrots however, will hear with difficulty a radio, TV set, or CD that is playing, and they will disregard all words and/or expressions and react most naturally by screaming loudly for a long time. They will even compete at screaming the loudest. And that doesn't apply to large birds only. Budgerigars, parrotlets, Fig Parrots, and small conures, too, are inclined to do this. For example, a couple of Canary-winged (Brotogeris chiriri) and White-winged Parakeets (Brotogeris versicolorus) in our home will persist in trying to scream louder than my daughter's piano playing. However, most birds seem to be very sensitive to soft, tuneful music, and I have often observed psittacines gently swaying their heads to the rhythm of my daughter's beautiful melodies.

If parrots continue screaming when a radio or TV set is on, then it is best to cover the cage with a thick cloth, and the screaming will soon stop.

Keep in mind, however, that little parrotlets, conures, Fig Parrots, budgerigars, and others do not usually pick up a large selection of words and expressions, with a few exceptions, when compared with many of the larger parrots such as African Grays, cockatoos (though not the best talkers around), and Amazons, but they are extremely capable of whistling tunes and speaking short, sharp-sounding words and many short sentences.

First Steps Toward Successful Training

The first few days in a new home (if it is one of your own birds) or new surroundings are most stressful for a parrotlet or small conure, but you must not give the bird you wish to train too much rest; start training immediately, and you'll have the best chance for success.

• As soon as the parrotlet sits in its ornamental cage, carefully put your hand inside. A strong leather glove on your hand would be a wise precaution for these initial overtures—even parrotlets and small conures know how to use their beaks. The parrot will soon accept your hand as being part of the "furniture" in the cage, especially if you move your hand slowly up and down. More than once, a young parrot has seated itself on my finger or hand within 15 minutes of its arrival in my home.

• Whenever you are occupied with your new parrot, call it by name, using a clear voice. Choose a short name like Bobby, Jacko, Polly, Peter, or Johnny so the bird will imitate this name without extra speech training. If this is not successful, you must think of other ways to teach the bird its name.

• As soon as the bird realizes that the hand inside does not change anything in the cage, or harm it in any way, it won't take long for the bird to accept your hand as a normal part of the cage. One parrot will accept your hand sooner than another; in the latter case you will have to continue your efforts. Don't lose patience under any circumstances, because any unexpected movement of your hand will be experienced as something new. Move your hand, after a while without a glove if you like, slowly and wait until the bird accepts it. As soon as the parrotlet perceives that the hand inside the cage is not a threat, it will examine it and after it has been approved your hand will be accepted without much ado as a "perch."

• Once the bird has come this far, put an index finger under the body very carefully, and press softly against the abdomen, just above the legs; the bird will then usually obligingly seat itself on your outstretched finger. If this does not work at first, and the bird flies away at the first attempts, continue the first exercise, using the hand as the old familiar seat. If, after a few days, the hand is once more accepted without fear, try the finger method again.

• Obviously, with large psittacines, just an outstretched finger is not enough. Two or three fingers work better, or else use an outstretched hand. With small parrots, however, move the index finger softly but "coercively" across the abdomen; under no circumstances must you withdraw your hand, as the bird may assume it has "scared away" your hand, and is likely to repeat the action.

Outside the Cage

Once the small parrot sits on your finger or hand without any difficulty, it is wise to teach it also to step back from your finger or hand to the perch. In order to accomplish this, hold the parrot resting on your finger with its breast against the perch. An order, such as *"Up,"* can be useful. When the bird fully knows this, it is time to take it out of the cage on your finger or hand. Several days may have passed. The first trip outside the cage must be of short duration. Of course, the parrot will probably first fly around the room and inspect things. After a few days, it will become evident that the bird chooses a special spot, preferably close to mirrors, windows, and other shiny objects in which it can see itself. Remember these places of preference so that you know where to look for it in the event the cage is accidentally left open. For that matter, letting birds fly around a room freely is quite risky, considering that

there may be fragile objects in the room. Also, even small parrots have a considerable wingspan and might easily injure themselves in the relatively small space of an average living room or den.

Returning to the Cage

A well-trained bird will return to the cage immediately if the trainer so wishes. At first, lure the bird back with some treats; later, of course, these treats will not be needed. Again, it is wise to use a fixed command like *"Come!"* If the bird refuses to come, despite repeated requests, use a thin bamboo stick or something similar, about ½ inch (13 mm) in diameter, or a perch shaped like a capital "T" of the same thickness.

The bird will usually climb onto it, especially if you press the stick softly against the abdomen—because the bird knows what that means. Slowly move back to the cage while the bird sits on the stick. It is still important to train the parrot so well that it returns to the cage immediately after the command *"Come!"* If you have to go "bird-catching" all the time, not only will it be unpleasant and tiresome for the bird, but it will be frustrating for you.

From One Hand to Another

Once the parrot will return directly to the cage whenever you wish, proceed to the next stage, which is teaching it to go from one hand to the other. Let the bird jump or step from one hand to the other as much as it wants.

Chapter Eight

The Species

Parrotlets

Spectacled Parrotlet—
Forpus conspicillatus conspicillatus
(Lafresnaye 1848)

There are two subspecies, *Forpus c. caucae* (Chassman) and *Forpus c. metae* (Borrero and Camacho).

Type: The body is slender and graceful, with clean lines; the posture is about 60°. The head is relatively small and round in form, while the rather hooked beak is held against the breast. The line of the back gradually curves into the tail base. The wings are held tightly against the body; well-proportioned specimens never have the wings crossed at the tip; they reach to the end of the keel-shaped tail.

Nominate Form: The nominate subspecies has a strongly accentuated eye ring that continues behind the eye, running into a point; this is, for example, never the case in the subspecies *F. c. metae;* in this subspecies a lighter line is visible.

The beak of the nominate form is more or less hidden among the "face feathers"; in other words it does not project far from the face and thus forms a harmonious line with the head. In *F. c. caucae,* however, the beak projects conspicuously out from the face and is somewhat larger than that of the nominate race.

Distribution: Colombia (the northern tropical range lies close to latitude 10 degrees), Gulf of Dariën,

All the secondary wing feathers and some of the primary feathers of the White-winged Parakeet (Brotogeris versicolurus) are white but the bird is nevertheless easily confused with the Canary-winged Parakeet (B. chiriri).

Spectacled Parrotlet *(Forpus conspicillatus conspicillatus)*

	Cock	Hen
Head & Face	• Face is vivid, dark green, merging at the edges into dark green washed with gray. • A cobalt blue edge above and below the eye merges at the back of the eye running into a point.	• Color above the beak is light grass green merging into dark green. Beneath and above the eye, a bright, dark green edge, merging behind the eye and running into a point.
Body	• Back, dark green. • Breast, yellow with a sea green wash. • Flanks and anal area, yellow with a sea green wash, somewhat lighter than the breast. • Lower back and rump, light violet.	• Back, dark green. • Breast, green with a yellow wash. • Flanks and anal area, bright, dark green. • Lower back and belly, bright, dark green.
Wings	• Scapulars, dark green with cobalt blue edges. • Wing coverts, dark green. • Primaries: outer four feathers have green borders. • Median wing coverts, violet edges. • Primary and secondary coverts, violet. • Underwing coverts, violet. • The edge of the wing-bend is cobalt blue. • Spurious wing feathers, sky blue.	• Wing coverts, dark green, may be somewhat "hammered." • Primaries, secondaries, and tertiaries, dark gray with dark green outers. • Primary wing coverts, dark green with lighter outers. • Underwing coverts, sea green. • Edge of wing-bend, dark green. • Spurious wing, yellow.
Tail	• Upper tail coverts, dark green. • Undertail coverts, yellowish green. • Tail feathers, dark green.	• Upper tail coverts, dark green. • Undertail coverts, green with a yellow wash, somewhat lighter than the belly color. • Tail feathers, dark green.
Eyes	• Dark brown iris, with a brown eye ring.	• Dark brown iris, with a brown eye ring.
Beak	• Light horn-colored; cere, flesh-colored.	• Light horn-colored; cere, flesh-colored.
Feet & Nails	• Feet, flesh-colored. • Nails, horn-colored.	• Feet, brownish gray. • Nails, horn-colored.
Length	• Minimum 5.1 inches (13 cm).	• Minimum 5.1–5.5 inches (13–14 cm).

eastern Panama, connected with the Magdalena River, and the western slopes of the eastern Andes to latitude 3 degrees south of the Nevado de Huila.

Subspecies: *Forpus c. caucae*

Male: Mainly distinguished from the nominate race by a larger and stronger-looking bill. The green plumage is somewhat lighter in color, but this is only easy to recognize when one has adequate comparative material. The blue feather patterns are more vague, with less obvious violet.

Female: In comparison with the nominate form, the hen has a stronger bill, but in general it is almost identical.

Distribution: Western Colombia, west of the Andes, near Cauca and Marino. To this day, I have seldom come across this subspecies in aviculture, perhaps because of its only minor differences from the nominate form.

Subspecies: *Forpus c. metae*

Distribution: Central Colombia, in the west, bordered by the eastern escarpments of the Andes mountains, near Bogotá, via Cundinamarca, east along the Meta River, into west Venezuela. The English common name is Metae Spectacled Parrotlet.

Mutations: At the present time birds with yellow feather parts are known: these can be regarded as *pied.* It seems that this mutation is sex-linked as the yellow patches are seen mainly in hens; very young

This is the male of the subspecies Forpus c. caucae, *which is more yellowish with less deep blue on wings and rump. The blue on the face is confined to the area behind and above the eyes.*

birds do not show it. Time will tell if this mutation can be perpetuated.

In the Wild: These beautiful but small birds, with an average weight of 1 ounce (25 g) live mainly in tropical and subtropical zones. The ornithologist Olivares reported that he could comfortably observe the nominate form around Bogotá; Miller, on the other hand, states that the form is "extremely abundant" in central Colombia. He observed the nominate form mainly in open forest and in bushland. Wetmore, however, saw the birds only now and again, usually in pairs, in Dariën in eastern

Metae Spectacled Parrotlet (*Forpus conspicillatus metae*)

	Cock	Hen
Head & Face	• Face is bright, dark green, merging into dark green, with a gray wash. • Above the eye a cobalt blue edge, running behind the eye to form a half-moon. Sometimes, a small blue edge beneath the eye.	• Above the beak, light grass green, merging into dark green. Beneath and above the eye, a bright, dark green edge, merging behind the eye and running into a point.
Body	• Back, dark green. • Breast, sea green with a gray wash. • Anal area, sea green with a light yellow wash. • Lower back and rump, cobalt blue with violet wash.	• Back, dark green. • Breast, green with a yellow wash. • Anal area and flanks, bright, dark green. • Lower back and belly, also bright, dark green.
Wings	• Scapulars, dark green with cobalt blue outers. • Wing coverts, dark green. • Primaries, dark gray, with green outers. • Secondaries, violet outers. • Tertiaries, blue with cobalt blue outers. • Primary and secondary wing coverts, cobalt with a violet wash. • Underwing coverts, cobalt, merging into black. • Edge of wing-bend, cobalt blue.	• Wing coverts, dark green and may be somewhat "hammered." • Primaries, secondaries, and tertiaries, dark gray, with dark green outers. • Primary wing coverts, dark green, with lighter outers. • Underwing coverts, sea green. • Edge of wing-bend, dark green. • Spurious wing feathers, yellow.
Tail	• Upper tail coverts, dark green. • Undertail coverts, yellowish green. • Tail feathers, dark green.	• Upper tail coverts, dark green. • Undertail coverts, green with a yellow wash, somewhat lighter than the belly color. • Tail feathers, dark green.
Eyes	• Brown iris with a gray eye ring.	• Dark brown iris with a brown eye ring.
Beak	• Upper mandible, light horn-colored. • Lower mandible with darker edge. • Cere, flesh-colored.	• Light horn-colored; cere, flesh-colored.
Feet & Nails	• Feet, brownish gray. • Nails, horn-colored.	• Feet, brownish gray. • Nails, horn-colored.
Length	• Minimum 5.1–5.5 inches (13–14 cm).	• 5.1–5.5 inches (13–14 cm).

Panama. Meyer de Schauensee found the birds in open woodland of the tropical zone in Colombia to an altitude of 5,240 feet (1,600 meters).

In the breeding season, from January to March, the birds live in pairs. High trees, tree stumps, and high fence posts are chosen as nesting sites, providing the interiors are sufficiently rotten to allow the birds to excavate their nest hollows.

Outside the breeding season, the birds forage together in small groups. Experiments with ringed birds have shown that the pairs stay together, but that the bond is not so great as during the breeding season; I have frequently seen various birds spend the night in nest holes or on twigs together. Their feeding habits vary with the situation (breeding season, feeding the young, and so on). When berries are ripe, they are eaten by the "barrow-load," together with other soft fruits. Grass seeds are consumed throughout the year; in the spring, leaf-buds and flowers are eaten. During my observations of these birds in the wild, I ascertained that they show a great preference for half-ripe grass seeds and rice; they are often seen in groups among the paddy fields. However, the damage they cause is only minimal because, as stated above, they operate only in small groups. While foraging, they will opportunistically take small spiders and insects. When observing birds feeding, one can only get the impression that they are very voracious feeders, a trait that is also apparent in cage and aviary: every possible food is inspected and tried. This means, of course, that it is relatively easy to introduce them to new foods such as various fruits and grains.

First Breeding: The first specimens of this species arrived in Europe during the 1960s. The Danish breeder, W. Langberg (Copenhagen) bred more than 30 youngsters between 1965 and 1973. The first breeding results, however, occurred in the United States when Mrs. A. R. Hood of California reported breeding results in 1931. In Germany, the first breeding results occurred in 1974: From a clutch of five eggs, three young were raised successfully by their parents; the two remaining eggs were infertile. In 1992 about 20 pairs

The all-green female Spectacled Parrotlet (Forpus conspicillatus). She does, however, have a more yellowish forehead than the male. In the wild she nests in tree cavities, fence posts, and palm fronds, usually 3–6 feet (1–2 m) but sometimes much higher from the ground.

were imported into the United States. A breeding cooperative was formed in order to ensure that the various pairs were bred by experienced breeders; this proved a great success. We must ensure that we keep a clean gene pool, so that the future of this wonderful, gentle bird is guaranteed. At the present time there are hundreds of these birds in America. In Europe, as well, especially in the Netherlands and Germany, the bird is well represented although demand still outstrips supply.

Hybridization, which has occurred through the last decade (especially with the Blue-winged and Mexican Parrotlets), must be strongly condemned. In this connection, it is interesting to report that a crossing of the nominate x. *Mexican* by the breeder Mrs. S. Thomlinson of Long Beach, California, in 1930 produced seven offspring. According to Rosemary Low in *The Parrots of South America,* during the cock's lifetime it reared 24 young.

Aviculture: With their graceful shape, soft colors, and charming behavior, Spectacled Parrotlets are not only suitable for an indoor or outdoor aviary, but also for a roomy cage in the den or living room. The birds are very loving to each other and soon become tame and trusting; at the time that imported birds still could be obtained, it was apparent that the reserve they first showed quickly diminished, and after two months they behaved as though they had been the best of pals with their owner for years. However, don't form a false opinion about this: this species is in no way easy to impress; on the contrary they will stand their ground; they are not timorous like the Green-rumped Parrotlets. It is recommended that pairs be kept singly, together in a large cage, or an aviary. Like all parrotlets, they like plenty of space, but a cage with a minimum length of 39.5 inches (100 cm) or 47.5 inches (120 cm) is adequate and successful breeding results are likely in such a cage. Trials have taught me that this species can be kept together with *different* parrotlet species in a large garden aviary; various waxbills and small finches *(Estrildidae)* can also be kept successfully with them.

Spectacled Parrotlets are less aggressive than Celestial or Pacific Parrotlets, though mature males will fight for the best nesting sites; these squabbles, however, usually take place at the beginning of the breeding season. When there is an adequate choice of nest boxes, these arguments will rarely cause problems, especially if the birds are kept in a large aviary with several feeding stations and room to avoid each other. Always place three or more pairs of parrotlets together and *never* two, in order to avoid fighting over nest boxes, food stations, and roosting areas. It is an open question as to whether pairs kept together really harm each other. In the more than 20 years that I have kept these parrotlets, in cages and aviaries, I have never witnessed any serious fights, only minor, harmless skirmishes.

When nest boxes are installed in cages or aviaries, the birds are encouraged to start the breeding process. My birds always exhibit breeding behavior within five days of when I make nesting facilities available (I leave my pairs together throughout the year). My nest boxes are 43 inches (110 cm) in length, 15.75 inches (40 cm) wide, and 24 inches (60 cm) high. Colleagues of mine have also had success with wooden budgerigar or parakeet nest boxes varying in size from 7.9 to 9.8 inches (20–25 cm) long, 6 to 9.8 inches (15–25 cm) wide, and 9.8 to 13.75 inches (25–35 cm) high. The entrance hole should be 1.6 to 2 inches (4–5 cm) in diameter. Situate the nest boxes horizontally, and make the entrance hole in the outer corner of one of the long panels; the nest cavity must, of course, be situated at the opposite end of the box, so that birds entering cannot damage the eggs. Rough sawdust or pine bedding can be used in the nest cavity, although it may not stay there. Many parents have the habit of turfing everything out. Try replacing it, but, if they turf it out again, let them go without. I have had much success using strips of willow bark about 9.8 inches (25 cm) in length. Before removing the bark strips, I scrubbed the twigs thoroughly with a hard brush to clean them (see page 61).

It is best to let your birds start breeding around May. Breeding pairs must be at least one year old, and should have had adequate calcium (cuttlefish) and appropriate vit-

A cinnamon (fawn or Isabelle) mutation of a male Spectacled Parrotlet—a somewhat surprising name as the bird doesn't show any beige colors.

amins (see page 49) during their first year. At least three months before the beginning of the breeding season, the prospective breeding pairs must be made accustomed to animal protein (see page 47) and a suitable rearing food available in pet stores. This preparation is, in my opinion, indispensable for the successful rearing of parrotlets and other small parrots.

Eggs are usually laid daily until a clutch of usually four to five has been produced. Frequently, some eggs will be infertile; the average hatch rate in my collection is three. The incubation period is 22–24 days. The hen stays mainly in the nest after one or more eggs have been laid. The male visits her frequently, to check that all is in order and to feed his mate from his crop, but otherwise

119

has little more to do, although from time to time I have seen males brooding eggs at night. You can observe birds in the nest by using a nest box with a glass window covered with a sliding wooden shutter. I have used a similar technique to study birds in the wild. After the breeding season, I have installed a "window" in the wall of a nest hollow and covered it with bark. This method relies on the fact that many birds return to the same nest hole when they are ready to breed again. When the hen leaves the nest to feed or defecate, the male guards the nest, or joins his mate at the feeding station.

The young, which have to be leg banded at seven to nine days of age, are generally raised without difficulty, especially if the correct food is available (see page 43). In addition to the commercially available soft food, you must ensure that an adequate supply of germinated seed and a variety of fresh greens are available. Don't forget to include carrot tops, grated carrot, and chickweed in the greens menu.

The young leave the nest at 32 to 34 days of age, but are fed by their father intensively for 8 or 9 more days, after which the pressure on the male gradually ceases. The young should be quite independent after another three weeks. The young will learn to feed themselves more quickly if you provide the right temptations such as millet spray (especially germinated) and a good variety of green food, including chickweed. For generations, parents have fed their offspring on such a diet and the young, once mature, will do the same for their offspring. Millet spray is essential, as it teaches the young how to efficiently dehusk seeds of all kinds.

If the weather is suitable, and the pairs are not unnecessarily disturbed, the parents may start a second brood after two to three weeks. The young from the first clutch can be safely left together with their parents for about two months. After this time, it is best to remove them in order to avoid possible trouble. If the parents have not yet started their second clutch, removal of the young will encourage them to do so.

Youngsters are similar in appearance to the female for the first few months, and should be banded so you don't make mistakes. Young males do have a blue tinge on the tips of their underwing coverts, but these can only be seen when the bird is taken in the hand and the wings examined closely. Full adult plumage develops by about six months of age. Well-colored males have a dark green face that contrasts sharply with the grayish blue breast; but, unfortunately, this is not always the case. Moreover, the eye ring that gives this bird its name is not always guaranteed in captive-bred birds. In show-quality birds, the eye ring runs completely around the eye, and behind the eye should run into a fine point, but never into the neck, which is a fault in some countries. A male may have a perfect eye ring in his first year, but this may extend into the neck in the following year, thus constituting a fault. From this, one can surmise that these birds take on their complete adult coloration in the second year and frequently show too much blue in the neck.

The second brood may start some time after the first, even as late as September or October. At this time it is often difficult to find adequate supplies of wild weed seeds and greens, so an alternative must be found. Plenty of germinated seed (see page 58) and commercial rearing food must be provided along with the normal seed mixture and the necessary vitamin/mineral supplementation.

Do not remove the nest box immediately after the young have fledged, because they still will spend the nights in it with their parents. I have always provided each of my breeding pairs with two nest boxes so that they can make a choice before the breeding season starts; this has the advantage that the unused box can be used as sleeping quarters. In this respect, it is interesting to know that the German aviculturist Karl Heinz Spitzer, in his book *Sperlingpapageien* (Ulmer, 1987), states that a pair of his birds had a late, second brood in October and that the fledged young regularly spent the night in the nest box. Noticing that the adult female seemed to be spending longer periods in the nest box, an inspection in the middle of January revealed five eggs there. As he had no spare accommodations at that time, and as

the young and their father were behaving well toward each other, the young of the second brood stayed in the aviary throughout the whole incubation period of the third brood. Moreover, the old male sat perched between his offspring, which, in the meantime, had almost stopped spending the night in the nest box. Shortly before the third brood hatched, the worst happened: The young had probably, for reasons unknown, been scared into quickly seeking safety in the old nest box, and they were driven out, without ceremony, by the father, probably with the help of the mother. Three eggs were broken in this process and lay shattered on the floor of the nestbox. Mr. Spitzer, of course, immediately removed the young after

A cinnamon (fawn or Isabelle) mutation of a female Spectacled Parrotlet. The mutation is recessive and autosomal.

this incident and the hen continued with the brooding process. The day after the young were removed, a single chick hatched and this was successfully raised; in the last (fifth) egg, the embryo had died in the shell. Of the three broken eggs, only one appeared to have been fertile.

The lesson we can learn from such an experience is that it is definitely safer to remove the young of a current clutch to their own flight at about two months of age as long as they appear to be independent and are not still being fed by the father. It should be obvious that a small cage is totally unsuitable for this. By removing the independent young, the parents are also likely to start on their next brood much earlier as long as the weather and other conditions are suitable. If you are using large breeding cages, it is even more important to remove the young as soon as they are independent.

In order to avoid the possibility of egg binding, it is extremely important that hens are not used for breeding until they are at least 12 months of age. Provide them with cuttlefish bone and the necessary vitamins/minerals throughout the year (most of the so-called fortified commercial mixtures contain pellets with the necessary vitamins and minerals mixed in with the usual seeds; but in spite of this, it won't hurt to give them an additional good-quality vitamin/mineral supplement, as well as egg food). Moreover, I would recommend that each pair be limited to three, preferably two, broods per season.

As long as you avoid inbreeding, you can usually expect healthy young from healthy parents, although, unfortunately, not all pairs make excellent breeders. Don't despair. Success can frequently be achieved by breaking up pairs; that is to say, the hen can be paired up with another (unrelated) cock, and vice versa. Furthermore, a hen that continuously lays infertile eggs is by no means unusable; it can just as well be the case that the cock is infertile. By changing partners you will soon learn how matters stand. Sometimes it can take a while for the new pair to accept each other completely, and a hen may not breed at all in the following season. It is thus important to ensure that the new pairs are "out of sight and sound" of their previous partners.

Spectacled Parrotlets are ideal companion birds due to the fact that they are very curious and not particularly timid; they have incredible personalities. One of my males gets enormous pleasure from sitting on my shoulder and nibbling at my ear lobe while chattering incomprehensibly (in spite of the fact that he can speak various words and even a few sentences). A female has the habit of tearing off strips of newspaper and piling them up next to the telephone. Nobody has taught the bird to do this. When I prepare food in the kitchen, both birds come and inspect every ingredient as if wanting to learn how to put a menu together. They should, perhaps, be called "Spectacular Parrotlets!"

Mexican Parrotlet—*Forpus cyanopygius cyanopygius* (Souancé 1856)

Sometimes called Turquoise-rumped Parrotlet, there are two sub-species, *Forpus c. pallidus* (Brewster) and *Forpus c. insularis* (Ridgeway).

Nomenclature: Fanciers know this parrotlet as the species with the most conspicuous turquoise blue rump. The ornithologist Finch first named the bird *Psittacus cyanopygius,* but this was soon changed to *Forpus cyanopygius* because the African Gray Parrot already possessed the generic name *Psittacus,* and there is no direct relationship between these two birds.

Type: In an old German book, I found the "type" described as "tear-shaped" and you don't need too much imagination in order to apply the description "tear-shaped and compact" when looking at the shape of the bird. The head is wide and somewhat bowed and the beak stands out somewhat from the face. The line of the back is set in a curve of 55–60°. The breast is robust, wide, and lightly bowed. The wing tips are not crossed, but close next to each other and extend two thirds over the tail.

Distribution: Western Mexico. In the west adjoining the Gulf of Mexico and the Pacific Ocean. In the east bordering the western slopes of the Sierra Madre to approximately Durango. In the north to the Sinaloa district and from there adjoining the Sonora district, where the sub-species *F. c. pallidus* is found. In the

The female Mexican Parrotlet (Forpus cyanopygius) *is all-green. The species is endemic to western Mexico.*

south, the habitat of the nominate race reaches to Colima. Finally, the race *F. c. insularis* occurs on the coast at Nayarit, and The Très Marias Islands.

Subspecies: *Forpus c. pallidus*

Distribution: Northwestern Mexico from the northern Sinaloan district to the southwestern Sonora district. Forshaw feels that this subspecies is not distinct from *cyanopygius.*

Subspecies: *Forpus c. insularis*

In the Wild: Mexican Parrotlets occur in coastal areas as well as at higher altitudes. In the coastal areas they are often seen in the vicinity of cotton plantations, but also in pastoral areas. The slopes of the Sierra Madre are covered with mixed, sub-tropical, broad-leaved and coniferous woodland. This type of terrain is the ideal habitat for these parrotlets but is, unfortunately, threatened due to

Mexican Parrotlet *(Forpus cyanopygius cyanopygius)*

	Cock	Hen
Head & Face	• Face is bright, grass green. • Back of head and neck, dull, matte green.	• Face is light grass green. • Head, green.
Body	• Lower back and rump, bright sky blue. • Anal area, flanks, and belly, grass green; feathers may be somewhat "hemmed" in older birds.	• Nape and back, green. • Anal area, flanks, and rump, light grass green with yellow highlights. • Lower back and breast, bright, grass green.
Wings	• Wing coverts, sky blue, merging into cobalt blue. • Outer four primaries and secondaries, green with dark green outers; the rest are all-blue. • Underwing coverts, sky blue. • Edge of wing-bend, sky blue with yellow spurious wing feathers.	• Primaries and secondaries, dark green with light green outers. • Underwing coverts, light grass green. • Edge of wing-bend, green. • Spurious wing feathers, yellow.
Tail	• Upper tail coverts, light grass green, with yellow-edged outers. • Undertail coverts, yellowish green.	• Upper tail coverts, bright, grass green. • Undertail coverts, yellowish green. • Tail feathers, green with yellow edges.
Eyes	• Dark brown iris with a gray eye ring.	• Dark brown iris with a gray eye ring.
Beak	• Silver-gray.	• Horn-colored with a silver-gray wash.
Feet & Nails	• Feet, gray. • Nails, horn-colored to light gray.	• Feet, gray. • Nails, horn-colored.
Length	• 5.1–5.5 inches (13–14 cm).	• 5.1–5.5 inches (13–14 cm).

habitat destruction. I have seen this species at altitudes of 1,000 to 1,680 feet (300–500 m) above sea level. The temperature averages 50 to 59°F (10–15°C) in January, and 77 to 86°F (25–30°C) in June. The nominate form is generally found in the approximate center of the distribution area, but only seen sporadically in the Sonora district, although Friedmann observed it at an altitude of 3,400 feet (1,000 m). The lowland coastal areas, it seems, are only visited by the birds outside the breeding season. Zimmermann reported that he observed the birds in the

Pale Mexican Parrotlet *(Forpus cyanopygius pallidus)*

	Cock	Hen
Head & Face	• Face is light green. • Crown and nape, dark green with a yellow wash. • Above the eye, a turquoise blue wash, running to the ear.	• Face is light green. • Head and neck, dark green.
Body	• Mantle and upper back, green with a yellow wash. • Anal area, flanks, and belly, green with turquoise blue wash. • Lower back and rump, deep turquoise.	• Mantle and upper back, dark green. • Anal area, flanks, and rump, light green, with a blue gray wash. • Lower back and breast, bright, dark green.
Wings	• Wing coverts, dark green with yellow highlights. • Primary wing coverts, deep, turquoise blue. • Primaries and secondaries, gray green with green outers. • Underwing coverts, turquoise blue. • Edge of wing-bend, turquoise; spurious wing feathers, yellowish white. • Secondary wing coverts, turquoise blue. • Scapulars, with a turquoise blue stripe.	• Wing coverts, dark green, washed with grayish blue. • Primaries and secondaries, dark gray with green edges. • Primary wing coverts, dark green. • Underwing coverts, bright, dark green. • Edge of wing-bend, green; spurious wing feathers, yellowish white.
Tail	• Upper tail coverts, light green, with yellow highlights. • Undertail coverts, greenish yellow. • Tail feathers, dark green.	• Upper tail coverts, bright, dark green. • Undertail coverts, green with yellow highlights. • Tail feathers, dark green with yellow edges.
Eyes	• Very dark brown to black.	• Very dark brown to black.
Beak	• Horn-colored to gray.	• Horn-colored to gray.
Feet & Nails	• Feet, gray to horn-colored. • Nails, gray to horn-colored.	• Feet, horn-colored to gray. • Nails, horn-colored to gray.
Length	• 5.5 inches (14 cm).	• 5.5 inches (14 cm).

Très Marias Parrotlet *(Forpus cyanopygius insularis)*

	Cock	Hen
Head & Face	• Face is bright, grass green. • Head, dark green with feathers edged in black.	• Face is greenish yellow.
Body	• Neck, mantle, and back, shiny dark green. • Anal area, flanks, and belly, grass green with a yellowish wash. • Lower back and rump, cobalt blue, with violet highlights.	• Mantle, back of head, nape, and back, dark green. • Anal area, flanks, and belly, greenish yellow with black edges. • Lower back and breast, bright, dark green.
Wings	• Wing coverts, glossy, dark green; frequently darker edges in older birds. • Primary wing coverts, cobalt blue. • Outer five primaries and secondaries, dark green edged, the remainder cobalt blue edged. • Underwing coverts, cobalt blue with violet highlights. • Edge of wing-bend, turquoise; spurious wing feathers, yellowish white. • Secondary wing coverts, turquoise blue.	• Wing coverts, dark green with black edges. • Primaries and secondaries, dark green. • Edge of wing-bend, dark green; spurious wing feathers, yellow.
Tail	• Upper tail coverts, bright, glossy dark green. • Undertail coverts, green with a yellowish wash. • Tail feathers, and upper tail coverts, dark green with yellow edges to the ends of the feathers.	• Upper tail coverts, dark green. • Undertail coverts, greenish yellow. • Tail feathers, dark green with yellow edges.
Eyes	• Dark brown iris with a gray eye ring.	• Dark brown to black.
Beak	• Gray.	• Gray.
Feet & Nails	• Feet, gray. • Nails, horn-colored.	• Feet, gray. • Nails, horn-colored.
Length	• 5.1–5.5 inches (13–14 cm).	• 5.1–5.5 inches (13–14 cm).

south of Autlan each morning in groups of 10 to 20, flying to their foraging area, a group of fig trees. I have personally observed that they are mainly active in the early mornings and evenings, as they fly with swiftly beating wings in a straight line, sometimes only a few feet above the ground, frequently accompanying groups of Petz's Conures *(Aratinga canicularis)*.

Forshaw reported flocks of up to 40 birds flying together in the same direction, without a single bird separating itself from the group. If you were able to observe them from above (as when flying in a small airplane), they are difficult to see as their green coloration matches almost exactly that of the tree canopy, grass, or brushland. Forshaw had to bang sticks against tree trunks in order to scare the birds into flight so that he could see them. It is very difficult, almost impossible, to observe the birds with the naked eye. You must locate them by their chattering calls, and view them from a safe distance through binoculars. This species constantly utters its contact call, whether flying or perching among the trees; the call sounds something like: "cc-veeg, cc-veeg." If they are disturbed or scared in any way, they also make this call. As with captive specimens, wild birds of this species are considerably less active than other parrotlet species. I have observed them perched quietly on twigs for hours; they twitter a lot, but seldomly preen each other's feathers or show other signs of affection. They also seem to

be somewhat finicky with their food; I have seen them, many times, pick up food items in their beaks, hold them for a while, then let them fall to the ground. In cages or aviaries, these birds can refuse certain fruits or greens that are eagerly accepted by other parrotlet species. It is interesting to note that, in the wild, parrotlets systematically test fruits with their beaks to determine their degree of ripeness.

Aviculture: Mexican Parrotlets were almost unknown in aviculture more than 100 years ago; the species was first described by Finch in 1868, in his well-known book about parrots. He said that the Mexican Parrotlet was larger than the other South American parrots he knew. Perhaps he had only badly prepared skin-specimens available. Russ also was not particularly correct in his descriptions and, indeed, based his on Finch's reports: He described their native range as "near the Amazon in Bolivia." The first correct statement of

Wing detail (top side) of the male Mexican Parrotlet.

the country of origin, West Mexico, was made by Dr. Reichenow in his book *Vögel ferner Zonen, Papageien*. None of the aforenamed authors or any of their contemporaries reported anything about breeding seasons, or gave further ornithological observations about the birds' habits in the wild. It seems that many authors in those days simply repeated what others had said, without making any of their own scientific observations.

These previously rarely seen parrotlets were increasingly imported just after the First World War, starting around 1920. E. Schütze in his journal of that time, *Vögel ferner Länder (Birds from Foreign Countries)*, reported that in June 1923 a large consignment of parrots arrived in Germany from Mexico. Among these were 15 parrotlets with a large, light blue patch on the rump, which differed markedly from other parrotlets known at the time. Schütze obtained a pair, which he housed in a 5.6-foot-long (4-m) out-door aviary, together with various exotic finches. For a whole year, nothing unusual happened. Only when he placed the pair alone in an indoor aviary did the birds show any seriousness about breeding. In September 1925, four youngsters left the nest box after a brooding time of 21 days. The young began to feed themselves after only eight days. At first, the young were similar in color, but after two months one of the youngsters developed some blue feathers in the rump. Schütze used egg-bread, hard-boiled egg, mealworms, and soaked millet as rearing food. The pair did not attempt to breed again that year. Schütze thus concluded that this species does not breed more than once per annum. It is interesting to report here that Schütze's brood was registered as the "first captive breeding" of this species, and, after some research on my part, I find this to be most probable. In England, Mrs. Goddard apparently bred this species in 1927.

These days, this species of parrotlet is common in aviculture. The breeding data given by Schütze do not tally with those experienced by other breeders. This species broods longer than the other parrotlets, that is to say, 24 days rather than 21. Newly fledged youngsters are more robust in build than other parrotlets, but they seem to take longer to grow. Fully grown birds weigh about 1.4 ounces (40 g). The best successes with this species can be achieved by placing three or more pairs together in a large flight, with a

Wing detail (underside) of the male Mexican Parrotlet.

good choice of nest boxes (at least two boxes per pair). Experience has shown that one clutch per annum is usual, and sometimes they will miss a season altogether. Because these birds remain somewhat flighty and nervous, it is important that they are left in peace during the breeding period. Stressed birds refuse to eat, or only eat a little, and are thus susceptible to fatal bacterial infections.

In the past, hybrids between Spectacled and Celestial Parrotlets have been bred, but such cross-breeding, as I have already stated, is to be strongly condemned. In general, the young are raised well when the birds are kept in quiet, peaceful surroundings and given the appropriate diet. My research into the literature has come up with the fact that this species can be housed together with budgerigars, weaver and wydah species, and lovebirds, but never with other parrotlet species.

For their diet, Mexican Parrotlets prefer millet, hemp (but only in moderation, or the birds will become too fat; this can cause egg binding in females—personally, I like to restrict this to a half teaspoonful per bird per day for aviary birds, and half this amount for birds in cages), and medium-sized black sunflower seeds. Oats should also not be missed, especially during the breeding season and in the winter months; the same also applies to canary grass seed and (in small amounts) various millet varieties. Willow twigs and twigs from apple or pear trees, half ripe corn (maize), and strips of ripe carrot will be gnawed at greedily. Weed seeds in various stages of development must also be available (see page 46).

Blue-Winged or Passerine Parrotlet *Forpus xanthopterygius* (Spix 1824)

There are five subspecies, *Forpus x. crassirostris* (Taczanowski), *Forpus x. flavescens* (Salvadori), *Forpus x. flavissimus* (Hellmayr), *Forpus x. olallae* Gyldenstolpe, and *Forpus x. spengeli* (Hartlaub).

Nomenclature: In older literature the Blue-winged Parrotlet is named *Forpus passerinus*. This scientific name is now used exclusively for the Green-rumped Parrotlet (see page 153); *vividus* has been replaced by *xanthopterygius.*

The male Blue-winged Parrotlet (Forpus xanthopterygius). *Among the various species of the Blue-winged Parrotlet there exist, unfortunately, a rather extensive variety of mixed colors due to the crossing in captivity of nominate with subpsecies and subspecies with subspecies. It is therefore rather doubtful to still find correctly colored species and subspecies, especially in European aviculture. Only the* **Forpus xanthopterygius flavissimus,** *as a pure subspecies, is still rather easy to recognize.*

Blue-winged Parrotlet *(Forpus xanthopterygius)*

	Cock	Hen
Head & Face	• Face is light grass green.	• All light green. • A small yellow band above the beak.
Body	• Mantle and back, dark green. • Anal area, flanks, and belly, light grass green. • Lower back and rump, dark cobalt with a violet wash.	• Uniformly light green, with a yellowish green beneath.
Wings	• Wing coverts are dark green with a violet wash. • The innermost five primary and tertiary feathers are green, the outermost, green with a cobalt wash. • Primary wing coverts are cobalt. • Underwing coverts are dark cobalt, with black tips. • The edge of the wing-bend is dark cobalt.	• Grass green.
Tail	• Upper tail coverts are light grass green. • Tail feathers are light grass green with yellow centers. • Undertail coverts are yellowish green.	• Tail feathers, grass green. • Undertail coverts, greenish yellow.
Eyes	• Dark brown iris with a gray eye ring.	• Dark brown iris with a gray eye ring.
Beak	• Horn-colored.	• Horn-colored.
Feet & Nails	• Feet and nails are gray-brown.	• Feet and nails are gray-brown.
Length	• 5.1–5.5 inches (13–14 cm).	• 5.1–5.5 inches (13–14 cm).

Type: This medium-sized parrotlet also has a tear-shaped body. The somewhat rounded head runs harmoniously into the somewhat undulated line of the back. The breast and belly are equally rounded. The wings are held tightly against the body; the tips of the wings do not cross, and lie close to the end of the tail. In comparison with the Mexican Parrotlet, the Blue-winged Parrotlet has relatively large eyes, a characteristic that makes it easy to distinguish the two species. Weight: 1.4 to 1.6 ounces (35–40 g).

Distribution: It occurs over an enormous area of central and eastern South America. It is interesting to note that this species, via the Netherlands (where it is still bred with great success), spread to other parts of Europe and Britain, where it was known in the avicultural business as the "Argentinian Parrotlet."

The nominate form, which has the greatest distribution, ranges deep into the southern part of South America from central and eastern Brazil (province of Bahia to the Rio Grande do Sul area in the south), in northeastern Argentina in Missiones and Corrientes, and from there into eastern Paraguay. In northern Bahia, the bird integrates with the subspecies *flavissimus.*

Subspecies: *Forpus x. crassirostris* (Large-billed Parrotlet)

This species is immediately recognizable by its large beak, in both sexes. The center of the upper mandible is compressed sideways, showing a conspicuous horizontal groove.

Male: The forehead and cheeks are emerald green. The back is dark grayish green. The rump, underwing coverts, and edge of the wing are deep, dark reddish violet. The primary tail coverts are a matte grayish blue, and the secondary tail coverts are violet-blue. Length: 5.1 inches (13 cm).

A female Blue-winged Parrotlet (Forpus xanthopterygius).

Female: Similar to the nominate form, but darker on the back. There is no yellow and it is somewhat smaller in build.

Distribution: Northeastern Peru to the Colimoës River (western Brazil), to southeastern Colombia along the banks of the Amazon River and its tributaries, to central Amazonas; northwestern Brazil (Forshaw).

Detail of the wing of the male Blue-winged Parrotlet.

Subspecies: *Forpus x. flavescens* (Salvadori's Parrotlet)

Male: This subspecies also is very similar to the nominate race, but is generally paler and has more yellow in the plumage. The forehead and cheeks are yellow, the underparts a striking yellowish green. The lower back, the rump, and the underside of the wings are pale blue, paler than in the nominate.

Female: Similar to the hen of the nominate form, the general impression is somewhat paler and there is more yellow in the plumage, especially on the forehead and face but *not* on the throat as in the following subspecies.

Distribution: In the provinces of Beni and Santa Cruz (the Germans call it the *Santa Cruz-Sperlingspapagei*), in eastern Bolivia; and in southeastern and central-eastern Peru (Forshaw).

The characteristic posture of the male Forpus x. flavissimus.

Subspecies: *Forpus x. flavissimus* (Ceara Blue-winged Parrotlet)

Male: Again, similar to the nominate form, but if you have enough comparative material you will see that this subspecies is paler and could be perhaps described as yellowish green. The forehead, throat, and cheeks are butter yellow; underparts are a striking emerald green and the rump and underside of the wings are lilac blue. Length: 5.5 inches (14 cm); weight: 1.06 ounces (30 g).

Female: Green, but darker on the back. Very similar to the nominate form, but with more yellow on the forehead, on the face, and on the lower underparts. The general impression is that of a lime green bird.

Distribution: Northeastern Brazil in the provinces of Marahao, Piauhy, and Ceara, south to northern Bahia.

Breeding: The first recorded breeding result came from Denmark and involved two pairs, each consisting of *F. x. flavissimus* (males) and *F. p. passerinus* (females). The young males were similar to the father after the first molt. The incubation period was between 21 and 23 days. All of the young developed very quickly and left the nest after one month. This subspecies is rather common in Europe and the United States.

Subspecies: *Forpus x. olallae*

Male: Very similar to *crassirostris,* only the rump, wings, and lower back are noticeably darker; the

Male (front) and female Forpus x. flavissimus.

The underside of the male's wing of the subspecies Forpus x. flavissimus.

underwing coverts, however, are paler blue and the shade of green on the upper parts is generally somewhat darker. Length: 4.5 inches (11.5 cm).

Female: Similar to the hen *crassirostris,* hence all the green is darker, especially above.

Distribution: Northern bank of the Amazon river (northwestern Brazil, in Codajas and near Itacoatiera). It is questionable whether this species is just a darker form of *crassirostris* and thus could be eliminated as an extra subspecies.

Subspecies *Forpus x. spengeli* (Spengel's Parrotlet)

Male: Very similar to the nominate form, though somewhat smaller in build. The essential difference lies in the lighter royal blue on the underside of the wings, and the pale turquoise on the lower back and rump. The secondary coverts and the bases of the secondaries are turquoise blue.

Female: Like the *xanthopterygius* female, but the yellow is more pronounced, especially on the forehead.

Distribution: Well apart from the areas of all the foregoing parrotlets, in northern Colombia on the Caribbean Sea near Santa Marta-Bergen and along the Magdalena River (northern Bolivia).

In the Wild: The Blue-winged Parrotlet and its subspecies have the largest range of distribution of all South American parrots. It is therefore understandable that this species occurs in many varied habitats from the rain forests of the Amazon, to high in the mountains of the Mata Grosso, and to the vast grassy plains of the Pampas. There are big differences in the climates of the various areas, from tropical to subtropical.

A pair of Forpus xanthopterygius spengeli; *these birds are considered a subspecies of the Blue-winged Parrotlet, due mainly to their distribution, anatomy, and behavior. Since* spengeli's *distribution area borders that of the* Forpus passerinus cyanophanes, *a subspecies of the Green-rumped Parrotlet, it could very well be possible that* spengeli *is synonymous to* Forpus passerinus.

The birds are not common in all of their areas; the numbers will vary depending on the availability of food. The birds move from location to location to forage and may be abundant in certain areas for a while, before they again disappear. In general, however, this species is relatively common throughout the range with the exception of the more arid areas. The birds are extremely abundant around the southern lakes and along the Magdalena River. The birds often are seen in groups of about 20 and, when food is plentiful, many birds may congregate in fruit trees. They are thus minimally welcome in orchards and plantations!

It was the nominate form that was first imported into Europe, which shouldn't surprise us, bearing in mind that this bird has the biggest home range of all South American parrots. I have been able to observe these birds fairly closely. They usually fly like a group of finches, in close formation, and move speedily over brush and grassland before finally landing in the top of a group of trees. This species seems to follow in the "footsteps of man" and is frequently found close to human habitations. I have even seen them in gardens and parks of big cities like Rio de Janeiro, São Paulo, and Santa Cruz.

The breeding season takes place in the dryer months of southern hemisphere spring, that is to say in September and October. During the breeding season, groups break up and form into individual breeding pairs. Research with ringed birds has shown that they probably pair up for life.

The birds feed mainly on ripe and semi-ripe seeds of various plants, as well as small fruits such as berries, leaf buds, and (according to Forshaw) possibly blossoms. The nest is usually in a hollow tree limb, but also is sometimes in the abandoned nest of the Ovenbird *(Furnarius rufus)*. Ovenbirds are shy birds, but you always know where they are because their "clay-oven" nests form a significant part of the landscapes in Argentina and adjacent countries. The ovens may be seen on walls, fence posts, tree stumps, and even on the roof gutters of buildings. Ovenbirds can be described as being similar to our thrushes, which forage for food on the ground. The clay nest is strengthened with grass and has walls about 1.6 inches (4 cm) thick. The nest is built in the winter, when the clay has been softened sufficiently by the rain to make it workable. Both sexes first build a bowl-like base before building up the walls and roof. The nesting chamber is lined with grass, and is accessible via a curved passage. The nest can last for two to three years before it is finally washed away by the rain, but the Ovenbird builds a new nest every year. The old nests are eagerly accepted by the parrotlets. Other animals also make use of these abandoned nests, for example, wasps, swallows, and cowbirds.

First Breeding: The first specimens were brought into France in 1682. The species was described even earlier by Marcrave (1648) and was also acknowledged by Carl von Linné (Linnaeus) in 1767.

The first reported breeding was in 1867 according to the well-known standard work by Dr. Karl Russ, *Die Fremdländischen Stubenvögel, Band III, Papageien (Foreign Cage Birds, Volume III, Parrots).* Dr. Russ did not make the mistake of his predecessors of regarding the green-colored hens as a separate species.

Aviculture: It is understandable that, because of their great natural range of distribution, not all Blue-winged Parrotlets can be kept for the whole year in an unheated outdoor aviary (although, in the wild, some of them are found in the mountains at an altitude of 10,200 feet [3,000 m]). Most fanciers thus keep their birds in indoor cages or aviaries. They cannot tolerate temperatures below 50°F (15°C) very well. Only when temperatures are above this limit will they thrive or breed. Because it comes from the temperate zones, it is not surprising that the nominate form of this species is so well suited to aviculture.

Experience has shown that only one pair of these birds can be kept together in a cage or aviary. The nest box should be affixed at least 6 feet (2 m) high—it seems the birds feel safest at this height; they will then regularly survey their surroundings from the entrance hole. It is generally not easy to recommend a particular style of nest box, especially as various breeders differ on the matter. Personally, I have found the birds to be not particularly fussy. Over the years I have found them ready to accept normal "square" nest boxes as well as the deep, parakeet nest boxes. They will also use natural hollow logs, or the nest box described on page 70. Give the birds a choice at the outset, and give them the same box to use again in the following year (keep records).

Before and during the breeding season, the birds must have access to a good brand of rearing food, plus germinated seed (for example, black sunflower seed, millet varieties, millet spray, canary grass seed, and niger), as well as their normal menu. They simply love millet spray, carrots, semi-ripe weed, and grass seeds. Chickweed is by far their favorite green food!

It is rather difficult to determine the sexes of the youngsters, although the males may show touches of blue in their plumage. They develop their adult coloration within six to nine months. In approximately 12 months, they are sexually mature and can be used for breeding. The clutch consists of four to five eggs; seldom more.

In her book *The Parrots of South America* (Gifford, 1972), Rosemary Low describes a fascinating breeding experience with Spengel's Parrotlet (sometimes called Barranquilla Parrotlet). She tells of a breeder, Mr. R. W. Drury, who had a pair of these birds. The birds gnawed a 3-inch tunnel into the decaying wood on the outside of their nest box. They were provided with a birch log, with the center chiseled out to form a cavity 2 to 3 inches in diameter and 9 inches long. The parrotlets gnawed through 4 to 5 inches of solid wood, widened

Wing and rump details of the male Forpus xanthopterygius spengeli.

out the hole at the end of the log, and then gnawed through its wall. Drury bred them successfully and fed them with soaked and sprouted sunflower seed, hemp, and oats throughout the year, in addition to their usual diet.

Celestial or Pacific Parrotlet—*Forpus coelestis* (Lesson 1847)

There is one subspecies, recently rediscovered, *Forpus c. lucida* (Pathe).

Immatures: Very much like their parents; in the young males the blue line behind the eyes becomes visible rather quickly but is obviously still somewhat paler and more restricted than that of their parents. All blue colors in young males are less prominent and still mixed with green. Weight (after leaving the nest), approximately 1.06 ounces (30 g); full-grown: 1.13 to 1.20 ounces (32–34 g).

Type: A rather compact bird with a straight bearing (55–60°). The head is evenly rounded, and the beak stands only marginally out from the face. The line of the back runs gradually to the tip of the tail. The breast is full, wide and rounded, but runs evenly into the tail. The wings do not cross and extend to one third the length of the tail. The tail itself is short, as in all *Forpus* species, and keeled.

This bird is, especially when viewed from a distance, very contrasting in color, with a sharp division between the light green mask and the dark grayish blue breast. A

Celestial or Pacific Parrotlet *(Forpus coelestis coelestis)*

	Cock	Hen
Head & Face	• Face light grass green. • Behind the face, a cobalt blue line running out from the eye. • The cobalt blue stops on the neck. • The neck is gray, with a cobalt wash.	• Face is light grass green. • Behind the face, a pale cobalt blue line running out from the eye. • The cobalt blue stops on the neck. • The cobalt blue is less obvious than in the cock.
Body	• Mantel and back, olive green above with a gray wash. • Anal, flank, and belly are light grass green with a blue wash. • Lower back and rump are dark cobalt blue with a violet wash.	• Mantel and back are dark green with a gray wash that is less obvious than in the cock. • Lower back and rump are dark green with a blue wash.
Wings	• Wing coverts are olive green with a gray wash. • Flight feathers are deep cobalt; outer edges of the outer five feathers are dark green. • Primary coverts are deep cobalt blue. • Underwing coverts, deep cobalt blue. • The edge of the wing-bend is cobalt with a blue wash.	• Primary wing coverts are light green with a yellow wash; they have yellow edges. • Wing coverts are dark green with a gray wash. • Flight feathers are dark gray with dark, green edges. • Underwing coverts are green. • Edge of the wing-bend is green with a blue shimmer.
Tail	• Upper tail coverts are olive green, running into a shiny dark green. • The tail feathers are dark green. • Undertail coverts are light green, with a darker green wash.	• Upper tail coverts are shiny green. • Tail feathers are dark green. • Undertail coverts are pale yellow with a green shimmer.
Eyes	• Dark brown iris with a gray eye ring.	• Dark brown iris with a gray ring.
Beak	• Horn-colored.	• Horn-colored.
Feet & Nails	• Feet light brown (beige). • Nails horn-colored, with a darker tip.	• Feet are light brown (beige). • Nails are horn-colored with darker tips.
Length	• Minimum 5.1 inches (13 cm).	• Minimum 5.1 inches (13 cm).

A pair of Celestial Parrotlets (Forpus coelestis). Note the stocky posture. These birds come originally from west Ecuador and northwestern Peru, and live in dry wooded habitats.

light green mask that extends into the breast is not tolerated in show birds because the contrast is not so great.

Nominate Form and Subspecies: The nominate form is very similar in appearance to the Yellow-faced Parrotlet *(Forpus xanthops)* (page 148), and it is therefore not surprising that the Celestial Parrotlet has been frequently misnamed in the literature. Until recently there were no subspecies recognized, although, in an article in 1932, Karl Plath, the Chicago Zoo curator of birds, mentioned the subspecies *Forpus coelestis lucida* that originated in Colombia and of which the *females*

had blue rumps. The blue eye ring in the subspecies (hence *lucida*) extends around the back of the head; in the nominate form it is lighter and shorter. The subspecies carries a gray-mauve band across its chest; the nominate form lacks such a band and has a dark green back, not a light one like the subspecies. And, last but not least, the subspecies has a lighter shade of blue on its wings. The subspecies turns up regularly in imports into Europe and America, but is seldom recognized as a subspecies. Thanks to their breeding experiences of the genus *Forpus,* Sandee L. and Robert Molenda discovered the subspecies among their own birds; their discovery was reported and illustrated with color pictures in *The AFA Watchbird* (Volume XXII, No. 5, September/October 1996, pages 20–22). They are adamant in stating that it is of greatest importance to keep the breeding of the nominate form and the subspecies *separate.* Unfortunately, mainly through ignorance, many hens of the subspecies are still being paired with cocks of the nominate race in order to produce young cocks with a more intensive blue rump. This is done mainly to help score high points in bird shows. Such breedings are strongly condemned now that we know that we are dealing with two different kinds of birds that need to be kept pure.

Distribution: Western Ecuador to northwestern Peru, along the west coast of South America from Bohia de Caraqueas, south to Trujillo. This area borders the Pacific Ocean in the west and the Talmanea Cordillera (Andes) in the east, approximately along 80-degree longitude. In the north, the area doesn't touch the equator, in the south it extends to approximately 10-degree latitude; this is in fact the most western coastal tip of South America. It is semi-open lowland habitat, ranging "from desert scrubland through to lighter woodlands and deciduous forest, even occurring locally in humid forest" (R. S. Ridgely, 1981. "The Current Distribution and Status of Mainland Neo-tropical Parrots," in R. F. Pasquier [Ed.], Conservation of New World Parrots, *ICBP Tech. Publ.,* No. 1: 233–384).

In the Wild: The birds tend to live in small family groups of five to ten birds once the breeding season is over. They are seen frequently in dry country, usually among shrubs and scattered stands of trees. Later, as the dry season approaches, groups of the birds come together and may form quite substantial flocks. Their high-pitched chattering helps bring more groups into the flock, but may also attract predators, especially when the birds are foraging on the ground in search of seeds and small insects. They are obviously safer in bushes or trees where they forage for berries and similar fruits. During the hottest part of the day they shelter among tree foliage, mutually preening each other (Forshaw).

The flocks of birds consist of many different families. When they take flight they can, like flocks of starlings or finches, swarm as one as they wheel around tree tops and other obstacles—an unforgettable sight! In the wild, these birds also are not particularly fussy with regard to their choice of nesting sites; I have found nests in abandoned woodpecker holes, in rotting fence posts, in holes in walls, in fact, in any hollow and cavity that is large enough (average 7.75 to 6.20 inches [20 × 16 cm]) to brood their white eggs in. The local people are very adept at finding their nests, and often remove half-grown young from nests in order to hand-rear them further. They feed them a gruel made of ground corn and germinated seeds. The birds are seldom exported, but kept in cages as pets. I have seen various birds that could repeat Spanish words adeptly.

In the wild the birds eat half-ripe grass and weed seeds, berries, and other soft fruits. Observation has shown that the birds don't relish feeding on the ground if they can help it; they prefer the trees (much safer).

Wing detail of a male Celestial Parrotlet.

Celestial Blue-mutation (Recessive and Autosomal)

	Cock	*Hen*
Head & Face	• Face is sky blue. • Behind the face, a cobalt blue line running from the eye and ending on the neck. • Back of head and nape are bluish gray.	• Face is light sky blue. • Behind the face, a cobalt blue line running from the eye and ending on the neck. • Back of head and nape, bluish gray. • The cobalt blue line is vague, and not always obvious.
Body	• Mantel is blue with a strong gray wash. • Anal, flank, and belly are dull blue, with a strong gray wash. • Lower back and rump are dark cobalt blue with a violet wash.	• Mantel is blue with a light gray wash. • Anal, flank, and belly are dull blue, with a light gray shimmer. • Lower back and rump are blue. Some hens have a turquoise wash here.
Wings	• Wing coverts are blue with a strong gray wash. • Flight feathers are deep cobalt; the outermost five feathers have white edges. • Primary wing coverts are deep cobalt blue with a violet wash.	• Wing coverts are blue. • Flight feathers are blue; the outer five have white edges. • Primary wing coverts are blue. • Underwing coverts are blue.
Tail	• Upper tail coverts are blue. • Tail feathers are blue with narrow sky blue tips. • Undertail coverts are sky blue.	• Upper tail coverts are blue. • Tail feathers are blue with narrow sky blue tips. • Undertail coverts are blue.
Eyes	• Dark brown iris with a gray eye ring.	• Dark brown iris with gray eye ring.
Beak	• Horn-colored.	• Horn-colored.
Feet & Nails	• Feet, light brown (beige). • Nails, horn-colored with darker tips.	• Feet, light brown with a gray wash. • Nails, horn-colored with gray tips.
Length	• Minimum 5.1 inches (13 cm).	• Minimum 5.1 inches (13 cm).

Aviculture: I consider the Celestial Parrotlet to be one of the prettiest members of the *Forpus* genus. It is also one of the easiest to breed, and is relatively inexpensive. As it is the most frequently bred species, it also has the largest number of mutations (for the most important ones, see Celestial Blue-mutation and Celestial Lutino-mutation).

Celestial Fallow-mutation (Recessive and Autosomal)

	Cock	*Hen*
Head & Face	• Face a bright, deep yellow. • Behind the face, a cobalt blue line, running from the eye. • The cobalt blue stops on the neck. • The neck is gray with a cobalt wash.	• Face is pale yellow. • Behind the face, a pale cobalt blue line, running from the eye, stopping at the neck. • The back of the head and nape are light sky blue with a gray wash.
Body	• Mantel and back are green with a strong brown wash. • Anal, flank, and belly are yellowish green with a strong brown wash. • Lower back and rump are dark cobalt blue with a violet wash.	• Mantle and back are green with a brownish gray wash. • Anal, flank, and belly, yellowish green, with an obvious brown wash. • Lower back and rump are light green with a gray wash.
Wings	• Wing coverts, green with a strong brown wash. • Flight feathers are deep cobalt, the outer five feathers with yellowish green edges. • Primary and underwing coverts are deep cobalt blue. • The edge of the wing-bend is cobalt with a light brown wash.	• Wing coverts green with a brown wash. • Flight feathers are brown with green edges. • Primary wing coverts are dull brown. • Underwing coverts are yellow-green with a dull brown wash. • The edge of the wing-bend is yellow with a light brown wash.
Tail	• Upper tail coverts are green with a strong brown wash. • Tail feathers are brown with a narrow beige border at the tips. • Undertail coverts are brown, with a yellowish wash.	• Upper tail coverts are green with a brown wash. • Tail feathers are brown, with lighter brown tips. • Undertail coverts are brown with a light brown wash.
Eyes	• Dark red.	• Dark red.
Beak	• Horn-colored.	• Horn-colored.
Feet & Nails	• Feet, flesh-colored. • Nails, horn-colored with dark brown tips.	• Feet, flesh-colored. • Nails, horn-colored with dark brown tips.
Length	• Minimum 5.1 inches (13 cm).	• Minimum 5.1 inches (13 cm).

A softer, somewhat lighter blue mutation of the Celestial Parrotlet. Note the dark hue in the head which is beautifully even. A beautiful bird!

The birds also make excellent pets if kept in cages or room aviaries in the living room or den; they can learn various tricks in a short time, and soon learn various words and short

A prize-winning lutino male Celestial Parrotlet.

sentences. In their native countries they are usually kept in cages and, apparently, breed quite readily, usually twice in rapid succession. The same holds true for the United States and Europe, where they use budgerigar (parakeet) nest.boxes quite successfully, as well as other types of boxes. Breeding usually starts when the birds are 12 to 14 months old; earlier breeding attempts should be strongly discouraged.

According to *Avicultural Magazine,* 1964, No.1, the first breeding results were achieved in 1963 when Mrs. W. Boorer of London, England, had success with a pair that was housed in a cage equipped for breeding. The pair spent most of their time in the top of the cage, so Mrs. Boorer promptly placed the feeding dish at the top also. After their arrival they only ate millet spray but soon started to include a mixture of canary grass seed, various millet varieties, groats, and hemp.

The parrotlets reared their brood entirely on millet spray. During the molt they became extremely fond of hemp and threw out all their other seeds in an effort to find it. They also had cuttlebone, grit, apple (which they ate sporadically), and seeding grass, of which they were very fond. Dried spinach, powdered yeast, and C.L.O. (an English soft food brand, similar to CéDé) were added to the seed mixture. They ignored sunflower seed, never used their feet to pick up anything, and also chewed up a lot of wood. When a budgerigar nest box was placed at one end of

Celestial Lutino-mutation (Recessive and Autosomal)

	Cock	Hen
Head & Face	• The face is deep yellow. • Behind the face, a white line runs from the eye into the neck. • Back of head and nape have an obvious gray wash.	(Colored similarly to the cock, with the exception of the white areas.)
Body	• Mantle and back, yellow with a light gray wash. • Anal, flank, and belly are yellow, but lighter than on the back. • Lower back and rump are white.	
Wings	• Upper tail coverts are yellow. • Tail feathers are yellow with light yellow tips. • Undertail coverts are light yellow.	
Eyes	• Red.	
Beak	• Light horn-colored.	
Feet & Nails	• Feet, flesh-colored. • Nails, light horn-colored.	
Length	• Minimum 5.1 inches (13 cm).	• Minimum 5.1 inches (13 cm).

the cage, the birds remained rooted to the perch at the other end for the next ten days. The cock finally investigated the box and shortly after this, the two of them used it for roosting. The hen started incubating on April 2nd. The eggs were white and laid every second day. It is not known whether incubation started with the laying of the first egg, but certainly the nestlings were all different in size and, when they finally flew, it was at three-day intervals. The cock spent much time in the nest box but, as he could always be seen sitting just inside the entrance hole, one could be almost certain that he took no part in the incubation. Seventeen days after the hen began incubating, a faint squeaking could be heard in the box, so one may presume the first egg had hatched. Four weeks later a chick was first seen at the nest entrance. Seven weeks after the first hatching, two nestlings were thrown out of the nest box. The larger was a young cock, with his blue quills just showing in his wings;

The cinnamon (fallow or Isabelle) mutation of the male Celestial Parrotlet. The mutation is recessive and autosomal.

the smaller was completely bald. Mrs. Boorer replaced these, and an hour later the young cock was again ejected, this time with both legs

A lutino male Celestial Parrotlet. The blue colors become white. This is a recessive and autosomal mutation.

bleeding. Shortly after this the mummified remains of another young cock were found on the cage floor. On June 23rd, eight weeks after hatching, the first young hen flew, to be followed at three-day intervals by three others. The fourth hen had been attacked in the nest box and had a crippled leg. As the adult hen was chivvying them, the fledglings were removed to a separate cage on the morning that the last one flew. Once they had left the nest, the youngsters were entirely self-supporting. The parents were never seen to feed them. There was also a large amount of millet and millet husks in the nest box, suggesting that the parents had been carrying whole millets into the box for some time before the fledglings flew.

The pair that Mrs. Boorer possessed was rather silent and shy. They were extremely reluctant to come to the floor of the cage and liked all their food hung up high. They never bathed, and disliked being sprayed. The birds went to roost very early; even in midsummer they would disappear into their box by 6:00 P.M. Perhaps the most noticeable feature was that the birds were always together. They were also very alert and suspicious and the lightest unusual sound caused them to draw themselves up very erect and peer around in all directions until they had located its origin. If one took flight, the other immediately followed. They sat pressed together on the perch and spent much time in mutual preening. When

Mrs. Boorer had to remove the hen, which became ill, they called out to each other for several hours. When they disagreed with each other, they made a high-pitched chattering, drawing themselves up very erect with feathers tight. They would bob and weave their heads and feint with their beaks open. The leg nearest their opponent was then raised, and the foot made vague grasping movements in the air. Mrs. Boorer never saw them touch each other during this display, which usually ended by one of the birds leaving the perch to fly around to the other side of the one left. Their threat display was rather impressive: With all feathers fluffed out and beaks open, they rocked very slowly backward. When it seemed they were about to fall off their perch, they lunged forward extremely fast. This was all done in silence and the strike forward was made long before the object they were threatening was in range. Mrs. Boorer never saw them do this to each other. It seemed to be directed solely at external dangers.

Mrs. Boorer, however, was not the first successful breeder; according to the literature, this was a certain Mr. R. F. Losky of Peru in 1938. In Europe, it was the well-known French biologist Dr. Jean Delacour who first raised an adaptive brood. In 1963, successes were reported for W. Grote of Hildesheim (Germany) and A. Jesen of Denmark.

Celestial Parrotlets were already extremely popular in the 1970s, and their popularity has not waned.

Two blue hens of the Celestial Parrotlet; the right bird has a so-called dark factor.

Indeed, it has probably increased. This is because this parrotlet is not at all fussy. It will make itself at home equally well in a large cage or in an aviary. The cage should be at least 3 feet (1 m) in length and placed in a well-lit area. In such accommodations, and especially in small flights, this species can be kept safely in pairs without mishap (such as toe nipping). In a large aviary, the young can be kept with each other during the breeding season (don't forget leg bands and, in particular, well maintained records). Singletons are seldomly really happy, even if you spend a lot of time with them; give them partners. In aviaries in which multiple pairs are kept, it can happen that they don't always get along well with each other. Their strong territoriality can lead to jealousy and squabbling.

In the breeding season, especially, this may develop into more serious fighting. In general the birds are not cowardly and are well able to hold their own. Pet birds should never be spoiled because if there is something they don't like they may become aggressive and won't hesitate to bite. Fortunately, this behavior is uncommon and the birds usually make ideal pets. They like to sit on your head or shoulder, or in a shirt pocket. One of my birds likes to nibble on my ear and gently pull my hair.

With regard to their diet, they will do very well on the diet recommended in the general feeding chapter (see page 42). They are particularly fond of germinated seeds, chickweed, and berries, especially bilberry and similar varieties. Additionally, they will take millet spray and grated carrot; it is recommended

A blue cinnamon female of the Celestial Parrotlet, offspring of a pairing of cinnamon × blue.

that grated carrot be mixed in with the soft food, especially in the breeding period. Don't forget to give them perches made from the twigs of willow or fruit trees, which they will gnaw passionately. Extra willow twigs are always welcome.

As stated at the beginning of this section, this species is far from fussy with regard to nest boxes; a horizontally mounted budgie nest box is, in my opinion, the best choice. The entrance hole is made in one side and, inside the other half of the box, a nest hollow with a raised edge is provided that will stop the eggs from rolling around. During the night the male likes to stay in the nest, and in a box such as described, there is plenty of space for him without unduly disturbing the brooding hen. The incubation period is 20 to 22 days. Because it is not always possible to tell precisely when the hen starts to brood (I have personally determined that captive hens usually start brooding after the second or third egg has been laid), it is difficult to say when the young will be ready to leave the nest. As copulation usually takes place in the nest box, it is also difficult to estimate when the first and following eggs are laid. Sometimes copulation takes place on a perch. This takes place "sideways"; the hen crouches on the perch and turns her rump toward the male, who holds on to the perch with one foot and places the other on the hen's back in order to keep balance. In this position, the cloacas are pressed against each other. Copulation also occurs "the other way around," both in captivity and in the wild; that is to say, the *hen* holds the perch with one foot and places the other on the cock's back. A sort of courtship dance usually takes place prior to copulation; the cock makes quick wing beats, stretches his body, and lets out rapid, high, fluting notes. This is frequently coupled with lunging movements, whereby the beak is tapped against the perch. Sometimes the birds tap their beaks together while making similar lunges. The whole performance seems to be rather aggressive but, a few minutes later, the pair will sit peacefully together and perhaps preen each other's plumage in a loving manner. During the courtship, the birds feed each other, but may also do so outside the breeding season so that the bond is kept intact.

After fledging (about four to five weeks), the offspring become quickly independent. The cock usually feeds them but, after eight to ten days, his task is finished and the young will feed themselves completely. Millet spray and soft food are essential, in addition to the normal food (see page 46). Place the food on a feeding tray, not on the floor, as these birds are naturally reluctant to feed on the ground. If kept in a large aviary, the young will tolerate each other well as they do in the wild; if one flies to the feeding base at the other end of the flight, the others will follow as one. They also like to preen each other's plumage as they sit brotherly (and

One of the latest blue mutations, without a name yet, of the Celestial Parrotlet. The bird looks like a cinnamon but has black eyes. Later pairings will tell us more about the genetics of this beautiful bird, bred in the Netherlands.

sisterly) together on a long perch. However, you will soon see a kind of order of rank (hierarchy) developing, and even the most inexperienced aviculturists can tell which birds are becoming "bosses." This pecking order is kept by "chopping-behavior" with the beak. As you can imagine, a bird newly introduced to the group will go through a tough period until the pecking order is reorganized. If the bird holds its own, it will show agitation for a few days and will frequently cry out in a quiet but concerned manner. Keep a close eye on the birds during this time and, if there seem to be any particular troublemakers, they are best moved elsewhere.

As the youngsters are so quickly independent, there is little point in leaving them with their parents for long; as soon as they are standing on their own two legs, they should be placed in their own flight. This is in case the parents become aggressive toward their young, especially when they want to start a new brood. In such cases the hen will drive the young away from the nest box and any perches close by. Should this concern youngsters that are still being fed by the cock, all you can do is place the young in a flight with some older, independent youngsters. These older birds will usually take the newcomers "under their wings" and feed them, although this feeding will never be as intensive as that performed by the father. Again, you must keep an eye on the proceedings, and, if the newcomers are not accepted, your last resort

The Yellow-fronted Parrotlet (Forpus xanthops) *lives in small flocks in the upper Marañón Valley in Peru. The bird in this picture is a male born and raised in captivity.*

will be to remove them for hand-rearing until such time as they are able to feed themselves.

Yellow-faced Parrotlet— *Forpus xanthops* (Salvin 1895)

Nomenclature: This species, the largest member of its genus, was long recognized by European ornithologists as a subspecies of *Forpus coelestis* (for example, by A. Reichenow in *Vögelbilder aus fernen Zonen, Papageien,* New Edition, 1955, Pfungstadt). This is not surprising, considering the close resemblance of the two species. At the present time, the Yellow-faced Parrotlet is regarded as a species in its own right (Wolters, Forshaw); no subspecies of *xanthops* are recognized. To prevent confusion with the previous species, however, I have supplied a color description (see page 149).

Male: Crown, forehead, cheeks, and throat intensive lemon yellow. The eye-stripe, which is blue-gray in color, is very pronounced and begins just behind the eye and runs far into the neck. The back and upper wing coverts are green, with a gray shimmer. The lower back, rump, and wing coverts are brilliant violet. Underparts are yellowish green. The undertail coverts are a light yellowish green. The beak is horn-colored, with dark, closely aligned dark brown stripes on the upper mandible. The feet are light flesh-colored, the iris black. Length: 5.5 to 6 inches (14.5–15 cm); weight: 1.76 ounces (50 g).

Yellow-faced Parrotlet *(Forpus xanthops)*

	Cock	Hen
Head & Face	• Head and face are yellow-green. • A gray-blue crescent from behind the eye and around the face. • Back of head and nape are green.	• Head and face, yellow-green.
Body	• Mantel and back are dark green, with a gray wash. • Anal, flank, and belly are yellow with a green wash. A little gray in the flanks. • Lower back and rump are violet.	• The mantel is dark green, gray edges. • Anal, flank, and belly are yellow, with a green wash; some gray in flanks. • Lower back and rump are weak violet (lighter than in the cock).
Wings	• Wing coverts are dark green with a light gray sheen. • Primary flight feathers are gray with dark green edges. • The remaining flight feathers are gray with violet edges. • Primary and secondary coverts are violet. • Underwing coverts are violet with black edges. • The edge of the wing-bend is violet. • Shoulder coverts are dark green.	• Wing coverts are dark green with a gray wash. • Flight feathers are gray with green edges. • Primary wing coverts are dark blue. • Secondary wing coverts are light blue. • Underwing coverts are blue-green, with black edges. • The edge of the wing-bend is cobalt blue. • Shoulder covers are cobalt blue.
Tail	• Upper tail coverts are violet. • Lower tail coverts, yellow with a green wash. • Tail feathers are dark green.	• Upper tail coverts are green, with sky blue edges. • Undertail feathers are yellow with a green sheen. • The tail feathers are dark green.
Eyes	• Black iris with a dark gray eye ring.	• The iris is black with a brown eye ring.
Beak	• Light horn-colored. The center of the upper mandible varies from dark gray to black (depending on the breeding condition).	• Light horn-colored. The center of the upper mandible varies from dark gray to black (depending on the breeding condition).
Feet & Nails	• Feet are gray scaled. • Nails, horn-colored with darker tip.	• The feet are gray scaled. • Nails, horn-colored with darker tips.
Length	• 5.5–6 inches (14.5–15 cm).	• 5.5–6 inches (14.5–15 cm).

The female Yellow-fronted Parrotlet (Forpus xanthops) has a smaller blue patch on her rump, and the yellowish underpart is less bright than in the male's. She doesn't have any blue on the upper-wing coverts and the flight feathers only have some blue hues.

Female: Similar to the male, but the blue on the back and rump is lighter. The underwing coverts are gray, tinged with some light blue. Primaries and secondaries are green, also tinged with blue. For more details see box.

Immatures: Similar to the female (see also page 149).

Type: Tear-shaped, with an upright stance (55–60°). The head is wide and strongly arched; the beak is carried close to the body. The line of the back runs straight into the short keel-shaped tail. The full breast is curved to the front; the wings are held tightly against the body, and cover about two thirds of the tail.

Distribution: It has a relatively small range—especially when compared with most other members of the genus: Northwestern Peru, especially in the valley of the Maranon

River, which is a tributary of the Amazon.

In the Wild: The birds inhabit the edges of tropical woodland that are divided by areas of tree and brush savanna. They sometimes may be found at altitudes between 2,000 and 6,460 feet (600–1,700 m) in the mountains. Unfortunately, herds of goats are decimating the sparse vegetation (source of various seeds) with the result that, sooner or later, general populations of birds probably will diminish. The presence of silver mines and similar land exploitations also do not help, as they destroy natural habitats of many species.

First Breedings: Literature on this species is sparse. This is perhaps understandable, bearing in mind that the birds only gained popularity (mainly in Germany) around the mid 1970s. In earlier years they were seldom seen, even in bird parks. As far as is known, the first pair in captivity was acquired by the breeder W. Heinrich of Mainz, Germany, who later passed them on to the famous bird park at Walsrode, apparently without having had any breeding success. In 1981, Peter Frenger was successful in breeding a pair of this species that he acquired in October 1980. In February 1981, the birds became interested in a square parakeet nest box that was provided and spent hours inspecting it. The first egg was laid on March 8th, followed by another five white eggs at intervals of two days. The first two hatchlings appeared on March 31st, the remaining four on the 1st, 4th, and 5th of April, respectively. The incubation period was about 21 days. The hatchlings were covered with an open, white down and each had a conspicuous egg-tooth (which is used to escape from the egg shell). After a further period of 32 to 35 days, the fully feathered young left the nest box. Three further successful broods were raised in 1981 (see *AZ Nachrichten,* February 1982, Osterholz-Scharmbeck, Germany). In the same journal, Mr. Friebe reported another successful breeding in 1981. His pair had laid five eggs, all of which hatched; unfortunately, one of the young died on the second day, but the remainder developed normally and left the nest at the beginning of August. A number of successes are also known from England. In 1979, the Midland Bird Garden-Park in Shropshire acquired 12 wild-captured birds. The first successful breeding occurred in the summer of 1980, when a hen raised three chicks. In 1985 the leading German magazine *AZ Nachrichten* conducted a small survey among eight breeders who, together, possessed nine pairs of these birds; 52 young were raised in that season.

From the end of 1970 to the beginning of 1990, the successes (especially in Germany, England, and the Netherlands), had steadily improved, and the Yellow-faced Parrotlet had become one of the most abundant "wild" aviary birds. In the United States, popularity of the bird also increased. Since late 1997, seven pairs have been committed to a regulated breeding program; many pairs in America have come via Europe.

Aviculture: Although the Yellow-faced Parrotlet is not yet readily available in the United States—as compared to Europe—the chances are high that this species will soon take a high profile in America. For successful breeding, the birds are best housed in roomy aviaries and, as so few birds are available in the United States, this is definitely the way to go. The birds are somewhat fussy in their choice of foodstuffs, especially with regard to seeds, soft food, and various berries. They will not pick up any food that falls to the floor. Their preference includes small black sunflower seeds, hemp, and millet spray. The first two should be offered only in small amounts, as their high oil content could contribute to obesity and liver problems. Personally, I give hemp seeds only once per week during the morning, and sunflower seeds every other day, also during the morning (only as much as the bird eats in 15 minutes). The daily fortified seed mixture consists of pellets, canary grass seed, various small millet varieties, and niger seed. Every other day they get, additionally, sprouted sunflower seeds, oats, and mung beans. In a special container, I place a mixture of grass and weed seeds. Millet spray is always available, as well as carrots (whole and in strips), chickweed, shepherd's purse, dandelion, sowthistle, seeding grasses, and a rich variety of berries. Willow and fruit tree branches are prized by the birds, as is corn on the cob.

As previously stated, the birds will do best in a large aviary; one pair per flight. If kept in a garden aviary (which is recommended), they must be brought indoors during the winter and placed in a breeding cage (minimum size 47.2 inches [1.20 m] long) and kept at a minimum temperature of 59°F (15°C) and a minimum humidity of 80 percent.

Acclimatized birds make excellent pets once they are accustomed to their surroundings. They easily learn to repeat words, perform tricks, and become very affectionate. Indeed, the Yellow-faced Parrotlet has the personality of a big parrot in a little body. Even birds kept in an outdoor aviary soon become very trusting, and some of mine eagerly accept tidbits offered to them in my fingers, even from between my lips. While some birds eat these tidbits, others land on my hand or shoulder, playing with my hair or ear lobe.

Wing detail of the female Yellow-faced Parrotlet.

Such trusting birds pose few or no problems during the breeding season, as long as each pair has its own accommodations. At least one month before the breeding season starts, I give them extra rations of germinated seeds and soft food. I mix a few drops of a commercial vitamin/mineral supplement into the soft food. It sometimes happens that newly acquired birds refuse to eat the soft food, but, by mixing some germinated seed or oats in with it, they will soon learn to take it.

The German breeder, K. Westen, is of the opinion that the black patch on the upper mandible of the male bird becomes larger and shinier as breeding time approaches. The incubation period I have recorded with my birds (six pairs) averages three days longer than most *Forpus* species, thus about 24 days. On leaving the nest, fledglings closely resemble the hen, though the colors are somewhat duller. The blue color in the male's plumage becomes visible at three to four months of age. During this period, the flesh color of the beak gradually changes to horn color and the dark patch on the upper mandible becomes gradually more apparent.

Finally, I would like to mention that, in the not-too-distant past, many newly imported Yellow-faced Parrotlets were infected with immature parasitic worms *(microfilariae)*. These worms occur in the circulatory system and were responsible for the sudden deaths of birds that otherwise appeared healthy. The disease was described as avian malaria. Newly acquired wild birds should be examined immediately by an avian veterinarian. However, prevention is certainly better than cure and captive-bred birds are a better acquisition. Even these, though, should be inspected if they have been in contact with wild-caught birds.

Green-rumped Parrotlet— *Forpus passerinus* (Linnaeus 1758)

There are four subspecies, *Forpus p. deliciosus* (Ridgeway), *Forpus p. cyanophanes* (Todd), *Forpus p. viridissimus* (Lafresnaye), and *Forpus p. cyanochlorus* (Schlegel).

Nomenclature: In older literature, further subspecies were placed under *passerinus,* including *vividus, crassirostris, flavescens, spengeli,* and *olallae.* At present, most biologists recognize only the four subspecies mentioned. *Forpus p. cyanochlorus,* however, is a "doubtful case" in that it almost exactly resembles the nominate species. I am personally not convinced either way, but will deal with it as a subspecies here.

Immatures: Similar to the female but the young males will soon begin to show the blue in their plumage.

Type: The Green-rumped Parrotlets are the smallest members of the genus. The body is slender, and they sit upright on their perch (55–60°). The head is characteristically rounded, the beak (which is rather small in proportion to the head) is held against the body and

The male Green-rumped Parrotlet (Forpus passerinus). *The rump is brighter green than the rest of the plumage. The subspecies* F. p. deliciosus, *however, has a rump with bluish tinge; the secondaries also have some blue.*

harmonizes with the outline of the skull. The line of the nape flows into the line of the back. The wings are held tightly to the body, the tips do not cross, and the wings run to the end of the keel-like, short tail. Weight: .71 to .99 ounce (20–28 g), though mostly .71 to .78 ounce (20–22 g).

Distribution: Northern Trinidad, through central Venezuela along the Orinoco River to eastern Colombia, and then from southeastern portion of the Rio Branco River to eastern Amazonas and to the Amapa River area in northeastern Brazil (near Nacapa in the Amazon Delta). This species has been introduced into Curaçao in the Netherlands Antilles, Jamaica, and Barbados. Introductions into Martinique were unsuccessful.

Green-rumped Parrotlet (*Forpus passerinus passerinus*)

	Cock	Hen
Head & Face	• Face is light grass green. • Behind the face running into dark green with a gray wash.	• Face is grass green with a small yellow triangle above the beak.
Body	• Mantle and back, dark green. • Anal, flank, and breast are light grass green. • Lower back and rump are light grass green.	• Anal, flank, and breast, light green; somewhat lighter than in the cock.
Wings	• Wing coverts are dark green. • Flight feathers are dark green, with some lighter edges. • Secondary wing coverts are dark green with light blue edges. • Primary wing coverts are violet. • Underwing coverts are dark violet. • The edge of the wing-bend is sky blue.	• Flight feathers are dark green. • Primary and secondary wing coverts are dark green with light edges. • Underwing coverts are light grass green. • Edge of the wing-bend is grass green.
Tail	• Upper tail coverts are dark green. • Tail feathers are dark green with a yellow tinge. • Undertail coverts are yellow with a green wash.	• Upper tail coverts are grass green. • Tail feathers are dark green with a light yellow edge. • Undertail coverts are light yellowish green.
Eyes	• Dark brown iris, with a brown eye ring.	• Dark brown iris with a brown eye ring.
Beak	• Upper mandible is light horn-colored.	• Light horn-colored.
Feet & Nails	• Feet are light brown. • Nails, horn-colored to brown.	• Feet are light brownish gray. • Nails, horn-colored.
Length	• 4.75 inches (12 cm).	• 4.75 inches (12 cm).

Subspecies: *Forpus p. deliciosus* (Delicate Green-rumped Parrotlet)

Distribution: Northern Brazil, in the area of the Amazon River to the Anapu River in Para, and further east, reaching Macapa in Amapa.

Subspecies: *Forpus p. cyanophanus* (Rio Hacha Parrotlet)

Male: Similar to *viridissimus,* but with much more intensive violet-blue on the bend of the wing. When the

Delicate Green-rumped Parrotlet *(Forpus passerinus deliciosus)*

	Cock	*Hen*
Head & Face	• The face is light, glossy grass green, running to dark green with a light gray wash behind the head.	• Face is grass green, with a small yellow triangle above the beak, running from eye to eye.
Body	• The mantle is green. • Anal, flank, and belly, light green with a yellow sheen. • Lower back and rump are light emerald green with a glossy blue wash.	• Mantle, light, glossy dark green. • Anal, flank, and belly are grass green with a yellow wash.
Wings	• Primary wing coverts are sky blue, running to cobalt. • Upper wing coverts are green. • Flight feathers are dark green. • Underwing coverts are sea green, running to cobalt and black. • The edge of the wing-bend is sky blue.	• Primary wing coverts are green with a blue wash. • Wing coverts are green. • The flight feathers are dark gray with green edges. • Underwing coverts are green with a yellow sheen. • The edge of the wing-bend is green.
Tail	• Upper tail coverts are light, glossy yellowish green. • Tail feathers are light grass green with yellow edges. • The undertail coverts are yellowish green.	• Upper tail coverts are glossy, grass green. • The tail feathers are grass green with yellow edges. • Undertail coverts are greenish yellow.
Eyes	• Iris, dark brown; eye ring, gray.	• Iris, dark brown; eye ring, gray.
Beak	• Light horn-colored.	• Light horn-colored.
Feet & Nails	• Feet, gray. • Nails, horn-colored.	• Feet, gray. • Nails, horn-colored.
Length	• 4.75 inches (12 cm).	• 4.75 inches (12 cm).

wings are closed, a round, violet-blue spot is visible; this blue occurs in the primary and secondary wing coverts. The underside of the wing has more violet-blue than the nominate race.

Female: Similar to *passerinus.*

Distribution: Northern Colombia, east of the Santa Marta Mountains in rather arid tropical habitat, extending into the Cesare River Valley and Camperucho.

Venezuelan Green-rumped Parrotlet *(Forpus passerinus viridissimus)*

	Cock	Hen
Head & Face	• Face is dark grass green. The cheeks are covered with a light blue wash. • Head and neck, dark green.	• Face is grass green, running into yellow on the forehead. • Head and neck are dark green.
Body	• Mantle and back are dark green. • Anal, flank, and breast are dark green with a yellow wash. • Lower back and rump are dark green with a cobalt blue sheen.	• Mantle and back are dark green. • Anal, flank, and breast are dark green with a yellow sheen.
Wings	• Wing coverts are dark green. • Flight feathers are gray with green edges. • Primary wing coverts are violet. • Underwing coverts are violet blue. • The edge of the wing-bend is violet. • Secondary wing coverts are light blue. • Shoulder coverts are dark blue, edged with light blue.	• Wing coverts are dark green. • Flight feathers are dark gray with green edges. • Primary and secondary wing coverts are dark green • Underwing coverts, green with a yellow wash. • The edge of the wing-bend is green.
Tail	• Upper tail coverts are grass green with a yellow sheen. • Undertail coverts are green with a yellow wash, lighter than the belly color. • Tail feathers, grass green with yellow edges.	• Upper tail coverts are grass green. • Undertail coverts are green with a yellow sheen; lighter than the belly color. • Tail feathers are dark green.
Eyes	• Black iris with a dark brown eye ring.	• Black iris with a dark brown eye ring.
Beak	• Light horn-colored.	• Light horn-colored.
Feet & Nails	• Feet, gray scaled. • Nails, horn-colored with darker tips.	• Feet, gray scaled. • Nails, horn-colored with darker tips.
Length	• 4.75–5.1 inches (12–13 cm).	• 4.75–5.1 inches (12–13 cm).

Subspecies: *Forpus p. viridissimus* (Venezuelan Green-rumped or Caralas Parrotlet)

Distribution: Introduced to Trinidad; further via northern Venezuela south to the Orinoco River, and east to the Zulia River Valley in Norte de Santander; possibly in northern Colombia (Arauca and Vichada). Introduced also into

Curaçao in the Netherlands Antilles, Jamaica, and Barbados.

Subspecies: *Forpus p. cyanochlorus*

Male: Similar to *passerinus* but with more yellow on the underparts; lower back and rump pale yellow tinged with pale blue. Smaller bill than nominate.

Female: Similar to *passerinus* but also with more yellow on the underparts. Various ornithologists would like to consider this subspecies as a somewhat lighter form of the nominate.

Distribution: Isolated to the upper Branco River, Roraima, in northernmost Brazil, Venezuela, Curaçao, and Surinam.

In the Wild: Due to the mainly green plumage, this species is difficult to observe or study in the wild. They keep mainly to the trees and can often only be located by the sound of their twittering. Many of the natives keep them in cages in their homes after having taken them out of their nests and hand-feeding them. Except for the breeding period, these gorgeous birds roam around in large groups searching for food, which consists of various seeds, berries, and soft fruits. Their chirping and soft chatter make one think of a group of twittering sparrows. If you should approach the trees in which they are chattering too closely, they will suddenly, as one, take off and wheel around the treetops and other obstacles, like a flock of starlings. F. Haverschmidt reports in *Birds of Surinam* (Boyd,

1968) that he was able to observe the birds frequently in open terrain, sparsely dotted with trees and tall shrubs. In Venezuela, I saw this species especially in pastured areas with copses of trees and shrubs. The birds breed in Surinam from June to August, in Venezuela from May to August; they use tree hollows and sometimes the nests of woodpeckers or tree termites. The hen lays two to seven eggs. The subspecies *viridissimus* was already described by G. J. Simons in *Description of the Island of Curaçao*. Nothing further was published about this subspecies until 1943 when M. de Jong was able to catch an exhausted specimen that landed on a wall in Willemstad, Curaçao. Apparently this bird had flown over from Venezuela. Personally, I feel that we are dealing here with a very interesting ornithological question:

Subspecies F. p. deliciosus *from the banks of the Amazon in Brazil, known as the Delicate Green-rumped Parrotlet.*

Have enough of these birds found their way to Curaçao in the course of time so that this subspecies has a breeding population there? I observed a number of these birds on Curaçao in 1998, but there is some question as to whether these were just a few individual specimens that had flown over from Venezuela, just like the one Mr. de Jong caught, or whether these were offspring from the group of 40 that were imported in 1940 and given free reign on the plantation "Klein Piscadera." Simons, by the way, calls this subspecies "bibitji" but the people of Curaçao refer to it as "bibitu."

First Breeding: As at one time there were some 11 subspecies recognized (now divided up), and as they are so similar to the Yellow-faced Parrotlet, it is difficult, though not impossible, to report on "first breedings." Dr. Karl Russ reported that in 1876 a Mr. Franken of Berlin received first prize in a bird show for a pair of Yellow-faced Parrotlets. These birds later attempted to breed but, due to disturbance, they were not successful in rearing young. Dr. Wildeboer reported a breeding success in 1926 (*Avicultural Magazine,* 4th. ser. 4); in this case the male was said to relieve the brooding female during the night, though this is very doubtful and could have arisen from mistaken observation. Personally, I have never observed this in wild or captive birds. More believable is the breeding success of C. af Enehjelm in 1951. This well-known aviculturist and director of the Helsinki Zoo had a

pair that laid seven eggs, all of which hatched; all the young were raised.

Aviculture: Pairs of these small birds can be housed in parakeet or lovebird breeding cages (minimum length 3 feet [1 m]). The temperature in the bird room must not drop below 59°F (15°C). Newly acquired birds should be handled with care as they are easily frightened when confronted with new (to them) situations. One of their first reactions is to refuse to feed, and they rarely (it is said) take millet spray. Give the birds adequate time to get accustomed to their keeper, surroundings, and so on. In this respect, Sandee L. and Robert Molenda give some useful advice in *Bird Talk* (November, 1997); it seems that this subspecies "often is prone to beak abnormalities, such as overgrowing and being misshapen. No explanation exists for this phenomena—nutritional deficiencies, genetic flaws, environment and medical problems have been excluded in most cases. One theory is that the birds in their native habitat use their beaks in some manner that wears them down quickly, therefore, they must grow rapidly to keep the beak healthy. Or, perhaps there are some trace minerals that the birds require that are not available in the captive setting. Fortunately, their beaks are easy to trim."

Experience has shown that the Green-rumped Parrotlets are pleasant birds that pose few problems. They are ideal as "pets" as they are not only intelligent, but also playful, comical, and always ready to take an active part in training and games. They are also good breeders. In Surinam, I have seen many natives keeping them as pets. They take the half-grown young from the nest and rear them further by hand with berries, half-ripe seeds, soaked seeds, cooked corn mixture, and various greens, although the birds do not particularly relish the latter. The specimens in my aviaries also usually refuse to eat green foods. However, they will eagerly take various millet varieties, sunflower seeds (small, black), hemp, and canary grass seed; fruit should be offered daily from a choice of apples, pears, bananas, and such, as well as various berries. During the breeding season you should offer a good commercial soft food and water-soaked wheat bread. In the wild, as soon as the breeding period arrives, the various pairs go off by themselves to find suitable nesting sites. They do not use nesting material. In the breeding cage or aviary they prefer a horizontal budgerigar nest box. Due to their nervousness (when compared to other species) it is best to place breeding cages fairly high up; 6 feet (2 m) is ideal. If you use battery cages placed in stacks, it is best to reserve the upper cages for the Green-rumped Parrotlets.

This species is well known for its large clutches of eggs; seven or more have been recorded both in the wild and in captivity. The Penard Egg Collection, housed in the Rijksmuseum of Natural History in Leyden, the Netherlands, shows a brood of two and one of five eggs. In captivity the number can vary even more since as many as nine eggs have been laid in one batch. All the incubation is done by the female and takes about three weeks, during which time the male provides her with food. The offspring stay in the nest box for 30 to 45 days, but even after they have flown out they will still be fed by the father for a short time. During this period it might be a good idea to keep an eye on the male since it is not unusual for him to start plucking out the feathers of his chicks, or worse, to even kill them, especially if they are housed in the same cage or aviary while the hen is ready for a new round. In such a case, you have to place the young in different accommodations.

As is the case with all parrotlets, the best breeding results are obtained when each pair is given its own abode where they can go about their business undisturbed. The birds can become quite aggressive toward other birds during the breeding season and they will aim for the little feet of their fellow inmates.

Cross-breedings have been achieved with the Blue-winged Parrotlet and Celestial Parrotlet, but such pairings should be avoided.

Sclater's Parrotlet—*Forpus sclateri* (G. R. Gray 1859)

Only one subspecies is recognized, *Forpus s. eidos* Peters.

Male: This species is the most green of the genus. Upper parts are dark green, the underparts somewhat lighter. The forehead and cheeks are also a lighter tone of green, with less blue suffusion. Undertail coverts are marked with yellow. The lower back and rump are very dark blue; the upper tail coverts are very dark green. Underwing coverts are bluish violet, as are the inner primaries at their bases. The upper surface of the tail is dark green, beneath bluish green. The top mandible is grayish black, the lower mandible light horn-colored. Legs brownish gray. Iris brown. Length: 5 inches (12.5 cm).

Female: Predominantly green, lighter than the male. Lower back, rump, and underwing coverts emerald green. Underside greenish yellow. Most females carry a clear yellow frontal band; cheeks yellowish, as is the throat. The female is somewhat smaller than the male.

Immatures: Males less bluish with green in lower back and rump; females resemble adult, but less yellowish.

Distribution: Southeastern Colombia southward via the Napo River and Sarayacu (eastern Ecuador) to eastern Peru and western Brazil (southern Acre) and northern Bolivia. Eastward to the Amazones in Belem and Para (northeastern Brazil).

Subspecies: *Forpus s. eidos*
Male: Lighter green with more yellow, especially on the underparts. Paler blue rump. Somewhat smaller in size.
Female: Smaller than nominate. Breast with more yellow.

Distribution: Northern parts of French Guyana, in Southern Surinam via Guyana and southern Venezuela to Rio Negro in western Brazil.

In the Wild: Little is known about this subspecies; it lives mainly in thickly wooded tropical areas and is thus difficult to observe. I have been able to establish that these birds can often be seen in the Para region, especially in the area around Belem, occurring in family groups of up to 30 individuals.

Aviculture: This race is unfortunately almost unknown in Europe or the United States; the only report in the literature states that one of these birds was imported into London in 1881, but no further information was available and it can be assumed that the birds were never bred. In view of the strict modern import/export regulations, it seems that this undoubtedly beautiful bird may never be seen in aviculture. The hen resembles a miniature version of a hen Celestial Parrotlet. The nominate is sometimes called the Dusky Parrotlet, and the subspecies is given the name Schemburgk's Parrotlet.

The Other Dwarf Parrots

Double-eyed Fig Parrot— *Cyclopsitta diophthalma* (Hombron and Jacquinot)
Nomenclature: The genus *Cyclopsitta,* formerly known as

Opopsitta, contains two species and numerous subspecies. There are six subspecies of this species that live in New Guinea, and three that live in Australia, namely *macleayana, aruensis, coccineifrons, coxeni, inseparabilis, marshalli, virago,* and *diophthalma.*

Male Nominate: Has a red forehead and cheeks and is orange starting at the crown going toward the back of the head. There is a small purple band bordering the back part of the crown. There is a curved line of bright blue feathers over the eyes. The beak is silver gray turning to black towards its tip. Length: 4.75 inches (12 cm).

Female: Like the male, only with paler, buff-brown cheeks.

Distribution: New Guinea, Papuan Islands, and northeastern Australia.

In the Wild: This species, like other Fig Parrots, is very peaceful both in the wild and in captivity, making very little noise while feeding and, consequently, being rather difficult to spot in the foliage. However, when someone gets too close to them, they let out high-pitched whistling sounds as if warning of danger. In the evening they leave the trees on which they are feeding and go to roost in eucalyptus trees in the savannas. At sun-up, they are off again to occupy themselves with the business of filling their tummies. Practically nothing is known about their breeding habits. Forshaw, however, found nests in Melaleuca trees some 30 feet (9 m) up. Each of the

The Double-eyed Fig Parrot (Cyclopsitta diophthalma) *is dependent on figs. The species lives in pairs or small groups, is very active, and has a chattering twitter. The picture shows a male; the female has buff-colored cheeks.*

nests that he found contained two white eggs.

Aviculture: Along with the nominate, the subspecies *C. d. aruensis* from Indonesia, the Aru Islands, and southern New Guinea, the *C. d. marshalli*—Marshall's Fig Parrot—also lives on the Cape York Peninsula, Queensland, Australia. Captain A. J. Marshall discovered the Marshall's Fig Parrot in 1942. The male has some pale red in the face and a soft purple color under the ear. There is a pale blue blotch above the eye. The crown area is a faded yellow. The female has no red in her plumage, and her head and neck are a bluish purple. Length: 5.5 inches (14 cm).

Several times during my various stays in Australia I have had the pleasure of seeing these birds in small or large groups—that is, about

150 to 200. They prefer to live in rain forests. They are fast fliers and constantly give voice to their shrill little cries during flight. While searching for food up in the trees, they communicate with each other by means of sharp whistling sounds. According to Forshaw, these birds eat fungus as well as fruit, as he has seen them remove it from the bark of trees; I have never seen this but give you the notation for what it's worth. The birds look for holes in trees, preferably high up, in which to make their nests. They might also carve their own hollow in soft or rotten wood. The female lays two white eggs. While in Australia, I did not come across any aviculturists who had any experience with this species. Taronga Park Zoo in Sydney had three of these birds at one time, but they were not particularly lucky with them: A pair went to nest, but at a certain time, a hawk scared the hen to such an extent that she failed to keep her single, two-day-old youngster warm and it died in the nest; the other eggs did not hatch. One of the adults was later stolen from the cage.

C. d. aruensis lives, as we have seen, on the Aru islands as well as in New Guinea. This is a very rare bird indeed both in the wild and in captivity. The males have a red forehead encircled by a yellow band. The cheeks are red also and have a thin red band that runs along underneath. The rest of the body is green. The female's cheeks are brownish instead of red.

C. d. macleayana, Ramsey's Lorilet or Fig Parrot, inhabits the rain forests of northern Queensland. Length: 6.5 inches (16 cm). This bird has a red blotch on the forehead as well as red cheeks. They have blue around the eyes, as well as where the cheeks end. The remainder of the body is primarily green with yellow underneath, paler on the belly and beneath the tail. The female lacks the red on the head.

Forshaw's pair started with one youngster, but they stopped feeding it after ten days; a second brood was also far from successful, when the two young died of a fungus infection on the day they left the nest. Four years later, in 1978, another youngster was born; this left the nest in December. Graham Taylor, the owner of the Australian Bird Park in Sydney, Australia, had greater success and bred at least 13 young. A pair would eat between 50 and 70 figs, but also fruit and seed; the hen laid three eggs in the first brood. After 27 to 30 days, the young left the nest. Thanks to the local folks, Mr. Taylor was able to feed his birds three different types of figs *(Ficus rasoma, F. ragerna,* and *F. glommerata).* Pieces of rotten wood, collected from the rain forest, were also given as gnawing material; the birds obviously enjoyed this luxury (Low). The bird is also known as the Red-browed Fig Parrot, for obvious reasons.

C. d. coxeni, Coxen's Lorilet or Fig Parrot, inhabits southeastern Queensland and the northeastern part of New South Wales. This is the largest bird of this group, measuring 6.75 inches (17 cm). There are very few of these birds in captivity. In the wild they live in tiny groups of three or four, usually in pairs. Due to the constant cultivation of the land that keeps infringing on their natural territory, these birds are being driven back into virtually impregnable regions. Their call is rather quiet, which also does not help in trying to locate them. Their beak is black; there is some blue on the forehead and in the cheek region. They are red around the ears and there are some red feathers on the face (my daughter once said that they appear to have a constant case of measles). The rest of their plumage is green. For more particulars see page 161.

Male Orange-breasted Fig Parrot (Cyclopsitta g. gulielmiterti) is also known as King of Holland's Fig Parrot, and is found in New Guinea as well as on Salawati (western Papuan islands) and the Aru Islands (Indonesia).

Orange-breasted Fig Parrot—*Cyclopsitta gulielmitertii* (Schlegel)

Male Nominate: Reddish black forehead; rest of back dark green. Yellow cheeks, orange breast, rest of underbody light grass green. Gray-black beak; green-grayish legs; brown iris. Length: 5.1 inches (13 cm), which is by far the smallest in the group.

Female: Yellow cheeks are bordered by a narrow black band, and below by a greenish blue one. Ear coverts orange; breast greenish.

Distribution: From Salawati and the coast directly opposite, in West Irian (Vogelkop); also the Aru Islands, Indonesia.

In the Wild: Although the birds mainly live a somewhat secretive life high in the treetops, they sometimes can be seen on the plains, often in large numbers. In some areas the birds are far from rare. Their constant twittering can be heard as they fly overhead, as well as when they forage for figs in the trees. They also breed in small holes in trees. It is thought that the birds, which live in family groups, reach full color at three years of age.

Aviculture: The first examples of this species reached Europe in 1908; in the late 1970s, the German Bird Park at Walsrode acquired five of the birds. No records of captive breeding can be found. The chances for American aviculture are small. In spite of the rarity of this bird in captivity, I will give a few specifics. First of all, as is the case with all Fig Parrots, they need to be provided

Female subspecies of the Orange-breasted Fig Parrot, **Cyclopsitta gulielmiterti suavissima.** *This subspecies is found along the western part of the Vogelkop, and in Salawati. The male has an orange-colored breast as in the nominate form, but is somewhat smaller in size.*

with plenty of fruit (especially figs, if available; as their name suggests, these are their favorite fruit), such as dates, grapes, pears, and bananas. As well as a usual parakeet seed mix, they should be given grass and weed seeds, soft food, and millet spray. Instead of "ordinary" water, you can sometimes give them a honey solution (but cover the container with mesh, so the birds cannot bath in it and ruin their plumage). Once a week give them fine grit (in the morning, free choice) and small pieces of charcoal should not be missing from the menu.

There are six subspecies that vary only in small color differences. They are seldom, if ever, seen in captivity. *C. g. melanogenia* from the Aru Islands, Indonesia. *C. g. nigrifrons* from the northern part of New Guinea, as is *C. g. ramuensis* (Ramu River). *C. g. amabilis* from northeastern New Guinea (from the Huon Peninsula east to Milne Bay). *C. g. fuscifrons* from the Snow Mountains and the Orange area of New Guinea. *C. g. suavissima* from the southern coast of southwestern New Guinea.

It is perhaps interesting to note here that the scientific name of the genus, *Opopsitta,* was a spelling error and was supposed to have been *Cyclopsitta* (now corrected), with *cyclops* meaning "with the round face" and *psitta* meaning "parrot." For details of this genus refer to page 160.

Salvadori's Fig Parrot— *Psittaculirostris salvadorii* (Oustalet)

Male: A stocky and very richly colored lorylike bird. Long and narrow elongated yellow head feathers that stand slightly away from the throat and cheeks. Grass green forehead, streaked with blue; yellow nape and neck. A small blue area behind the eye. Red breast. The underside is yellowish grass green; rest of body is dark green. Some orange on the inner wing coverts. Beak black; legs grayish; iris dark brown-orange. Length: 7.5 inches (19 cm).

Female: No red on breast; dark sky-blue instead. Yellow face feathers; less bright, however. In general darker bluish green.

Immatures: Similar to the female but duller green. The sexes are only easy to determine after a year, but a little red may shimmer in the breast of young males earlier.

Distribution: New Guinea, from Humboldt Bay to Geelvink.

In the Wild: Mainly in lowland rain forest; usually in small family groups, breaking up into individual pairs in the breeding season. They like to spend a lot of time high in the trees and behave much like lories.

Aviculture: This species (and the same goes for all other members of the genus) must have a sleeping box (horizontal nest box) into which they can retire at night to sleep. Even in the wild, these birds frequently seek out a cozy nook in which to spend the night. The sleeping holes may also be used for nesting in the breeding season. These birds are known for their curiosity, both in the wild (inspecting all kinds of nooks and crannies) and in the aviary, inspecting every nest box with great interest; if they can creep inside, all the better.

Salvadori's Fig Parrots were first introduced into Europe, as well as into America, in 1977. Although their lifestyle is very similar to that of the lories, they also will eat a wide variety of seeds (especially black sunflower seeds, various millets, canary grass seed, and some millet spray) as well as figs, rice, lots of fruits (apples, bananas, oranges, berries, pomegranates), insects, soft food, weed and grass seeds, and greens (chickweed). Unfortunately, these birds are mostly seen in the better parks, and rarely come into the hands of hobby aviculturists. This

The male Salvadori's Fig Parrot (Psittaculirostris salvadorii) has a scarlet breast band; the female is duller and has a bluish green band. Parent birds like to nourish their young with mealworms, especially the first 20 or so days.

also applies to all of the species and subspecies listed on page 11. Rosemary Low, in her book *Parrots, Their Care and Breeding,* gives a very interesting and comprehensive report of her experiences in the care and breeding of Salvadori's Fig Parrots and I heartily recommend it to those who are interested.

In 1978 I possessed a pair of this species that I kept in a room aviary maintained at a temperature of about 71.6°F (22°C). The aviary was 9 by 6 feet (3 × 2 m) and had a nest box that was 7.9 inches high, 15.75 inches wide, and 7.1 inches deep (20 × 40 × 18 cm). The birds bred successfully several times. Two

The female Salvadori's Fig Parrot (Psitta-culirostris salvadorii) *often has some red on the shoulder. The species is considered vulnerable, and the world population is estimated at approximately 10,000 birds.*

eggs were laid for most of the time, but three times, three were laid. The young left the nest at two months of age and after another 10 to 14 days they were quite independent. For rearing food I used soaked seeds (especially black sunflower seed, millet varieties, millet spray, canary grass seed, and niger seed), soft food, hemp seed, berries, bananas, oranges, apples, and insects (fly maggots, ant "eggs" [pupae], and enchytrae). In the soft food, which was well used by the parents, I mixed a few drops of a commercial vitamin/mineral supplement; extra vitamin K was also added to the soft food every other day. Full-grown

birds were mad about small meal-worms. Edward's and Desmarest's Fig Parrots (see page 11) require the same care.

Guiaiabero—*Bolbopsittacus lunulatus* (Scopoli 1786)

There are four subspecies, all confined to the Philippine Islands. *Bolbopsittacus l. lunulatus,* found in Luzon. *Bolbopsittacus l. intermedius* found in Leyte. Males are darker green on top and the blue color is deeper. *Bolbopsittacus l. callainipic-tus,* found in Samar. Similar to the preceding subspecies, but with a green wash through the blue. Less blue in the cheeks. Females with lots of yellow; the collar is rather bright. *Bolbopsittacus l. mindanensis,* found in Mindanao and Panaon Islands. The male has green cheeks and a very dark blue collar. Females similar to nominate.

Male: Grass green with dark green wing coverts; primaries blue. Sky blue face and neck collar. Yellowish green on underparts, rump, underwing coverts, and upper tail coverts. The bulbous beak (see scientific name) is bluish-gray; legs grayish; iris brown. Length: 6 inches (15 cm).

Female: Blue face color confined to throat and lower cheeks. The blue neck collar is well mixed with yellow. All the green coloration is less vivid than that of the male. Black or dark crescent markings on neck, rump, and tail tips.

Immatures: Like females, but beaks are pale grayish.

Distribution: The Philippine Islands.

In the Wild: Inhabits thin or open forests in small flocks, but sometimes ascends to some 2,000 feet (600 m) in the mountains. The birds feed on all kinds of berries and, obviously, guavas (berrylike fruits of a tree that is a member of the myrtle family); they frequently raid orchards, though as they operate only in small groups (up to about 20 individuals), they don't do much damage.

Aviculture: Almost unknown in captivity (see page 15). Even in their country of origin, they are seldom kept in spite of the availability of fruit. This is because in captivity they tend to die in a few weeks or months. It is suspected that, in the wild, they feed on various fungi and insects that cannot be offered in captivity. Their behavior is somewhat reminiscent of the Fig Parrots, which, according to some ornithologists, are closely related. Little is known about their breeding habits. Dr. R. Burkard acquired some of the birds in 1965 but these lived only for a short time; the same applied at around the same time at the San Diego Zoo, when a pair of the birds also died after a few weeks.

Brehm's Parrot—*Psittacella brehmi* (Schlegel 1873)

There are four subspecies, all native to New Guinea. *Psittacella b. brehmii,* found in northwestern New Guinea (the mountains of Vogelkop). *Psittacella b. intermixta,* found in west and central New Guinea (Weyland and Snow Mountains, Mount Goliath in West Irian). More yellow, especially on underparts, back, mantle, and upper tail coverts. Females paler, with more yellow; subspecies is somewhat larger than the nominate. *Psittacella b. harterti,* found on the Huon Peninsula, east New Guinea. Males have a paler head with olive-green coloration. Smaller bill. Females are duller, and also have yellow colors in flanks and sides of abdomen, with some black barring. *Psittacella b. pallida,* found in south and southwestern New Guinea, westward to the Sepik region. Like the nominate but with more yellow, and some blue on the abdomen. Rather narrow beak. Females with much yellow and black bars on flanks and sides of abdomen.

Male: Mainly green, which is darker on the wings and back. The head is a dark, blackish brown with a vague olive green shimmer. There is a conspicuous yellow stripe on both sides of the neck, but these do not form a collar. There is black barring on the mantle, back, and upper tail coverts. The undertail coverts are red. The tail feathers are dark green, as are the underwing coverts, with a blue edge. The beak is steel gray with a creamish tip to both mandibles; legs dark gray; iris red. Length 7.5 to 9.5 inches (19–24 cm).

Female: The most obvious difference is the absence of the yellow neck stripes. The upper breast has narrower markings.

Immatures: Like female, but with a green breast and dull yellow barrings.

In the Wild: Generally found in mountain areas to 8,840 feet (2,600 m); usually solitary, or in pairs. It is a generally peaceful bird that can spend long periods sitting on the same spot on a branch while slowly examining its perch. The flight is similar to that of the Blue-rumped Parrotlet, and is noisy and straight. It has been suggested that this species can remain in breeding condition throughout the year.

Aviculture: Sir Edward Hallstrom kept some of the nominate race in his aviaries at Nondugli (New Guinea), and sent a pair off to the San Diego Zoo in 1966. They did not seem to tolerate aviary life, and died shortly afterwards. The birds were given sunflower seed and a rich variety of fruit. The name "tiger" refers to the barring on the back and rump; in older literature it is sometimes called Brehm's Tiger Parrot. Another name, Brehm's Ground Parrot, makes no sense. The birds are seldom seen on the ground, but forage for food in trees and tall shrubs; they also never breed close to the ground. In the wild I have seen them in tall grass and along road edges, looking for small stones and grit. It seems that these birds also eat half-ripe grass and weed seeds. The other members of this genus listed on page 16 are unknown in aviculture.

Blue-rumped Parrot—
Psittinus cyanurus
(Forster 1795)

There are three subspecies. *Psittinus cyanurus cyanurus,* found in southwestern Thailand, as well as Malaysia, Borneo, and Sumatra. *Psittinus c. pontius,* found in Siberut, Sipora, and North and South Pagi (Mentawai Islands; Indonesia). This subspecies is somewhat bigger than the nominate race. *Psittinus c. abbotti,* found in Simalur and Siumat Islands (off the west coast of Sumatra, Indonesia). Bright blue crown and green around the eyes, and on the forehead. Green mantle, back, rump, and upper tail coverts; underparts yellowish. Female has a green head; both sexes are larger than the nominate race.

Male: Red upper mandible; lower mandible grayish brown. Black mantle and back; grayish blue head; whole lower back and rump grayish blue or deep blue. Partly red wing coverts; each green covert feather with yellow edges. Legs grayish green; iris pale yellow. Length: 7.5 inches (18 cm); weight: males 2.19 to 2.30 ounces (62–65 g), females 2.65 to 3 ounces (75–85 g).

Female: Much paler, without much blue or red. Mainly green with brownish head and yellowish ear coverts. Same red underwing coverts and a little blue on the lower back. Grayish-brown beak.

Immatures: Resemble the female; young males, however, soon show some blue on the head and back. Horn-colored beaks.

Distribution: Borneo, Sumatra (Indonesia), and offshore islands; further from Tenasserim and southwestern Thailand to Malaysia.

In the Wild: It is frequently seen accompanying Long-tailed Parrots

(Psittacula longicauda) in tropical rain forests. Blue-rumped Parrots tend to keep to the lower areas of the trees, where they forage for fruits, berries, insects, and other edibles. They may also be seen in palm oil plantations and orchards, sometimes assembling in large flocks. They are very cautious in their manner. Therefore, in the aviary they carefully study the area around them before taking any action. This is not meant to suggest that they are lazy, "lifeless" birds; on the contrary, they are quite active once accustomed to their new surroundings. They like to clamber around on the aviary wire and will soon damage any wooden parts of the structure if these are not protected. After breeding, the birds migrate to other areas. When feeding, these birds are rather quiet and, due to their colors, are difficult to observe. This coloration is excellent camouflage against predators. Their flight is fast, and during flight they keep contact by chirping. They feed mainly on soft fruits, berries, blossoms, grass and weed seeds, and, of course, unripe oil palm fruits.

Aviculture: This species was first exhibited to the public at London Zoo in 1866, and was then irregularly imported until the turn of the century. At the present time, the species is available only sporadically. It is advisable to give newly imported specimens a rich variety of berries (such as redcurrants, pyracantha, or rose hips). Experience has shown that they will acclimate best in roomy accommodations, where they should be disturbed as little as possible. The well-known English veterinarian George A. Smith relates in his fascinating book, *Lovebirds and Related Parrots* (London: Paul Elek Ltd., 1979), that one of his six birds (five hens, one male) was extremely tame. After it walked over to eat the offered tidbits, if another Blue-rumped Parrot made any approach, it would flash its eyes and shrug its wings as a warning for the other to keep its distance. He placed two birds in an enclosed aviary with plenty of climbing branches. In the breeding season the birds became very territorial and the hen voiced a pleasant four-note call while she sat in her nest; the male usually perched close to the nest box, also calling pleasantly, and fanning his tail. Smith worked the colony system with various birds and it was this that made it possible to ascertain that the hens incubated at night; during the day, they would chase off any other of their species that came too close. The hen normally lays three eggs 1.01 by 0.82 inches (26 × 21 mm).

In addition to fruit, the captive birds would eagerly take millet varieties, spray millet, canary grass seed, small black sunflower seeds, a little niger and hemp, pine, and peanuts. Due to their gnawing disposition, they should be provided with plenty of willow twigs. A variety of green food and vegetables is also welcome. They will eagerly take elderberries, corn flakes, the bark of pine and pine needles, raw mushrooms, maggots and other small insects, hard-boiled egg, soft food, raw scraped red meat, sprouted and soaked grass and weed seeds, fortified seed mixtures, and cuttlebone. The birds seem to appreciate as wide a variety of food as possible and, according to many aviculturists, they are seldom happy with the same food offered for more than two days. A regular variety is therefore a "must." It has also been noted that the beak and claw growth of this species is very fast and, if insufficient gnawing material is available, you will have to trim or file the beak at least twice a year.

In general, this bird is difficult to keep. In the not-too-distant past there were a number of keepers in Germany, but they all discovered that at least 90 percent of the birds did not survive, probably due to stress, inadequate variety of food, and other factors. It is therefore probably best not to attempt keeping these birds in aviculture.

Vernal Hanging Parrot—
Loriculus vernalis
(Sparrman 1787)

Male: Mainly green; darker on the top of the head, sometimes with a bluish tinge. Throat light blue; upper tail light yellowish. Upper tail coverts red to brownish red. Wing coverts darker, primaries dark olive green. Beak coral red to brownish red with a yellowish tip; legs orange; iris yellowish white. Length: 5.1 inches (13 cm).

Female: Duller; no blue, or very little, on throat. Both sexes of this species show some small color vari-ations, depending on where they originate in their range. The iris can sometimes be brown.

Immatures: Forehead and cheeks grayish brown; the rump has no, or only a few, red feathers. Beak pale orange; iris brown, like the legs.

Distribution: Southwestern India from north of Bombay and eastern Bengal and Bangladesh and the eastern Himalayas to eastern Nepal, Assam, Burma, Thailand, Cambodia, southern Laos, and South Vietnam; also on the Andaman Islands and the islands in the Mergui Archipelago.

In the Wild: These birds occur in pairs and small groups mainly in thickly wooded areas and planta-tions. They usually roost, like bats, hanging upside-down from their perches. When trees are in blossom, these birds may form large flocks. They feed on soft fruit, berries, figs, nectar, insects, and seeds. They have a quiet "chi-chi-chi" call that can also be heard when they are in flight. Their flight is finchlike, that is to say, fast wing beating, inter-spersed with short pauses with both wings closed. This causes a "dip" in the flight. Newly fledged youngsters sleep like other parrots, sitting upright on the perch, but after a few days, they too start to "hang" by their feet when sleeping. They are typically arboreal birds, and are sel-dom seen on the ground. When sit-ting together in the foliage, they keep a distance from each other and make so-called threat movements to keep their colleagues at bay should they approach too closely; this behavior also occurs in the Blue-crowned Hanging Parrot.

Aviculture: This friendly little bird has been long known in aviculture, but the first recorded captive breeding dates from 1966 when a pair owned by Mr. Paolo Bertagnolio went to nest. The birds had been fed on a commercial insectile food mixture to which was added minced silkworm pupae, sugar, Mellin's Food, and powdered liver. They also were given a syrup compounded with sugared water and a proprietory vitamin-antibiotic mix, plus raw minced meat and mealworms. In practice it has been ascertained that these birds (and the other Hanging Parrots) indeed require a high proportion of animal protein, vitamin B complex, and vitamins C and K in their diet.

Courtship begins with a strutting walk (see Blue-crowned) and little head movements. Both sexes cut nesting materials (for example, various leaves and bark) into a "C" shape, and carry them to the nest chamber tucked under the breast and rump feathers; the female, however, is the most active in this nest building. Copulation may last up to ten minutes. The clutch consists of two to five eggs; incubation lasts about 20 days. The chicks are born with some pink-colored down. The eyes open at two weeks, and at six weeks they leave the nest.

These birds make good household companions, being peaceful and far from noisy. Their call is reminiscent of that of many finches. They should not be overwintered in an outdoor aviary; the cold, damp conditions are not tolerated. They are best kept indoors at room temperature. In the summer months, this species can be kept in a well-planted outdoor aviary. However, you should protect them from predators that may try to attack them through the wire roof should the parrots hang upside down from it. This can be done by placing an additional fine-mesh cover over the main roof, with a gap of several inches between.

It is thought by many ornithologists that this "upside-down" roosting is a form of defense, especially against tree snakes. The snakes move along the top of the branches (of course) and thus are less likely to encounter a bird that is hanging beneath.

In addition to the foodstuffs previously mentioned (see also page 8), the birds must be provided with seeds (canary grass seed, millet, spray millet, rolled oats, boiled rice), greens (chickweed, etc.), a commercial lory food, a rich variety of fruit (berries, bananas, figs, oranges, etc.), and insects. Make sure that commercial soft food does not spoil. If you keep more than one pair in an aviary (three or more, never two), it is advisable to supply several feeding stations to prevent fighting. It is also recommended that the birds be given a daily supply of fresh poplar, willow, or fruit tree twigs on which they can gnaw. In cages, you should place perches as high as possible, as the birds will roost as high as they can.

Blue-crowned Hanging Parrot—*Loriculus galgulus* (Linnaeus 1758)

Male: Mainly green; darkest above, becoming yellowish beneath. Crown deep blue. Yellow triangular patch on mantle. Yellow band across lower back. Throat, rump, and upper tail scarlet. Undersides of wings and tail greenish blue. Beak black; legs brown; iris dark brown. Length: 5.1 inches (13 cm). Weight: 0.71 ounce (20 g).

Female: Rather duller than the male with more yellow beneath. The red throat and the yellow band on the back are absent. The blue crown is smaller and less marked. Older hens can occasionally develop a red spot on the throat.

The Blue-crowned Hanging Parrot (Loriculus galgulus) *can easily be housed in spacious cages indoors, but like to roam outside their abode. Keep the bars of the cages scrupulously clean, as these birds expel liquid droppings onto them.*

Immatures: Very similar to the female, but duller. Forehead grayish blue. The rump is green with some red feathers on the sides.

Distribution: Malaysia, Borneo, and Sumatra (Indonesia); also Singapore and various outlying islands in the region; Thailand.

In the Wild: This species is quite abundant throughout most of its natural range. It may be found along the edges of forests, and also in parks and gardens; they seem to have little fear of humans. In the wild they eat small insects, small seeds, soft fruits, flowers and their nectar, and pollen; in captivity they enjoy greens and other "pet bird" foods, like various soft foods that you should enrich with various insects (mealworms, pupae, enchytrae, etc.). Mr. S. G. Eade reported in *Parrot Society Magazine* (No. 11, 1977) that a male would catch bees to take the pollen sacs from their legs to eat. It is quite possible that this also occurs in the wild; in Sumatra, I have seen these birds close to bee hives, though I have not caught one doing this. This species also sleeps like a bat, usually hanging by one foot, the other foot tucked in the plumage. As they sleep, the head is held up close to the body and the feathers are puffed out (thus, the head is not tucked beneath a wing or on the back). Defecation doesn't soil the feathers and, as George A. Smith, DVM, says: ". . . the birds pull themselves forwards at an angle and lower the tail and then squirt the contents of the lower bowel out with some force well away from the body."

Aviculture: Like the preceding species, the Blue-crowned Hanging Parrot shows geographical color differences. In young imported birds, the adult plumage appears only in the second year. This is probably due to the stress involved in catching, confining, and traveling. The bird has been quite familiar for a long time and has been regarded as the prototype for all Hanging Parrots. Carl von Linné (Linnaeus) described it back in the late eighteenth century. After leaving the nest it takes about three months for color to develop so that the sex can be determined. However, captive breeding of this species poses few problems.

As nest material you can supply the bark of willow, birch, hazel, and fruit trees, plus grass, hay, and green leaves (privet). The nesting material is carried between the breast and rump feathers by the hen. She lays two to five white eggs, which take 21 to 22 days to hatch in captivity. The young leave the nest at four to five weeks. They develop rather slowly and are first sexually mature after two years. If they are kept in indoor cages (which is recommended), the floor must be cleaned frequently because of the fluid consistency of their droppings. In aviaries, the birds regularly take a shower in the rain, spreading their wings with obvious pleasure. Caged birds can be given a regular spray, in addition to their normal "bath."

This species was first bred in Germany (1907); in 1966 the San Diego Zoo in California reported a success.

Female Blue-crowned Hanging Parrot (Loriculus galgulus).

Courtship behavior of the male is very interesting and starts with the so-called "strutting": The throat feathers are fluffed out and the tail is spread to show the red rump; the wings are drooped so that the yellow and crimson colors are displayed. In this position, the male runs with his long, strong legs up and down the perch, nods his head, and chews at the white frothy paste that he regurgitates, like a kid with bubblegum. Then he feeds the hen with this paste, after which he lets out a "yeat yeat" call.

There are a few other species in the genus (see page 7), but they are not available at the present time. Now and again the Ceylon Hanging Parrot, *Loriculus beryllinus* (J. R. Forster) from Sri Lanka turns up. This species is about 5.1 inches (13 cm) long, is mainly green in color, darker above, lighter beneath. The

The Plain Parakeet (Brotogeris tirica) can be found in wooded habitats and cultivated country, low- and uplands, forest canopies, parks, gardens, and city plazas with high, mature trees, as I encountered in São Paulo and Rio de Janeiro.

coverts are red; there is a little blue visible on the side edges of the rump. The underside of the wings is blue. The beak is orange-red; the feet orange; the iris brown. This bird is somewhat larger than the preceding species, that is, 5.5 inches (14 cm). The female has no red throat/breast patch, and there is a little blue around the beak and on the face. These birds live high in the treetops in the Philippines and the Sulu Archipelago. The female incubates three eggs for 20 days. The young are rather naked on hatching and for the first nine to ten days, but then quickly become covered in a gray down. At two weeks the eyes open, and a week later the first green feathers appear. Red and orange coloration becomes visible after about 25 days. The young leave the nest at 34 to 36 days of age.

Plain Parakeet—*Brotogeris tirica* (Gmelin)

Adults: Wholly green, with a little yellow on the upper side and blue wing feathers. The central tail feathers also have a bluish tinge, as does the neck and mantle. Beak brownish, much lighter toward the base; legs pinkish; iris dark brown. Length 9 inches (23 cm).

Immatures: Like the adults, but with some blue tinge on the green primary coverts and outer secondaries. Beak darker.

Distribution: Eastern and southeastern Brazil (southern Bahia to São Paolo and inland to southern Goias).

Aviculture: The species is quite abundant in its native lands as well

forehead and crown are light red, the eye ring red. Throat is bluish green, red around the rump. Wings are somewhat darker, primaries are olive green. Bluish green beneath the tail. Beak is orange; legs yellow-orange; iris light yellow. The hen has no blue-green throat patch.

In the larger bird parks of Europe and America these birds are occasionally exhibited; in spite of this, breeding successes are few. Should one acquire a breeding pair, they must be cared for and fed in the same manner as the Blue-crowned. The same applies to the Philippine Hanging Parrot, *Loriculus philippensis* (P. L. S. Müller), which has (possibly) 11 subspecies. The bird is grass green with a red forehead and front of crown, and a bright red throat/breast patch. There is a yellow/orange band on the nape. The rump and upper tail as in our aviaries, although the numbers are rapidly declining due to Brazil's strict export regulations. The first examples were imported into Germany in 1873, and the first breeding successes were reported in 1882. A blue mutation has been reported from Brazil. The hen lays four to five eggs; the incubation time is 22 to 23 days.

White-winged Parakeet—
Brotogeris versicolurus
(P. L. S. Müller)

Adults: This species is very similar in appearance to the Canary-winged Parakeet, but is grayer and more olive, especially on the head. There is a blue sheen around the eyes. There is a white bar (from which the name arises) with a yellow tinge in the wings, but the latter is less obvious than in the Canary-winged Parakeet. Usually, the white is visible only when the wings are spread. Bill horn-colored with a yellow tinge; legs grayish pink; iris dark brown. Length: 8.67 inches (22 cm); weight: 2.12 ounces (60 g).

Immatures: Primaries are less white, and green tipped; secondary coverts yellow with green edges.

Distribution: Native to French Guyana, through the Amazon Valley to eastern Ecuador and northeastern Peru. They are also found on the islands of Pará and Mexicana, have been introduced on Puerto Rico, and probably occur in Surinam. For quite some years this species has been very common in the suburbs along the southeastern Florida coast; less common around Los Angeles, California.

Aviculture: This species is sometimes called Canary-winged or Yellow-winged Parakeet. Unfortunately, many of the birds in captivity were, at one time or another, hybridized with the Canary-winged Parakeet. Most of these hybrids have a well-feathered facial area, and are more greenish in color. The importation of this and other South American parrots is extremely doubtful. Nevertheless, the bird is very popular and not particularly noisy. Tame birds are adept talkers. They are rather bold and will challenge a colleague two to three times their own size. I know of birds that have been "potty trained" successfully; the birds are taught a key word and, when they hear it, they must return to their cage to deposit their droppings. Another way is to repeat the word only when the bird does "its thing" in the correct spot.

This species can, indeed, be one of the finest family pets, if it is properly trained. It learns to speak words clearly, and soon masters various tricks. I regard these birds as one of the most intelligent members of the parrot family. A pet bird must, however, receive lots of attention. If you don't have the time to spend four to five hours daily with the bird, you should consider another kind of pet, or at least get a partner for the bird. Provide chewable toys so that the bird keeps its beak in trim, although it may still be necessary to have it trimmed by a veterinarian or experienced aviculturist.

The Canary-winged Parakeet (Brotogeris chiriri) nests in arboreal termitaria (e.g., Nasutitermes) and tree hollows in gallery forests. But I also saw the species in parks and large gardens.

They love to bathe in a large bowl of water, and a daily bath, especially in the summer, will be welcomed with a great deal of chatter. A single pet is by no means noisy, as long as you don't teach him to scream (or at least to get away with it). For example, don't reward him for screaming by letting him out of his cage!

This species can be safely kept in a community aviary with other small birds, but not with psittacines. They are not particularly destructive. They sometimes hang like bats from the roof of the aviary. The nest box should be 9.75 by 9.75 by 13.75 inches (25 × 25 × 35 cm), with an entrance hole 2.25 inches (7 cm) in diameter. They are somewhat aggressive during the breeding season. A blue mutation has been reported in Brazil.

Canary-winged Parakeet— *Brotogeris chiriri* (Vieillot)

Adults: The body is mainly green, darker above than beneath, where there is a black and yellow shimmer. There is a bright yellow epaulet on the wings. The face is totally feathered; while *B. versicolorus* has some bare facial areas. The beak is light horn-colored; the legs are grayish pink; the iris is dark brown. Length: 8.50 to 8.67 inches (21.5–22 cm). Weight: 2.12 ounces (60 g).

Immatures: Like adults.

Distribution: Native to northern and eastern Bolivia, northern Argentina (Chaco, Missiones), Paraguay, and Brazil. Until 1977, when Brazil stopped its exports, this was one of the most commonly imported South American psittacines.

Aviculture: This species was exhibited at the London Zoo as early as 1868. Over the years it has turned out to be an exemplary aviary inmate and an excellent family pet. The hen lays three to five eggs, occasionally six, and incubates them unaided for 26 days. The young leave the nest at about two months of age. A good variety of green food is necessary throughout the year, but especially at breeding time. Grass and weed seeds, apples, pears, cherries, soaked raisins, and bananas can supplement the diet.

It is unfortunate that these beautiful parrots have such nerve-shattering voices, usually used when not wholly contented, but they should not be too much trouble if kept in a roomy outdoor aviary. The best kind of nest box is a natural birchwood log. Alternatively, you can use a homemade box with the dimensions 17.75 by 9.75 by 9.75 inches (45 × 25 × 25 cm). A layer of humus or peat about 1.6 inches (4 cm) thick should be laid at the bottom. The box should be affixed high in the aviary for best results. The birds can winter in the outdoor aviary provided they have a draft-free, dry shelter.

The subspecies *B. c. behni* (Neumann), which is slightly larger, is no longer available and is less common in Europe as well as in the United States.

Gray-cheeked Parakeet— *Brotogeris pyrrhopterus* (Latham)

Adults: Primarily green, lighter on the belly. The crown is grayish, the forehead and cheeks are pale gray. There are orange patches both above and below the wings. Therefore, the bird is often called the Orange-flanked Parrot (as well as Pocket Parrot and Orange-winged Parrot). Bill horn-colored, tinged with some orange; legs pale pink; iris dark brown. Length: 7.88 inches (20 cm); weight: 2.12 ounces (60 g).

Immatures: Like adults, but with a green crown without any blue tinge.

Distribution: Native to western South America, from Bahia de

The Gray-cheeked Parakeet (Brotogeris pyrrhopterus) *lives in pairs or flocks in mainly wooded habitats, farmland with mature trees, and in banana plantations.*

Caraques to northwestern Peru. They frequently form large flocks and can cause severe damage to banana and other plantations.

Aviculture: Once frequently available in the trade and well-known as excellent pets. They should have conditions similar to those described for *B. jugularis* (see page 178). In the wild they nest in termite mounds, but will also use a hollow limb. Four to six eggs are laid on a layer of damp moss. The hen incubates the eggs unaided, but the cock keeps guard close to the nest.

These birds have an interesting habit of assembling in huge flocks at certain times of the year, just like

European starlings. They are quite intelligent little birds; with patience you can teach them to repeat a few words, or even to "cry" or "laugh."

A breeding pair should have access to a nest box 13.75 by 11.75 by 11.75 inches (35 × 30 × 30 cm) in size with an entrance 3.5 inches (9 cm) in diameter. A thick layer (2.33 to 3.25 inches [6–8 cm]) of damp moss, peat, or similar material should be placed on the floor of the box. The box should be affixed as high as possible, with the entrance facing the north. The birds should be kept in individual pairs for breeding, but other small birds, such as

In the wild the Tovi Parakeet (Brotogeris jugularis) *has the habit of roosting in large groups (communes), in a palm tree or such. They nest in tree hollows (for example, woodpecker nests) and arboreal termitaria.*

finches, doves, and quail, may be kept with them without any problem.

Orange-chinned, Tovi, or Bee-Bee Parakeet— *Brotogeris jugularis* (P. L. S. Müller)

Adults: Primarily green, but with a yellow sheen on the underside and blue on the lower belly. There is a little blue on the head, back, rump, wings, and tail. There is a round orange mark on the chin. The underside of the wings is yellowish, the flight feathers are blue. Beak light horn-colored; legs pale yellow-brown; iris dark brown. Length 7.13 inches (18 cm); weight: 2.19 ounces (62 g).

Immatures: Similar to adults.

Distribution: The birds range from southwestern Mexico to northern Colombia, west of the eastern Andes, and eastwards to Norte Santander. They usually live in partially open habitats in groups of about 20 individuals, but sometimes they live in single pairs. They feed freely on nectar and on flowers, fruit, and half-ripe seeds. They have particular roosting and resting sites where hundreds of birds may gather. They breed in termite mounds and in tree hollows, often in dead limbs. Sometimes two or more pairs may breed in the same tree. A clutch of eight to nine eggs is not unusual. The incubation time is about 22 days.

Aviculture: Although these parrots are relatively easy to breed in captivity, they are not bred as much as they should be (especially now that exportation has stopped). The genuine fancier on a limited budget still has the opportunity to buy pairs, as they are available. Clutches in captivity usually are smaller than in the wild (three to four eggs per clutch), but a pair may frequently rear two or three clutches per breeding season. During incubation, a diet of soaked corn, rice, fruit, fresh twigs and buds, and soaked stale bread (with the excess water squeezed out) should be given in addition to their normal seed and green food diet. The birds should always have access to a sleeping/nest box: 11.75 by 11.75 by 15.75 inches (30 × 30 × 40 cm), with a 3.25-inch (8-cm) entrance hole. Newly imported birds (if available) remain nervous for a while, but they soon settle down and, with kindness and patience, can be finger-tamed quite easily to become excellent family pets. Subspecies *B. p. exsul* is unknown in aviculture.

Cobalt-winged, Blue-winged, or De Ville's Parakeet—*Brotogeris cyanoptera* (Pelzeln)

Adults: A predominantly green bird with a little blue sheen on the head and neck. Frequently there is a yellow eye stripe, and the chin is orange. The secondary flight feathers are blue, the underside of the wings is blue-green, and the central tail feathers are blue. Beak horn-colored; iris dark brown; there is a naked white ring around the eye. Length: 7.88 inches (20 cm); weight: 2.19 ounces (62 g).

The Cobalt-winged Parakeet (Brotogeris cyanoptera) has a less scratchy call than the Golden-winged Parakeet. The Cobalt is one of the most popular pet birds in Peru.

Immatures: Similar to adults; duller, and upper mandible with a dark gray base.

Distribution: Native to Venezuela, Colombia, and the upper part of the Amazon basin. The birds are found at altitudes of up to 6,800 feet (2,000 m) in the hills of the tropical rain forests, where they live in small groups high in the trees.

Aviculture: These birds are rather sensitive to frost and must not be kept below 53°F (12°C). They should always have access to a sleeping/breeding box, in which they spend their nights. The hen usually lays four to five eggs (occasionally six), which are incubated for 23 to 24 days. These birds are excellent breeders and will repeat their performances year after year. The young leave the nest after seven to eight weeks but are still fed by their parents for about a month. The two subspecies (*B. c. gustavi* and *B. c. beniensis*) are unknown in aviculture.

Golden-winged Parakeet—
Brotogeris chrysopterus
(Linnaeus)

Adults: Primarily green with a brownish patch on the chin. The primary flight feathers are deep orange. The undersides of the wings are blue. Beak light horn-colored; legs yellowish brown; iris dark brown. Length: about 6.33 inches (16 cm); weight: 2.26 to 2.83 ounces (64–80 g).

Immatures: Similar to adults, but duller and with green primary coverts.

Distribution: They occur in eastern Venezuela, Guyana, Surinam, and French Guyana to the northern Amazon area. They are especially common along the coast of Guyana

The Golden-winged Parakeet (Brotogeris chrysopterus) *is declining in the wild due to local deforestation. During the day they like to play high in treetops; they are rather noisy, even in flight.*

on coffee plantations, where they feed on the flowers of *Erytrina* trees and the fruit of the *Ficus frondosa,* among other fruits, seeds, berries, and greens. They nest in hollow limbs, laying eggs. In captivity they seem to be "difficult" breeders, thus posing a challenge for the more enthusiastic fancier. Three of the four subspecies (*B. c. chrysosema, B. c. solimoensis,* and *B. c. tenuifrons*) are practically unknown to aviculture.

Tuipara Parakeet—
Brotogeris chrysopterus
tuipara (Gmelin)

Adults: This subspecies is mainly green in color, with a lighter underside. There is a blue-black sheen on the head. There is a yellow-orange stripe across the forehead and an orange stripe on the chin. There are yellow feathers on the wings and on the tail. The primary flight feathers are a shiny blue-black, edged with dark green. The beak is whitish gray; legs are pink; iris brown, with a naked, greenish blue eye ring. Length: 7.3 inches (18 cm); weight: 2.01 ounces (57 g).

Immatures: Similar to adults with blue and yellow.

Distribution: Found in the lower Amazon Basin and along the northern Brazilian coast, sometimes in groups of about 40 individuals. They feed largely on the fruit of the tree *Bombax monguba.*

Aviculture: This species is available only occasionally from the better importers in Europe. They are unquestionably extremely enticing birds worth our attention. They soon become tame, but have a rather overbearing screech. They are best suited to a roomy outdoor aviary with minimum dimensions of 13 by 8 by 6.5 feet (4 × 2.5 × 2 m), and should have access to a nest box with dimensions of 8.67 by 8.67 by 19.5 inches (22 × 22 × 50 cm). They can be kept in a community aviary with other species (finches, doves, quail, and so on). Since the birds climb and clamber a lot, they should be given natural branches and twigs to keep them amused.

Tui Parakeet—*Brotogeris sanctithomae* (P. L. S. Müller)

Adults: Primarily green, with a lighter (yellow) underside. The forehead, the front part of the crown, and the areas below the eyes are yellow. The slender wings have a shading of blue. The underside of the tail is green with a yellow tinge. Beak a shiny chestnut; legs flesh-colored; iris gray. Length: 6.7 inches (17 cm); weight: 1.75 ounces (49.5 g).

Immatures: Like adults.

Distribution: This bird occurs in eastern Ecuador, northeastern Peru, and eastward to western Brazil, northern Bolivia, and parts of Amazonian Colombia. In the wild it nests in termite mounds as well as in hollow trees. The hen lays four to six eggs, which she incubates for 21 days. The young leave the nest after 45 days.

This species, which is available on a regular basis, is known for its peaceful and trusting nature. Sur-

The only subspecies of the Tui Parakeet is the approximately 6.7-inch (17-cm) Brotogeris sanctithomae takatukasae. *The subspecies is immediately recognizable due to the clear yellow streak behind (and sometimes below) the eyes. The bird lives in northern Brazil in the immediate vicinity of the mouth of the Madeira River, and further in lower eastern Amazones, east to E. Pará and Amapá, and south to the Curuá River. In the wild these birds are rather noisy, always chattering; they use termites' nests or tree hollows; the 4 to 5 eggs are incubated for approximately 24 days and the young leave the nest when 45 days old. Care and management are the same as for the Tui Parakeet.*

prisingly, however, these are not the easiest birds to breed in captivity. They require a nest box 8.67 by 8.67 by 24 inches (22 × 22 × 60 cm) in size, with an entrance hole of 2.75 inches (7 cm) in diameter. The one subspecies *(B. s. takatsukasae)* has a yellow streak behind the eye, but is almost unknown in American aviculture.

Sierra Parakeet—
Bolborhynchus aymara
(d'Orbigny)

Adults: Mainly dark green. The forehead, crown, and upper section of the "ears" are brownish gray. The remainder of the head, neck, and throat is whitish gray. The abdomen, the undersides of the tail coverts, and the lesser wing coverts are yellowish green. The slender wings show a bluish sheen. The beak is whitish gray or pinkish, often somewhat darker in the hen. Iris brown; feet and legs brownish. Ornithologists rightly find this bird similar in appearance to the budgerigar, especially with regard to the tapered tail. Males usually have a darker crown and a silvery breast. Length: 7.5 to about 9 inches (19–20 cm).

Immatures: Similar to adults, but tails are much shorter.

The Sierra Parakeet (Bolborhynchus aymara) *is an elegant, terrestrial bird, living in small flocks in the hills and mountains of the Andes.*

Distribution: Eastern slopes of the Andes from central Bolivia to northwestern Argentina and probably also to northern Chile.

In the Wild: The birds live in groups, sometimes at over 6,560 feet (2,000 m) altitude. As they are rather common in the lands of the Aymara Indians, the German and Dutch names of the bird are Aymarasittich and Aymara parkiet, respectively; note also the scientific name. Some English authors refer to it as Aymara Parakeet. The birds feed largely on berries, fruits, and seeds. They are far from shy and I have seen them in gardens and parks, as well as on farms. These birds can be regarded as gregarious in that I have seen groups of 20 to 40 individuals in the Sierra de Velasco, a rather dry area in northwestern Argentina, usually congregating around waterholes. They have a rapid flight and the group sticks close together. During flight, as well as on the ground or in the trees, the birds frequently let out a high-pitched twittering.

The nest is usually situated in old hollow tree limbs, or in self-excavated tunnels in river banks. Nests I have inspected both in trees and in river banks contained sparse linings of wood chips and roots. In the wild, the hen lays four to six eggs. Forshaw reports that a certain Mr. Woods observed about ten birds nesting in small holes in a large cactus at an altitude of 10,000 feet (3,000 m), near La Paz, eastern Bolivia.

Aviculture: In 1959 the first specimens were brought to England by the late naturalist and writer Gerald Durrel. One of the eight birds was kept in the Parrot House at the London Zoo. The bird quickly became affectionate and amused the public. For example, if a person stuck a finger through the cage mesh, the bird would come and perch on it, and would nibble gently on the finger while uttering quiet chattering noises. The bird lived for about ten years at the zoo.

With an outdoor aviary and a choice of nest boxes a pair of this species is almost certain to breed. Give them small black sunflower seeds, a variety of millets and millet spray, and the usual commercial parakeet seed mixture, fortified with vitamins and minerals, as well as apples, grass and weed seeds, berries, and so on. The birds frequently refuse certain seeds, except sunflower seeds; sometimes even millet spray is ignored. It is thus important to note what foods they accept eagerly. It is very important to offer a large variety of food choices so that the birds get a balanced diet. Don't let them become too addicted to sunflower seed; it is bad for the birds' health if the menu is "one-sided." (See also page 46.)

Sierra Parakeets are peaceful cage and aviary birds; many people like to keep one or more pairs in the house. They make more than reasonable pets with their charming appearance and attractive finchlike chatter.

A good breeding pair will give the fancier enormous satisfaction. The female lays 4 to 6 eggs, 10 to 11 in exceptional cases. A 1-inch (2-cm) layer of humus laid in the base of the nest box is recommended. The boxes, 8 by 8 by 12 inches (20 × 20 × 30 cm) with a 2-inch (5-cm) entrance hole, should be affixed about 6 inches (12 cm) from the floor. The incubation time is 21 to 22 days, and the young leave the nest at five to six weeks old. Apart from the short tail, they are very similar in appearance to the adults.

According to the literature, newly imported specimens of this species occasionally die for no apparent reason. One reason could be the change from a high altitude to a lower one, resulting in breathing difficulties. You should thus take very good care of breeding pairs so that as many young as possible are reared in captivity. This species is worth it. During breeding the males should have access to their own sleeping boxes.

Mountain or Golden-fronted Parakeet—*Bolborhynchus aurifrons* (Lesson)

There are four subspecies, *Bolborhynchus a. aurifrons* (Lesson), *Bolborhynchus a. robertsi* (Carriker), *Bolborhynchus a. margaritae* (Berlioz and Dorst), and *Bolborhynchus a. rubrirostris* (Burmeister).

Nominate Male: The forehead, the area between the eye and the beak, part of the cheeks, and the whole throat are golden yellow. There is also some golden yellow on the breast and flanks. The flight

A pair of Mountain Parakeets (Bolborhyn-chus aurifrons). In the wild they nest in holes and crevices of inaccessible rocky outcrops or high banks.

feathers are greenish blue. Both sexes have a dark green back and a lighter underside. Beak horn-colored; iris dark brown; feet and legs brownish pink. Length 7.1 inches (18 cm).

Female: All yellow is absent on the head, but some yellow on the breast and throat. Underparts darker green.

Immatures: Like the female.

Distribution: Native to the Andean slopes of southern Peru, southwest Bolivia, northern Chile, and northwestern Argentina. The birds are found at relatively high altitudes in the mountains, but also in bushland, sometimes reaching the coast. Since they also occur in agricultural areas, they can cause significant damage. They are also seen in gardens and parklands of urban areas, often in close proximity to humans. During the winter months, the birds often take refuge in thickly wooded areas. The *robertsi* variety is somewhat darker, especially on the underside, and there is no yellow wash; restricted to Soquian (Maranon Valley) and Libertad in northwestern Peru. The *margaritae* is somewhat larger in size and has a shorter tail; the beak is horn-colored in the male, dusky gray in the female; restricted to southern Peru and central-western Bolivia south through Tarapaca and Antofagasta (northern Chile), and northwestern Argentina. The *rubrirostris* looks very much like the previous race, without much yellow or with no yellow at all, and with a pinkish beak in the male, a dusky gray one in the female. Restricted to the eastern slopes of the Andes (northwestern Argentina) and central Chile.

Aviculture: The species is now imported infrequently especially because of its high mortality rate. The birds are rather timid and not very loud. Supplementary food should include millet spray, hemp seed, small dark sunflower seed, safflower seed, apples, grass and weed seeds, pieces of carrot, bananas, oranges (half an orange spiked on a nail will amuse the birds), and a rich variety of green food. Newly acquired birds must be left in complete peace and quiet; otherwise they may refuse to feed. The birds are extremely sensitive to changes in air pressure, temperature fluctuations, humidity changes, and stress. Many of them

The Barred or Lineolated Parakeet is often very prolific in captivity, and various mutations are now available. Sky blue (top left). Lutino (top right). Olive green (middle left). Cobalt blue (middle right). Mauve (bottom left). Dark green (bottom right).

die within the first days or months from lung infection.

The birds are mainly active during the evening or night (if you leave the light on, that is). Kept in a quiet indoor aviary, a pair will sometimes breed. The female lays two to five eggs that are incubated for about 24 days. A Dutch aviculturist, A. Veldink, has had a pair of these birds for about ten years. They use a nest box 3.25 feet (1 m) long by 6 inches (15 cm) wide and high. The inside of the box is divided into four compartments, each with an entry through a small hole. The two deepest compartments are obviously very dark and are used for nesting (probably reflecting the birds' preference in the wild). The pair seems quite comfortable in the outdoor aviary. When breeding, the birds must be given adequate rearing food, including soaked weeds (with some liver oil), soaked and squeezed out wheat bread, grass and weed seeds, various fruits and berries, and green food. When they are kept together with other members of the same species, it can happen that they spend the day in the nest box, only coming out in the evening to feed. Sometimes it seems that you are dealing with nocturnal parakeets. By artificial lighting they will indeed stay active well into the night, although I have been able to observe many pairs, kept in a quiet aviary with perhaps a few finches as companions, to be quite settled and active. Rosemary Low in *The Parrots of South America* (London: Gifford, 1972) gives some very interesting information on practical experiences of European breeders with this species.

Lineolated or Catherine Parakeet—*Bolborhynchus lineola* (Cassin)

There are two subspecies, *Bolborhynchus l. lineola* (Cassin) and *Bolborhynchus l. tigrinus* (Souancé).

Nominate Male: Mainly green with black scallop lines along the head, neck, back, rump, and wings. The wing feathers are black-edged. The eyes are yellowish brown; the beak is grayish yellow; and the feet and legs are gray-black.

Female: Usually somewhat smaller, green with black markings on the back but these are less sharply profiled than those of the male. The tips of the tail feathers are less black and in some females the black is absent altogether. Length about 6.33 inches (16 cm), including the 2.33-inch (6-cm) tail.

Immatures: Like the parents, but somewhat paler and with more bluish tinge on the head.

Distribution: Native to Central America from southern Mexico to western Panama. They are especially prevalent in the mountains and along the Talamanca Cordillera. They often travel in pairs but also in groups of 70 or more individuals. Because of their small size and cryptic coloration, they are difficult to observe in the wild. They live in wooded country interspersed with meadowland, and have regularly even been seen close to volcanoes.

Aviculture: These birds are usually available commercially and may be kept in aviaries or large cages with other small exotics since they are peaceful and nonaggressive. They spend much of their time on the ground, both in the wild and in captivity, seeking seeds and insects. It is recommended that the flight floor be regularly (and deeply) raked to prevent worm infestation. The worm eggs adhere to sand particles (literally dozens on a grain of sand). Obviously, a concrete floor is recommended since it is the most hygienic.

These attractive little hookbills are not at all destructive in their aviary; they climb slowly up branches, preferably 1.50 inches (4 cm) in diameter, or hang head downward in careful acrobatics. They are sensitive to low temperatures and must be kept in mildly heated indoor accommodations during the fall and winter. Supplementary food includes sunflower seed, hemp (not too much, as it makes them too fat), all kinds of millet varieties (including millet spray), and a regular multivitamin/mineral supplement. They love apple and other fruits.

With good husbandry a pair should go to nest. A lovebird or parakeet nest box should be accepted. They frequently carry nest material into the box as lining (sometimes as much as 1.6 inches [4 cm] deep) for the floor. They prefer strips of willow bark, small soft feathers, and similar materials. Hang the nest box out of the glare of the sun since these birds seem to avoid sunshine

as much as they can, a behavior I have also seen in the wild. Rosemary Low tells about her pair (in *Parrots, Their Care and Breeding*) that "went into ecstasies of delight at their first sight of snow, hanging upside down from the perch, flapping their wings, then opening them wide." These birds breed most successfully if kept together in groups of three or more (never two) pairs. The hen lays five or six eggs.

They will also breed fairly readily in a large cage, as was proven by M. G. Stern of Ropley, Hampshire, England, when his pair, between November 1972 and May 1975, reared 34 young. The birds' menu consisted of sunflower seeds, panicum, millet, and groats; as the young were weaned, chickweed, seeding grasses, twiggy branches of hazel and hawthorn, especially in bud, were relished (Low). Incubation time is about 21 days; breeders recommend leg banding at about 12 days (ring .21 inch [5.4 mm]). The young leave the nest at about eight weeks of age. A few days before fledging, give them an additional nest box so that the hen can rest away from the young when they return to roost at night. Hens should not be allowed to breed (and it's not necessary to do so) before they are at least 14 months old. Unless you put a stop to it, a pair is likely to breed for most of the year. To allow them to do so is, of course, dangerous to the health of the hen. You can't remove the nest boxes since they sleep in them at night, nor can you separate the sexes since they pair for life. At appropriate times, I place my birds in a separate enclosure with a different nest box, and this seems to make them want to "take a break" from breeding.

As you will have noted, I said "about" when referring to the incubation time. This is because various breeders have reported different times: from 18 to 25 days. My birds also did not provide me with a concrete answer to this question. In several cases, it seemed that the hens did not start incubation at any set time; some began after laying the first egg, others after the third.

Quaker or Monk Parakeet— *Myiopsitta monachus* (Boddaert)

Male: Forehead, crown, and occiput grayish blue; cheeks, throat, and lores pale gray. Back of head, neck, back rump, wings, and tail are all parrot green. Length: 11.5 inches (29 cm); weight: 5 to 5.7 ounces (125–142 g).

Female: Generally somewhat lighter in color, but in many instances there is no difference at all.

Immatures: Similar to adults, but with some green tinge on the forehead.

Distribution: East and middle Argentina (Buenos Aires, Entre Rios, Santa Fé, Cordóba), Urugauy, and introduced to Puerto Rico. A large feral population in southeastern New York, New Jersey, and Connecticut; nests have been recorded also in Massachusetts, Virginia, and Florida.

Also introduced in Europe (Berlin, Austria, and Mediterranean).

In the wild: This abundant bird— not only in its native countries—lives in thin woodland, farmland, orchards, parks, and gardens. At harvest time, these birds fly out in flocks of hundreds or thousands into the fields, where they cause so much damage that the whole harvest can be ruined. The flight is rapid and impetuous. They live mainly on seeds, fruits, millet varieties, corn, fresh twigs, and buds. The species is well known for its gigantic nests, which are constructed loosely in the treetops, usually on the outermost branches. They usually use thorny twigs as nest material. Nests frequently have a diameter of 3 to 9 feet (2–3 m). In the Berlin Zoo, I once saw a nest with a diameter of 75 cm (30 in); in the neighborhood of Buenos Aires, I have examined nests with a diameter of 35 to 122 inches (90 cm–3.1 m). Karl Neunzig wrote in his famous *Fremdländische Stubenvögel* about a nest that had a diameter of 3.5 feet (1.15 m). Needless to say, such nest-building is fascinating. There is often an entrance to the nest that is completely protected with a little portico; the parents often sit here to watch the world go by and to keep a lookout for possible danger (using it as a guard post). The nest itself usually consists of two rooms. The eggs are hatched in the back room, while the room that leads to the portico could be considered a living room since the parents spend most of their time there, including the night. When the young are bigger, they too will move into the living room so that the female can start laying a new clutch. The inside of the nest, which in the first phase is usually built by the female, is lined with thin twigs and strips of bark.

Aviculture: Behavior in the wild and in captive care was first documented in the eighteenth century. Since these parakeets are easy to keep and are strong in constitution, they are popular in aviculture, but, probably because of their loud, screeching calls (especially if the bird is kept as a household "pet," which is quite possible since they make excellent pets), they are frequently set free—and the result is that many birds have now set up home in areas outside their natural territory. Young birds can become exceedingly tame and can learn to repeat a few words. Compared to many other birds, they are somewhat aggressive, especially in the breeding season; thus, it is better to keep them in single pairs, or together in groups of three or more pairs (colony nesters). They can be kept in a roomy aviary with well-protected woodwork. They can live to up to 18 years of age. Kept like homing pigeons (which is presently illegal), they will return "home" even after excursions of several miles. They damage fruit trees by gnawing and removing new growth and buds.

A single bird kept in a large cage will soon become tame and affectionate, especially if it is a young

The Quaker Parakeet (Myiopsitta monachus) *can be rather destructive to timber. It is obvious that garden aviaries should be strongly built. Use 16 G wire gouge (mesh size: .5 by 1 inch [12.5 × 25 mm]).*

one. Breeding cages with minimum dimensions of 39 by 28 by 59 inches (100 × 70 × 150 cm) can be used. In an outdoor aviary (9 feet by 6 feet by 6 feet [3 × 2 × 2 m]), a few pairs can be extremely entertaining. They can spend the winter outdoors and temperatures as low as −13°F (−25°C) don't seem to worry them. They just creep into their nest or sleeping box early in the evening. A timber aviary is not recommended; strong mesh should be used. Up in one corner of the aviary you should erect a timber cross-shaped shelf, or affix, high up, an open box platform with dimensions of about 19.5 by 24 inches (50 × 60 cm). As nest material, provide them with large quantities of 8-inch to 3-foot (20–100-cm) long twigs of

The blue mutation of the Quaker was established in Belgium in the early 1950s by aviculturist M. J. Bruyneel.

willow, aspen, birch, oak, and fruit trees, which are placed on the aviary floor. At first, both sexes build, but the hen does most of the initial work. The nest is held together with fine slivers of wood and bark. The first eggs are laid about 14 days after mating. The clutch consists of four to six, sometimes seven, white eggs and these are brooded by the hen, but the male also spends the night in the nest. During the incubation process, the cock feeds the hen and he continually brings additional nest material to add to the nest. The eggs hatch after 23 to 25 days; the young are covered with yellow down; after one to two weeks, this becomes whitish. Rearing food consists of soft food mixed with ant pupae, extra boiled egg, grated carrots and spinach, various seeds and greens, buds, young twigs (willow), endive, chickweed, chicory, and sprouted grass and weed seeds.

The young leave the nest after 40 to 45 days; they are fully independent three weeks thereafter. Nest inspections won't harm the birds, but they will certainly protest with their loud screams. At first, the fledglings return to the nest each night, but they are usually "thrown out" by their parents after 10 to 14 days, after which they sleep on the nest. The pairing of the adults is interesting to study: The male holds himself with one foot on the hen's back, the other foot on the perch or branch on which the hen is sitting. He lets out soft chirping sounds. Copulation usually occurs in the morning. At pairing time these birds frequently scream loudly but quiet down once brooding begins. The named subspecies (see page 24) are unknown in aviculture.

Useful Addresses and Literature

Books

Athan, Mattie Sue. *Guide to a Well-Behaved Parrot, Second Edition.* Hauppauge, New York: Barron's Educational Series, Inc., 1999.

Avian Medicine. Lake Worth, Florida: Wingers Publishing, 1997.

Axelson, D., D.V.M. *Caring for Your Pet Bird.* New York: Sterling Publishing, 1989.

Burgemann, Petra, D.V.M. *Feeding Your Pet Bird.* Hauppauge, New York: Barron's Educational Series, Inc., 1993.

Doane, Bonnie Munro. *The Pleasure of Their Company: An Owner's Guide to Parrot Training.* New York: Howell Book House, 1998.

_____. *The Parrot in Health and Illness: An Owner's Guide.* New York: Howell Book House, 1991.

Forshaw, Joseph M., and W. T. Cooper. *Parrots of the World.* Third edition. Melbourne, Australia: Lansdowne Editions, 1989.

Juniper, Tony, and Mike Parr. *Parrots.* New Haven, CT: Yale University Press, 1998.

Low, Rosemary. *Parrots, Their Care and Breeding.* Poole and Dorset, England: Blandford Press, 1995.

Vriends, Matthew M., Ph.D. *Conures, A Complete Pet Owner's Manual, Sec-ond Edition.* Hauppauge, New York: Barron's Educational Series, Inc., 2000.

_____. *Hand-feeding and Raising Baby Birds.* Hauppauge, New York: Barron's Educational Series, Inc., 1996.

_____. *Lovebirds, A Complete Pet Owner's Manual, Second Edition.* Hauppauge, New York: Barron's Educational Series, Inc., 1995.

_____. *The New Bird Handbook.* Hauppauge, New York: Barron's Educational Series, Inc., 1989.

Bird Magazines and Newsletters

Bird Talk
P.O. Box 6050
Mission Viejo, CA 92690
714-855-8822
Fax: 714-855-0654

Bird Times
7-L Dundas Circle
Greensboro, NC 27407
336-292-4047
Fax: 336-292-4272

World of Birds
Seacoast Publishing
850 Park Avenue
Monterey, CA 93940
800-864-2500

Bird Breeder On-Line
Web site: http://www.birdbreeder.com

National Bird Clubs

Bird Clubs of America
Dick Ivy
P.O. Box 2005
Yorktown, VA 23692
804-898-5090

International Parrotlet Society
Sandee L. Molenda, Secretary
P.O. Box 2428
Santa Cruz, CA 94063-2428
831-688-5560
E-mail: ips@parrotletranch.com
Web site: www.parrotletranch.com/IPS

Society of Parrot Breeders and
  Exhibitors
P.O. Box 369
Groton, MA 01450

Bird-related Associations and Organizations

The American Federation of Aviculture
P.O. Box 7312
N. Kansas City, MO 64116-0012
816-421-2473

The Association of Avian Veterinarians
P.O. Box 811720
Boca Raton, FL 33481-1720

Cornell Laboratory of Ornithology
159 Sapsucket Woods Road
Ithaca, NY 14850
607-254-BIRD
Web site: http://www.ornith.cornell.edu

International Aviculturists' Society
P.O. Box 2232
LaBelle, FL 33975
941-674-0321
Fax: 941-675-8824
Web site: http://www.mecca.org/
  -rporter/PARROTS

Index

Dedication

For Kimy and Korrina Lindsey, Terry Williams, and William F. Treuber, J.D.

Soyons fidèles à nos faiblesses.

Photo Credits

Pieter van den Hooven: pages vi, vii, viii, x, 2, 4, 5, 8, 9 top right, 10, 12, 13, 22, 27, 36, 46, 48, 49, 50, 53, 57, 58, 60, 68, 69, 97, 115, 117, 119, 121, 123, 127, 128, 129, 131, 132, 133, 134, 136, 138, 139, 142, 144, 145, 146, 147, 148, 150, 152, 153, 157, 161, 163, 164, 165, 166, 173, 174, 176, 177, 178, 179, 180, 181, 182, 184, 185; B. Gardiner: pages 9 bottom right, 33, 172; Matthew M. Vriends: pages 19, 21, 23, 24, 37 top right, 38, 40, 41, 43, 44, 45, 47, 56, 59, 72, 189, 190; J. G. Blasman: pages 26, 28, 30, 37 bottom right, 66.

Cover Credits

Front cover: Pieter van den Hooven and Matthew M. Vriends; Inside front: Matthew M. Vriends; Inside back: Matthew M. Vriends; Back cover: Pieter van den Hooven.

All inquiries should be addressed to:
Barron's Educational Series, Inc.
250 Wireless Boulevard
Hauppauge, New York 11788
http://www.barronseduc.com

ISBN-13: 978-0-7641-0962-1
ISBN-10: 0-7641-0962-6

Library of Congress Catalog Card No. 99-30560

Library of Congress Cataloging-in-Publication Data

Vriends, Matthew M., 1937–
    The parrotlet handbook / Matthew M. Vriends ; illustrations by Tanya M. Heming-Vriends.
        p. cm.
    ISBN 0-7641-0962-6
    1. Parrotlets. 2. Parrots. I. Title.
    SF473.P3 V73   1999
    636.6'865—dc21   99-30560
                                              CIP

Printed in China
15 14 13 12 11 10 9

About the Author

Matthew M. Vriends is a Dutch-born biologist and ornithologist whose advanced degrees include a Ph.D. in zoology. Dr. Vriends has written more than 100 books in three languages on birds and other animals. He has traveled extensively in South America, Indonesia, Australia, Africa, the United States, and Europe to observe and study birds and other animals in their natural environment, and is widely regarded as an expert in tropical ornithology and aviculture. Dr. Vriends lives on Long Island, New York. He is the author of several Barron's pet books.

Acknowledgments

I'm grateful to all my friends who gave me encouragement, assistance, and their time, especially Arthur Freud, Sandee L. and Robert Molenda, Robbie Harris, and my dear friend and colleague John Coborn for his valuable suggestions and extensive annotations. I would also like to thank H. E. Branje of the Dutch Parrotlet Society, J. G. Blasman, K. Hammer, P. Konkelaar, T. Lansink, E. Woltman, B. Gardiner, and especially Pieter van den Hooven.

Thanks to my daughter, Tanya M. Heming-Vriends, for her invaluable assistance during the preparation of the text; without her, this book never could have been written. Finally, thanks to Grace Freedson and Mark Miele of Barron's.

All the opinions and conclusions expressed in the following pages are my own, and any errors must be my own responsibility.

Important Note

The subject of this book is how to take care of parrotlets and other miniature parrots in captivity. In dealing with these birds, always remember that newly purchased birds—even when they appear perfectly healthy—may well be carriers of salmonellae. This is why it is highly advisable to have sample droppings analyzed and to observe strict hygienic rules. Other infectious diseases that can endanger humans, such as psittacosis and tuberculosis, are rare in parrotlets. However, if you see a doctor because you or a member of your household has symptoms of a cold or the flu, mention that you keep birds. If you have any doubts, consult your physician before you buy a bird.

Many insects used as food by birds are pests that can infest stored food and create a serious nuisance. If you decide to grow any of these insects, be extremely careful to keep them from escaping from their containers.

The
Parrotlet
Handbook

Matthew M. Vriends, Ph.D.

With Full-color Photographs
Drawings by Tanya M. Heming–Vriends

BARRON'S